D1259775

THE RISE OF URBAN AMERICA

ADVISORY EDITOR

Richard C. Wade

PROFESSOR OF AMERICAN HISTORY
UNIVERSITY OF CHICAGO

AMERICAN CITY GOVERNMENT

Charles Austin Beard

ARNO PRESS

&

The New York Times

NEW YORK · 1970

Reprint Edition 1970 by Arno Press Inc.

Reprinted by permission of Hawthorn Books, Inc.

Reprinted from a copy in The University of Illinois Library

LC# 70-112522
ISBN 0-405-02435-5

THE RISE OF URBAN AMERICA
ISBN for complete set 0-405-02430-4

Manufactured in the United States of America

AMERICAN CITY GOVERNMENT

Municipal Bathhouse, East 23rd Street, New York City.

AMERICAN CITY GOVERNMENT

A SURVEY OF NEWER TENDENCIES

BY

CHARLES A. BEARD

ASSOCIATE PROFESSOR OF POLITICS IN COLUMBIA UNIVERSITY

NEW YORK
THE CENTURY CO.
1912

TABLE OF CONTENTS

LIST OF ILLUSTRATIONS

PREFATORY NOTE

This volume, as its subtitle indicates, is not a systematic treatise on municipal government, but a survey of recent leading tendencies. Its reason for existence, in view of the several works already available, is in the distribution of emphasis, in the stress which it lays on the social and economic functions of city government. Less than one-third of the space is given to politics and administration. There is also some difference in the point of view, for the position is here taken that, strictly speaking, there can be no such thing as "municipal science," because the most fundamental concerns of cities, the underlying economic foundations, are primarily matters of state and national, not local, control.

These pages are in a way supplementary to my "American Government and Politics." They are not addressed to professed experts in city affairs, but to students and citizens who wish a general survey. In preparing the text I have relied upon standard treatises and drawn largely upon *The American City* and the *National Municipal Review*. . I have studiously avoided the use of footnotes on account of the popular aversion for them. Whoever would carry his investigations beyond the bare suggestions of these pages will find some help in the brief bibliographies at the end of the volume.

CHARLES A. BEARD.

New Milford, Conn.,
    August, 1912.

AMERICAN CITY GOVERNMENT

AMERICAN
CITY GOVERNMENT

CHAPTER I

THE PEOPLE OF THE CITY

WHEN George Washington was inaugurated in Wall
Street on April 30, 1789, the city of New York was an
overgrown village of 33,000 inhabitants — about as
large as Cedar Rapids, Iowa, in 1910. Greater Philadelphia, in her vaunted superiority, claimed that more
than 42,000 people dwelt within her borders. Boston
had a population of 18,000, Baltimore, 13,000, and Richmond, 3,761. At that time only about three per cent.
of the people of the United States lived in towns of
more than 8,000 inhabitants. And those towns differed
so fundamentally in their industries and their markets
from the modern American city that they would really
be called trading hamlets to-day.

When Lincoln began his administration, as he so aptly
put it, in a palace all on fire, the United States was still
fundamentally rural. For nearly twenty years the politics of the country had been dominated by the slave
power — eminently rural in its political economy and
national outlook. But during those years a new force
was growing up that was destined to wrest from slavoc-
racy its scepter. That force was composed of the cap-
tains of steel and steam and capital, whose centers of

operations were not on the plantations nor the open prairies of the West, but in the cities — New York, Pittsburgh, Chicago. Their supremacy in economics and politics would have come, had there been no Civil War.

Within forty years of the firing on Sumter a great change had come over American life. Chicago had grown from 109,260 to 1,698,575; Greater New York from 1,174,779 to 3,437,202; and San Francisco from 56,802 to 342,782. At the close of the nineteenth century, about one-third of the people of the United States dwelt in cities of over ten thousand; and the latest survey shows that the drift city-ward continues unabated.

The census of 1910 classifies as urban all thickly populated areas of 2500 or more inhabitants, including New England towns which are in part rural in character, and on this basis reports 46.3 per cent. of the total population of the United States as urban and 53.7 per cent. as rural. The following table shows the comparative growth of such urban areas since 1890:

Class of Places	Number of Places, 1910	Population, 1910	Per Cent. of Total Population		
			1910	1900	1890
Total Population........	.....	91,972,266	100.0	100.0	100.0
Urban Territory.............	2,405	42,623,383	46.3	40.5	36.1
Places of —					
1,000,000 or more........	3	8,501,174	9.2	8.5	5.8
500,000 to 1,000,000......	5	3,010,667	3.3	2.2	1.3
250,000 to 500,000.......	11	3,949,839	4.3	3.8	3.9
100,000 to 250,000.......	31	4,840,458	5.3	4.3	4.4
50,000 to 100,000........	59	4,178,915	4.5	3.6	3.2
25,000 to 50,000........	120	4,062,763	4.4	3.7	3.7
10,000 to 25,000.........	374	5,609,208	6.1	5.8	5.5
5,000 to 10,000.........	629	4,364,703	4.7	4.3	4.0
2,500 to 5,000..........	1,173	4,105,656	4.5	4.4	4.3
Rural Territory..............	.....	49,348,883	53.7	59.5	63.9

At the head of the States having the largest urban population in 1910 are the eastern commonwealths. Massachusetts reports 92.8 per cent. as urban, Rhode Island, 96.7, New York, 78.8, Pennsylvania 60.4. In the Southern and West North Central States the rural population continues to hold the balance of power. North Carolina returns 14.4 per cent. as urban, Mississippi, 11.5, North Dakota, 11, and South Dakota, 13.1. It must be noted, however, that the highest percentages of increase are to be found in the Pacific, West South Central, and Mountain States, showing that the western commonwealths are following in the wake of the older States in the building of cities.

The remarkable feature of this urban growth is that rapid increase is not to be found in the transformation of rural hamlets into small cities, but in the additions made to the cities of considerable size and to the already huge metropolitan districts like New York, Chicago, San Francisco, and Cleveland. In twenty-five metropolitan districts, centering around New York, Chicago, Philadelphia, Boston, Pittsburgh, St. Louis, San Francisco-Oakland, Baltimore, Cleveland, Cincinnati, Minneapolis-St. Paul, Detroit, Buffalo, Los Angeles, Milwaukee, Providence, Washington, New Orleans, Kansas City, Louisville, Rochester, Seattle, Indianapolis, Denver, and Portland, are to be found twenty-two of the ninety-two millions dwelling in continental United States. It is the cities of smaller size, however, that seem to be gaining more rapidly; for the increase of the ninety cities ranging in population from 50,000 to 250,000 was over forty per cent. between 1900 and 1910, while the five cities ranging from 500,000 to 1,000,000 show an increase of only about twenty per cent.

These figures illustrating the growth of municipalities are not merely significant in themselves. They point to the growing predominance of the city dwellers over the rural population and mark the shifting of the balance of political power from the farm to the forge and market place. Of the total increase in the inhabitants of the continental United States during the past decade, 1900–1910, seven-tenths was in urban areas and three-tenths in the rural areas. Moreover, the last census reports that "the *rate* of increase for the population of urban.areas was over three times that for the population living in rural territory." Furthermore, in running over the returns for the rural counties in even prosperous agricultural States like Indiana, Illinois, Iowa, and Michigan, one cannot help being struck with the number which are reported as having lost in population during the past few years, and particularly with the number which show a steady decline in population from census to census since 1880.

No mere statistics of population, however, furnish a statement and interpretation of the problems which confront modern city governments. These are to be sought in the modes by which urban dwellers gain their livelihood and in industries, wages, housing, markets, transportation, and communication.

Here we find the most significant fact to be not merely a movement from the country to the towns, but the reconstruction of our economic system by the Industrial Revolution, brought about by steam and machinery — a reconstruction which transfers the basis of our modes of living from a rural economy to the capitalist system of production and distribution. The machine process which it involves is conquering ever larger areas of business and manufacturing and carries in its train certain positive results which must be taken into account by every student who would not reduce the science of municipal government to barren abstractions or the mere description of political and administrative measures.

The first of these results is the separation of the workman from the ownership and control of his tools and instruments of production and the creation of two rather sharply marked classes in society — the capitalist class, deriving its incomes from the ownership, management, and manipulation of industries, franchises, and public utilities, and the working class, dependent upon the sale of labor power for a livelihood. It is this class division and its manifestation in labor conflicts that are most distressing to those Americans who like to look upon their country as a land where all are equal.

Because this social conflict is repugnant to old-fashioned American ideas, attempts are made to gloss it over, to minimize its importance, or to deny its existence altogether. Of course it is easy to show that working men are constantly rising out of their class — Rockefeller, Carnegie, McCormick, and Jay Gould were poor men once and their achievements show what any man can do in America. This view, in its cheerful optimism, ignores the fundamental fact, however, that what any single man may do is no indication of the condition of the masses who, by the very nature of the circumstances, must stay behind. Individual working men may rise out of their class but the class remains and must be regarded as a permanent factor when the functions of municipal government are under consideration.

And this working class, which forms the bulk of the population of the great industrial centers, is in the main a landless, homeless, and propertyless proletariate. The exact percentage of those who are propertyless in the cities is a matter of much speculation and little exact knowledge, but that it is very large there can be no doubt. The modern system discourages the accumulation of property by the proletariate: wages are not far above the margin of subsistence; the ownership of homes in cities of tenements is well-nigh impossible, and it is, as we shall see, in many respects a handicap in smaller cities; and the discovery of "safe" investments is difficult for the poor man who has a little laid by but knows nothing about the ways of finance — except, of course, the postal savings banks which pay a small rate of interest.

In the matter of wages of the proletariate, we have, unfortunately, no splendid survey of even a single city comparable to that which Charles Booth made for London; and consequently there is much vague guessing as to the earnings of the working class. It should be pointed out, however, that reports on "average" wages are meaningless, and that the only really valuable statistics on this subject are those which show the number of persons and percentage of the whole receiving a given rate of wages per day and per year.

Happily for the cause of a real municipal science, there are a few careful studies which show how low are the wages and how precarious the existence of a vast mass of the proletariate of our great cities. For example, a survey of the Polish working people of Buffalo,

recently made under the direction of the Russell Sage
Foundation, yields some figures of genuine significance.
That city had 135 Poles in 1870 and it now has over
80,000 — one-sixth of the entire population. The survey mentioned above included 2429 Polish women and
11,609 men. "Of the women, eighty-four per cent. are
in factories and the others in hotels, laundries, junk and
rag shops. Of the men, eighty-seven per cent. are in
manufacturing and twelve per cent. are employed by
railroads, lumber yards, and contractors. It is close to
the facts to estimate that the Poles contribute one-fifth
of the entire labor supply of the city, one-fourth of the
labor outside of the mercantile and clerical lines, and
fully one-third of the rough labor in manufacturing.
They are in Buffalo's elemental industries . . . and
these industries are vitally dependent upon them for
their operation."

A study of the wages of the Polish men made by the
survey showed that sixty-four per cent. earned not over
$1.75 a day; thirty-two per cent. from $1.75 to $2.50
a day; three and seven-tenths per cent. from $2.50 to
$3.50 per day, and the balance over $3.50 a day. De-
ducting the loss of wages due to intermittent unemployment, the survey concluded that the average yearly earnings of the first group was $375 and of the second group
$525. At the same time, a study of the cost of living
in Buffalo for a typical working-class family showed
that from $635 to $735 per annum was necessary for
the maintenance of a decent standard of life. "The
fact emerges, therefore," says Mr. Daniels, the director
of the survey, "that sixty-four per cent. of the Polish
laborers are receiving less by $260 and another thirty-

two per cent. less by $110 than the minimum yearly wage required for family subsistence." Certain things are obvious: such a working man cannot support a family in decency and if he marries his family must live in dire poverty or his wife (and the children as soon as they are old enough) must work outside of the home.

This condition of affairs for such a large per cent. of the working men and women of a city like Buffalo can hardly be very exceptional; although, of course, other evidence is not forthcoming to prove that it is typical. Enough evidence is available to show that a very large proportion — very probably sixty per cent.— of the people of American industrial cities receive wages which are barely sufficient to cover the pressing needs of life and permit no accumulation of capital worthy of mention.

On the subject of home ownership and the working class we have more positive information. Under the authority of an act of Congress an investigation was undertaken into home owning by the census authorities in 1890. Again in 1900 the returns were taken in great detail and are printed in the census for that year. At the head of the list of considerable cities stood Detroit where 39.1 per cent. of the population owned homes — 22.5 per cent. free of mortgage. "Of all the cities considered," reports the census, "the largest proportion of hired homes, 87.9 per cent., is found in New York City. In Manhattan and Bronx Boroughs the proportion is even higher, 94.1 per cent. as compared with 82 per cent. for Brooklyn Borough. . . . There is also a very large proportion of hired homes in Boston, Fall River, Jersey City, and Memphis, constituting in each of them four-

fifths of all the homes in 1900." Of the larger cities of
the country, Los Angeles, Toledo, Detroit, Scranton,
Rochester, Syracuse, and Cleveland in the order named
have the smallest proportion of hired homes. Three-
fifths of the owned homes in Manhattan and the Bronx
are encumbered. In the eighth assembly district of
Manhattan, fourteen out of 13,662 families owned their
homes free of mortgage, and only forty-two, including
those with encumbered property, owned homes. Returns show that there are about 5000 evictions a month
in New York for non-payment of rent.

When we deduct, from the number owning homes, the
well-to-do and the lower middle class, we find that the
working-class families who are "homeless," in the sense
that they are renters, must be extremely large. And,
strange as it may seem, it is often disadvantageous for
the working man to own his house, because he is thereby
less free to resist wage reductions in his neighborhood,
is under greater stress in periods of unemployment because he cannot move freely to other places in search of
work, and in general is prevented from following the
higher grade and better paid industries which may rise
in other parts of the country. The working man who
owns a home encumbered with a mortgage is less liable
to join with his fellows in resisting a wage reduction and
an increase in the onerous conditions of labor.

Another significant feature of industrialism in the
cities is extensive employment of women. The census
(1909) reports [1] that 19.5 per cent. of the industrial
wage-earners are women, and the proportion of women

---

[1] Females sixteen years of age and older included in the report.

who are breadwinners steadily increases. The proportion of females who were engaged in gainful pursuits was 14.7 per cent. in 1870, 16 per cent. in 1880, 19 per cent. in 1890, and 20.6 per cent. in 1900. At the last date about one-third of the females over ten years of age in Philadelphia were engaged in gainful pursuits and one-eighth were employed in industries. At the same time about 18,000 out of 42,000 women at Fall River, Massachusetts, were employed — about 15,000 of them in industries. The recent federal report on women in industries in the United States says: "The story of woman's work in gainful employments is a story of constant changing or shifting of work and workshop, accompanied by long hours, low wages, unsanitary conditions, overwork, and the want on the part of woman of training, skill and vital interest in her work. . . . The most surprising fact brought out in this study is the long period of time through which large numbers of women have worked under conditions which have involved not only great hardships to themselves but shocking waste to the community."

Not only is the urban working class toolless and homeless and recruited largely by women whose duties are traditionally supposed to be domestic; it is also dependent upon conditions of employment beyond the control of the individual worker. The industries in which the urban working class is engaged are subject to the expansion and contraction which accompany modern business methods and consequently there are constantly returning periods in which the amount of unemployment is very large. The effects of cycles of business depression on the workless urban dweller are demoralizing in the extreme and are always accompanied by an increase in crime, vagrancy, and domestic difficulties.

These economic factors only serve to intensify the helplessness which characterizes a large section of the working class of our great cities. Without reserve capital, and dependent upon a labor market beyond his power to control in any way as an individual, the most energetic and foresighted person is likely to lose heart and join the great army of the hopeless who live from day to day. But it should be remembered that our cities have been built up of people conscious of no definite purpose and power of achievement, but rather of people of every race and clime driven there by blind economic and social forces, and often unprepared by training or native talents for the stress of city life. Indeed, a very small proportion of our population has come to America out of what may be loosely termed " free choice." During the colonial period, our laboring population was largely recruited by slaves torn from African wilds for the profit of slavers and planters, and by indentured servants induced by the hard poverty of England or the Continent to sell themselves as bondmen in order to receive passage to the New World. The Irish driven out by famine and desperate poverty, the Jew fleeing from the wrath of Russia, the Italian in search of an escape from the bitter want and burdensome taxes, and all the other races of Europe hunted out of their native lands by grinding necessity are, from the point of view of economic freedom, but little removed from the condition of the black bondmen or the indentured servants of colonial days. Only a small per cent. of them are trained for any special high-grade work in the United

States, or are looking forward to a definite place in the life of the land of their adoption. They simply come and take their chance at things, hoping, somehow, to find a foothold above the poverty line.

The whole complex of industrial conditions under which the urban working man must live and labor is such as to exercise a deteriorating effect upon his home. Low wages of themselves mean inadequate housing; absentee landlordism means the management of property on a profit or rental basis only; and the non-ownership of the home undermines the incentive to improvement. The result of these circumstances is that in every large industrial center there is a vast area in which the conditions of living are such as to make them detrimental to the health, physical comfort, and morals of the inhabitants — to say nothing of esthetic considerations.

Although the word congestion is constantly used by municipal reformers, it is very difficult, if not impossible, to define it accurately. Obviously, the number of persons inhabiting a block is not a test of their physical well-being. For example, in a district of monster apartment houses equipped with all the sanitary and other conveniences of modern science, a far higher degree of congestion, numerically speaking, will be found to exist than in the most densely populated areas of overcrowded India, and yet the comfort and health of the inhabitants may be nearly perfect. Neither is a crude death rate an accurate test of congestion, although all recent writers agree that there is a more or less direct relation between congestion and mortality in modern industrial life. Where there are so many other factors influencing the death rate — accidents and diseases incident to dangerous trades — the effect of congestion upon health cannot be separated and studied as a single force.

The conditions of living, the number of persons per room, the air space per head, methods of ventilation, the amount of sunlight and the sanitary conveniences — these afford tests for congestion, or rather for overcrowding, which is a better word to use in this connection. It is after all the effect of the conditions of living upon physical and moral well-being that counts, and the mere concentration of population does not necessarily imply, although it is generally associated with, what we may term, overcrowding.

For instance, there is more overcrowding in thousands of small shanties scattered over the hills in the anthracite coal region of Pennsylvania than in the thickly populated areas of the better residential districts of New York City. The homes of the miners described by Mr. Peter Roberts in his remarkable study of the anthracite regions, present conditions which are more deteriorating in their effects upon the physical and moral well-being of the coming generations than are millions of homes crowded together in the great cities, where the number per acre is tenfold greater than in some of the mining areas. This fact makes it apparent that the land question is not the sole, or even the most important, factor in undue overcrowding.

It must be observed also that the amount of overcrowding (tested by the standard laid down above, that is the physical and moral well-being) does not necessarily bear a direct relation to the number of inhabitants in a given city. In some of the smaller of the purely industrial towns, the percentage of inhabitants living in what may be correctly termed an overcrowded condition is greater than in some of the larger cities where industries are more diversified, factories are more widely scattered and the home-owning population relatively greater. Of course this should not obscure the fact that the overcrowding in our great cities like New York, Pittsburgh, and Chicago is not only a menace to our civilization, but evidence of the disgraceful state of our public morals.

Concerning the city of New York, the distinguished housing expert, Mr. Lawrence Veiller, wrote in 1905:

No conception of the existing conditions can be obtained from any general statements. To say that the lower East Side of New York is the most densely populated spot in the habitable globe gives no adequate idea of the real conditions. To say that in one section of the·city the density of population is 1000 to the acre and that the greatest density of population in the most densely populated part of Bombay is but 759 to the acre, in Prague 485 to the acre, in Paris 434, in London 365, in Glasgow 350, in Calcutta 204, gives one no adequate realization of the state of affairs. No more does it to say that in many city blocks on the East Side there is often a population equal to that of a good-sized village. . . . The limits have not only been reached but have long been passed.

Five years later Mr. Veiller could report no fundamental changes in the condition of affairs described above in spite of the vigorous efforts of one of the best-equipped tenement-house departments in the United States, for in his " Housing Reform " he writes:

We have to-day the tenement-house system prevalent throughout New York as the chief means of housing the greater part of the city's population, over two-thirds of the people living in multiple dwellings; we have to-day over 100,000 separate tenement houses; we have a city built up of four- and five-story buildings, instead of two-story and three-story ones; we have over 10,000 tenement houses of the hopeless and discredited " dumb-bell " type with narrow " air shafts " furnishing neither sunlight nor fresh air to the thousands of people living in the rooms opening on them; we have over 20,000 tenement houses of the older type in which most of the rooms are without light or ventilation; we have over 100,000 dark, unventilated rooms without even a window to an adjoining room; we have 80,000 buildings housing nearly 3,000,000 people, so constructed as to be a standing menace to the community in the event of fire, most of them built with wooden stairs, wooden halls, and wooden floors, and thousands built entirely of wood.

Over a million people have no bathing facilities in their homes; while even a greater number are limited to the use of sanitary conveniences in common with other families, without proper privacy; over a quarter of a million people had in the year 1900, no other sanitary conveniences than antiquated yard privies; and even to-day 2,000 of these privy sinks still remain, many of them located in densely populated districts, a source of danger to all in the neighborhood, facilitating the spread of contagious disease through the medium of the common house-fly.

Here we have conditions of congestion of population unparalleled elsewhere in the civilized world. In one small portion of Manhattan Island, the district south of Fourteenth Street and east of Broadway, dwell over 500,000 human beings, a population in itself greater than the entire population of any other American city except Chicago, Philadelphia, St. Louis, Boston, and Baltimore; a population greater, indeed, than the population of each of the following States: Arizona, Delaware, Idaho, Montana, Nevada, North Dakota, Oregon, New Hampshire, New Mexico, Rhode Island, Utah, Vermont, and Wyoming.

The demoralizing effects of congestion upon the people have been so marked in England where the transformation from rural to urban life has been most thoroughgoing that English statesmen and scientists are profoundly disturbed as to the future of " the heart of the Empire "; and the United States cannot longer afford to ignore the development of factors so menacing to the strength of the nation.

There is no doubt that undue congestion increases mortality; but we should be careful about applying the crude death rate as a test of the degree of a city's wellbeing; for the death rate of a city depends upon many factors in addition to overcrowding. For example, the number of children under five years — a period at which the death rate is particularly high — may be far greater in one city than in another. Again, the population of a given city may contain a large proportion of selected and healthy adults recently drawn from rural districts in the United States and Europe, and its death rate — even though the conditions of overcrowding are as bad as can be imagined — may be lower than in another city where the congestion is less.

Furthermore, the vital statistics in most American cities are so deficient as to be worthy of little respect as compared with those of European cities. The health officers are frequently political officers who have a particular interest in making the salubrity of the city appear as nearly perfect as possible. Landlords, merchants, politicians, and chambers of commerce in any city are not anxious to advertise to the world the fact that their community has an abnormally high death rate. It is a favorite occupation of departments of health to point with pride to low death rates.

A more accurate test of the relation of congestion to health can be applied in some of the older English cities that are not growing so rapidly. One of the results of Rowntree's investigation of the city of York, published a decade ago, was a demonstration of the fact that there was a direct relation between the degree of congestion and room overcrowding on the one hand, and the physical well-being of the people on the other.

Dr. Antonio Stella, who a few years ago studied six congested blocks in New York City inhabited largely by Italians, reported that while the death rate for the city at large was 18.35 per 1000 and for children under five 51.5 per 1000, it varied in those particular blocks from 22.3 to 24.9 per 1000 for all ages, and from 59.5 to 92.2 per 1000 for children under five years of age.

The study recently made in Glasgow of 72,857 school children belonging to families living in one, two, three or four rooms respectively, showed that the weight and stature of boys and girls of a given age varied directly with the number of rooms occupied by their families — those living in one room being at the bottom of the scale and those in four rooms at the top. Further statistical materials could be adduced — if it were necessary — to demonstrate the obvious truth that persons living in conditions that deprive them of fresh air, sunlight and proper sanitary conveniences, suffer more than their due portion of the ills that flesh is heir to.

Realizing the fact that a mere high mortality due to congestion will not seriously disturb a nation that com-

placently slaughters more people on its railways and in
its factories and mines than any other country in the
world, mathematically minded reformers are trying to
reach the heart of the public through its purse by pointing out that there is a great economic loss in the death
of persons of working age. An ingenious statistician,
Professor Irving Fisher, of Yale University, has figured
out the net worth in dollars of the average person at
various periods in his life — ranging from $950 at the
age of five to $4100 at the age of thirty, after which time
there is a gradual decline. The death of any person at
a given age is a net loss of a certain amount to the community; and the loss, if due to preventable illness and
the lack of physical stamina, might be roughly figured
in dollars and cents. According to Professor Fisher:
" The actual economic saving annually possible in this
country by preventing needless deaths, needless illness
(serious and minor), and needless fatigue is certainly
far greater than one and a half billion dollars, and may
be three or four times as great." The amount of
economic loss due to overcrowding alone would be difficult to estimate; but if we had the data they might be
translated into dollars and cents.

The most destructive of all diseases is tuberculosis.
The annual mortality from it in the United States is
almost as great as the total number of men killed and
mortally wounded during the four years of the Civil
War. And from special studies of tuberculosis in our
great cities, a distinct relation has been established between congestion and the number of those destroyed by
the white plague. Those who fall before this dread

disease are, in a large measure, the sons and daughters of the poor.

An immediate connection between overcrowding and the growth of crime, particularly juvenile crime, seems also to be fairly established. It is apparent that children belonging to families crowded into one or two rooms must be driven out into the streets to play at a very early age. The great majority of them, of course, can receive relatively little attention from their mothers, who are busily occupied with the housework or are in some factory.

It is the general testimony of those connected with juvenile courts that playing in the streets is directly responsible for the development of crime among children. Mr. Ernest K. Coulter, clerk of the Children's Court of New York County, recently stated that in his opinion congestion was responsible for a vast number of cases that came into the juvenile courts of the city, and that environment counted for nine-tenths of the juvenile delinquency. He added: "The children often come to feel that they are not wanted in their so-called homes and they are really forced to the streets. The most skilful pickpockets in New York City are children. The ranks of these young thieves are constantly being recruited from the districts where there is the greatest congestion. The reason is that the homes of these children are so crowded and wretched that there is little attraction for them there, and these little unfortunates, when given the first taste of easy money, have little desire to live in the old way."

This testimony is supported by the Honorable William McAdoo, formerly police commissioner of New York, now chief city magistrate, a gentleman of large experience in handling crime of every kind. In his view, " there can be no question but that the connection between congestion of population, especially in that form which it takes in the tenement houses, particularly the old-style tenements, and crime and delinquency is very marked. The crowded living conditions in these small rooms, lack of personal privacy and separation of the sexes, must, in the very nature of things, beget conditions which conduce to immorality and the lack of self-respect."

Overcrowding also has a most disastrous effect upon the mental development of children and adults. With the family washing drying in the room, the baby crying in one corner, and the air heavily laden with the odors of many kitchens, it requires an extraordinary effort upon the part of the tenement dweller to undertake any serious reading or study. No doubt a great deal is done even under these adverse conditions, but certainly the weight of circumstances is against any intellectual improvement. The children instead of having an opportunity to read and prepare their school lessons at home are driven out on the streets, and the adults are encouraged to read only trashy fiction or the sensational news of the yellow journals.

In addition to the unhappy working and living conditions which characterize modern urban centers generally, the American city has special problems of its own on account of the large percentage of foreigners embraced in its population. According to the last census —

There are in all 229 cities which had in 1910 more than 25,000 inhabitants, with an aggregate population of 28,543,-816. Of the combined population of these cities native whites of native parentage number 10,149,145, or 35.6 per cent.; native whites of foreign or mixed parentage 9,219,-007, or 32.3 per cent.; foreign-born whites 7,479,033, or 26.2 per cent.; negroes 1,625,640, or 5.7 per cent.; all other 70,991, or 0.2 per cent. For continental United States as a whole the equivalent numbers and percentages are: Native whites of native parentage 49,488,441, or 53.8 per cent.; native whites of foreign or mixed parentage 18,900,-663, or 20.6 per cent.; foreign-born whites 13,343,583, or 14.5 per cent.; negroes 9,828,294, or 10.7 per cent.

The combined population (28,543,816) of the 229 cities taken together constitutes 31 per cent. of the entire population (91,972,266) of continental United States in 1910. In the case, however, of native whites of native parentage the number in these cities constitutes only 20.5 per cent. of the total number in the United States, while for native whites of foreign or mixed parentage the percentage is 48.8 and for foreign-born whites, 56. For negroes the percentage in the principal cities is 16.5.

The foreign-born white element is mainly concentrated in the Northern and Eastern States and in many of the cities in these States the proportion of foreign-born whites in the total population is very large. Passaic, N. J., has 28,467 foreign-born whites, representing 52 per cent. of its total population (54,773). This is the largest proportion of foreign-born whites in any of the principal cities, and Lawrence, Mass., with 41,319 foreign-born whites in a total population of 85,892, has the next largest proportion, 48.1 per cent. There are eleven other cities in each of which the foreign-born whites constitute more than 40 per cent. of the total population, namely, Perth Amboy, N. J., 44.5; New Bedford, Mass., 44.1; Woonsocket, R. I., 43.4; Fall River, Mass., 42.6; Chelsea, Mass., 42.4; Manchester, N.

H., 42.4; New Britain, Conn., 41; Lowell, Mass., 40.9; Shenandoah, Pa., 40.6; New York, N. Y., 40.4; Holyoke, Mass., 40.3.

Negroes constitute one-fourth or more of the total population in each of twenty-seven principal cities, and in four of them the proportion is more than half, namely, Charleston, S. C., 31,056 negroes, or 52.8 per cent.; Savannah, Ga., 33,246, or 51.1 per cent.; Jacksonville, Fla., 29,293, or 50.8 per cent.; Montgomery, Ala., 19,322, or 50.7 per cent.

Our larger cities are in fact foreign colonies.

In thirteen of the nineteen cities of 250,000 inhabitants or more in 1910 the foreign-born whites constitute between 25 and 40 per cent. of the total population. These cities, with their respective percentages, are: New York, 40.4; Boston, 35.9; Chicago, 35.7; Cleveland, 34.9; Detroit, 33.6; Newark, 31.8; San Francisco, 31.4; Milwaukee, 29.8; Jersey City, 29; Minneapolis, 28.5; Buffalo, 28; Pittsburgh, 26.3; Philadelphia, 24.7. In these cities taken together the foreign-born whites constitute 34.7 per cent. of their combined population, but for the remainder of the country outside of these cities the percentage is only 11.2; for continental United States as a whole the percentage is 14.5.

If the native whites of foreign or mixed parentage, as well as the foreign-born whites, are considered it appears that the proportion of the total population represented by white persons of either foreign birth or foreign parentage is very large in most of the nineteen cities named; in each of fifteen cities the percentages for these two elements, taken together, represent more than half the total population and in eleven of them it is more than two-thirds. These eleven cities, with the percentage of their population represented by these two elements, are: New York, 78.6; Milwaukee, 78.6; Chicago, 77.5; Cleveland, 74.8; Boston, 74.2; Detroit, 74; Buffalo, 71.3; Newark, 69.9; Jersey City, 69.7; San Francisco, 68.3; and Minneapolis, 67.2.

There are obvious reasons for this tendency of the

foreign population to concentrate in the larger cities. Diversified opportunities are afforded for earning a livelihood, and foreign immigrants find there a larger proportion of their fellow countrymen. The Scotch, English, and Scandinavians go to our country towns and to the farms in large numbers; but the Irish, Jews, and Italians prefer to take their chances in the city. A large proportion of the latter group are poverty-stricken, and do not possess the means — even if they had the incentive — to establish themselves on the land.

While no fair-minded American sanctions the gratifying notion that the evils of our city governments are due to the foreigners, it is no doubt true that certain evils are aggravated by the alien character of the voting population. There has been a marked tendency on the part of many foreign groups to fall under the domination of leaders of their own nationality, not always to their own advantage. There is also a natural tendency among them to retain their own customs and traditions in a manner that prevents their taking a large and generous view of city government as a whole. They are too often satisfied with sops thrown to them in the form of the nomination of " one of their own race " to office, and are frequently the victims of the demagogues who play upon race pride and prejudice. To assume, however, that American municipal government would have been much better if the cities had been inhabited only by " native " stock is not warranted by theory or practice.

When all the several factors — number of inhabitants, races, industries, and location — are taken into consideration, it is evident that the cities must vary among themselves in the character of the governmental matters

which they are required to take up. On the basis of
population alone there is no little variation. According
to the census of 1910 there are three cities — New York,
Chicago, and Philadelphia — with more than a million
inhabitants; five cities — St. Louis, Boston, Cleveland,
Baltimore, and Pittsburgh — with between five hundred
thousand and a million inhabitants; fifty cities with over
one hundred thousand; nearly two hundred cities with
between twenty-five thousand and a hundred thousand.

The great cities — New York, Chicago, and Philadelphia — stand in a class by themselves, presenting peculiar problems on account of the bulk and the diversity
of their population. Greater New York, by the census
of 1910, has 4,766,883 inhabitants, and the urban center
of New York, embracing Westchester and New Jersey
suburbs, boasts a population of 6,474,568 — nearly twice
the total population of the United States in 1790
(3,929,214). "In New York, computations based on
the census (1900) show 785,053 persons of German
descent, a number nearly equal to the population of Ham-
burg, and larger than the native element in New York
(737,477). New York has twice as many Irish
(710,510) as Dublin, two and one-half times as many
Jews as Warsaw, half as many Italians as Naples, and
50,000 to 150,000 first and second generations from
Scotland, Hungary, Poland, Austria, and England.
Chicago has nearly as many Germans as Dresden, one-
third as many Bohemians as Prague, one-half as many
Irish as Belfast, one-half as many Scandinavians as
Stockholm. The variety of races, too, is astonishing
New York excels Babel. A newspaper writer finds in
that city sixty-six languages spoken, forty-nine news-

papers published in foreign languages, and one school at Mulberry Bend with children of twenty-nine nationalities. Several of the smaller groups live in colonies, like the Syrians, Greeks, and Chinese. But the colonies of the larger groups are reservoirs perpetually filling and flowing."

Again, the anthracite mining towns of Pennsylvania so graphically described by Dr. Peter Roberts in "The Anthracite Coal Communities" form a class by themselves. At least fifty per cent. of the miners and laborers in the anthracite collieries are Slavs and seventy per cent. of the total population in the anthracite counties which he investigated are either of foreign birth or native-born of foreign parents. More than twenty-five different nationalities were represented — Welsh, Germans, Swedes, Slavs, Hebrews, and Poles, full of race pride and devoted to their peculiar customs, dwell side by side in shanties and work together in collieries and breakers. Here we find a constant shifting of the population; special kinds of distress due to strikes, mine disasters, and lockouts; an excessive number of saloons, evictions on a large scale due to the number of miners' houses owned by the companies; most trying educational problems on account of the variety of races and religions represented; and from the point of view of esthetics, the most unrelieved hideousness.

The iron, steel, and coal center at Pittsburgh, embracing that city and the surrounding areas of Allegheny, McKeesport, Duquesne, Homestead, Braddock, Wilmerding, and minor places, represents another type of urban life — in some ways, the worst on the continent. Pittsburgh was characterized by an English member of Parliament as "hell with the lid off," and another English observer has added that Homestead is "hell with the hatches on." These generalizations are more than borne out by recent investigations — the most famous of all being "the Pittsburgh Survey" made by the Russell Sage Foundation. There the grime and squalor of the mining regions are enhanced by a never-ceasing pall of black smoke; labor conflicts with capital have been bitter and prolonged — marked by the famous riots of 1877 and later by the bloody work at Homestead, the seat of Carnegie's main plants; hours of work in many branches are almost unlimited; accidents are frequent and ghastly; and political ideals are at a low ebb — notwithstanding the recent stirring of the "civic conscience."

There is another important type of American municipality represented by the smaller manufacturing towns — ranging in population from ten to one hundred thousand — towns like Akron, Ohio; Fort Wayne, Indiana; Kalamazoo, Michigan; Des Moines, Iowa; and Topeka, Kansas. These towns are based upon more or less diversified industries; their populations are, as a rule, more homogeneous and recruited largely from native stocks; they depend for their trade not a little upon the surrounding rural districts; and a considerable percentage of their inhabitants are home owners.

The political implications of the industrial revolution and the growth of our cities in size and complexity are manifold. The working class is developing a solidarity and consciousness of identity of interest which is manifesting itself in the trade union and socialist movements whose demands are all collectivist in character. The clerical and shopkeeping sections of the bourgeoisie are willing to approve such communal enterprises as waterworks, gas and electric plants, and street railways, if it can be shown that they promise a reduction in taxes and rates. Moreover, enlightened leaders among the middle classes, either because they fear the development of a purely proletarian movement, or regard the economic and human waste of the present state of affairs as intolerable, are advocating the assumption of new and vital functions by the municipalities. To all appearances, the age of tinkering with political machinery and spectacular " wars on bosses " is passing into an era of constructive municipal undertakings on a large scale.

From city to city and type to type, the problems of government must vary. Education in New York, with its thousands of foreigners is one thing, and in Des Moines recruited largely from native stock it is another Housing in the anthracite coal regions does not involve the problem of congestion in a small area, but of providing decent, sanitary homes in the place of the miserable shanties — hideous to look at and demoralizing to live in. Housing in Manhattan, pinched as it is in a narrow island, is another matter altogether. The question of transportation where the inhabitants are scattered over an open plain is quite different from transportation in closely crowded cities where the people live in six- and ten-story tenements. And so on through the whole range of the administrative problems which the city must attack.

Nevertheless, each municipality must deal with some aspects of great problems common to them all: election of officers, efficient management, police, education, housing, transportation, recreation, city planning, and the like.   And the experience of each city throws light on the questions of all other cities.   The positive gains of one are an encouragement to the workers in all; and out of the combined gains in our common municipal experience have come some of the finest achievements in our political life.   It may be, after all, that the American city, which Mr. Bryce thought to be our greatest failure, will prove to be " the hope of democracy."

CHAPTER II

HOME RULE

It is apparent from our examination of the diversities among the cities of the United States that no single plan for municipal administration or municipal functions can be universally adopted. Nearly every city has its own peculiar problems which cannot be met by general laws applicable to all other cities of its size, even in the same State. If our legislatures were made up of representatives from municipalities and the rural members excluded entirely, it may be doubted whether they could deal satisfactorily with the municipal problems of the separate cities under their jurisdiction.

Nevertheless, the municipalities in a great majority of the commonwealths are almost completely at the mercy of the state assembly. The legislature not only makes the charters of the cities and amends them from time to time, but it constantly interferes with minor details in their administrative affairs by creating new offices, or imposing special burdens on finances. For example, the New York Legislature in 1911 added $350,000 to the annual pay rolls of New York City and the boroughs and counties embraced within its limits; and, in addition, passed other bills for special claims against the city which will ultimately total into the millions — bills giving to private persons and property owners the right to present or recover claims against the city for damages resulting from changes in street grades, or for relief from public improvement assessments, which could not be secured by general law.

Not only do legislatures interfere with the fundamental rights and pettiest details of city affairs; their consent is required for some of the most insignificant undertakings on the part of municipal governments. Take, for example, the following list of statutes, compiled by the New York Municipal Government Association, from recent legislation relative to cities and villages in that State, all of which pertain to matters that should normally be within the competence of the city to decide for itself, subject to the general limitations later enumerated:

Hudson, to issue bonds for care and improvement of cemeteries. Laws 1898 (ch. 188).

Binghamton, appointment of stenographer by corporation counsel. Laws 1910 (ch. 67) amending L. 1907 (ch. 751).

Newburg, city funds for band concerts. Laws 1910 (ch. 74) amending L. 1907 (ch. 203).

Ilion, money by taxation for Ilion hospital. Laws 1910 (ch. 246).

Cohoes, to borrow money for equipping fire department. Laws 1910 (ch. 385).

Mt. Vernon, to borrow money for buildings for fire and police department. Laws 1910 (ch. 390) amending L. 1905 (ch. 87).

Johnstown, compensation of chief of police and policemen. Laws 1910 (ch. 661) amending L. 1905 (ch. 447).

Ossining, Westchester County, to issue bonds for certain street improvements. Laws 1910 (ch. 666).

Oneonta, sprinkling and oiling streets. Laws 1911 (ch. 186) amending L. 1902 (ch. 572).

Auburn, sidewalks, curb-stones and gutters. Laws 1911 (ch. 560) amending L. 1906 (ch. 185).

An excellent example of the way in which city authorities are hampered by state constitutions, laws, and judicial decisions is afforded by the following list of measures which the Cleveland council was prevented from carrying into effect under the constitution as in force in 1911. The council discovered that it was not authorized:

To exercise the right to control the use of sub-surface of public highways as a means of obtaining revenue.

To prevent disfigurement of streets by signs and advertisements.

To regulate the architectural appearance and character of buildings fronting upon public highways.

To manufacture ice for charitable distribution.

To prevent the invasion and depreciation of residence sections by the location there of industrial establishments.

To banish chickens and other noise-making animals from the city.

To banish dogs from the city.

To prohibit the erection and maintenance of bill-boards.

To require the erection of gates at grade crossings.

To require the isolation of patients afflicted with tuberculosis.

To provide public lectures and public entertainments.

It is to remedy just these evils that a new constitutional amendment providing a measure of home rule was adopted by the voters of Ohio in September, 1912.

Ordinarily the streets and property of the city are at the mercy of the state legislature, subject only to constitutional limitations. In Massachusetts, for instance, " the legislature may take from a city all control of its streets and provide for work upon them at the expense of the city, but through other agents than those appointed by it. The legislature may authorize a street railway company or a gas company or an electric light company to occupy the streets of a city, even if owned in fee by it, without its consent and without payment to it. In this way, a large proportion of the streets in the cities of Massachusetts are given over to private corporations; and the locations cannot be revoked without the consent of the State." It required a special act of the Massachusetts legislature to secure for cities the use of school buildings as social centers; but, under the constitution, the legislature cannot authorize, and the municipality of its own right cannot provide for, the purchase of wood and coal for sale to its inhabitants, even if they are freezing to death.

Legislatures interfere in the administration of cities as well as in their law making. They create bureaus and commissions endowed with powers to control some of the most fundamental matters within the city's gates. They often create jobs for the weary politicians who are put out of office by city elections, and legislate out of office (by exercising the power of abolition) those in whom the people of the city have placed their trust. They may shorten terms of municipal officers or lengthen them to suit "the needs of the party" with slight consideration for the needs of the city.

For example the state public service commission is imposed upon the city of New York by legislative act, and the substantial control of public utilities, thus taken out of the hands of municipal authorities, is vested in officers appointed by the Governor and senators of the commonwealth. The approval of the state civil service commission is required for all important rules and regulations adopted by the municipal commission. The valuation of special franchises subject to taxation in the city is fixed by a state board of tax commissioners. Thus, in every important matter relative to public service corporations — street railway, gas, electric light, telephone, and other utility concerns — the city is under the control of state boards. And, as if to add insult to injury, the city must pay all of the expenses of the public service commission, and these expenses are not limited by statute; that is, the city of New York must pay any bill which is presented.

In summarizing the principles controlling city government generally (except in the States which have adopted " home rule "), we may say that (1) the city has no general powers of government, but only those powers expressly conferred upon it by the legislature or the constitution of the State; (2) that the courts will usually construe narrowly as against the public and in favor of private parties and corporations the powers enjoyed by cities, such as they are; and (3) that the system of government existing in the city, except in minor details, is the work of the state legislature; and (4) that the rights, powers, and privileges enjoyed by the city by gift of the legislature are only held on sufferance and may be swept away at any time. If, for example, a legislature grants a franchise to a private corporation, it at once becomes a contract under the Federal Constitution and the substantial property rights created by it cannot be taken away without compensation; but if a legislature grants to a city the power to establish its own water-works, it may at any time seize the plant, and transfer it to a private corporation, on such terms as it may choose to provide.

Out of the oppression and exploitation of cities by partizan state legislatures has grown the movement for what is called " municipal home rule. " Defined in the abstract, home rule means that the city should have the power to establish its form of government, create its own offices, and decide upon its public functions. The doctrine is admirably stated in the " Government of American Cities," by Mr. Horace E. Deming as follows:

A city is not a province to be administered by some outside authority, but a government.

A city should have all the powers requisite to satisfy the local needs of the community within its corporate limits.

Within its corporate limits a city should be invested with all the powers of government not inconsistent with the state constitution or general state laws.

The qualified voters of a city subject to the state constitution and to general laws applicable to all the cities of the State (and, as a consequence, not liable to alteration or amendment at the caprice of the state legislature) should be free to make and amend their own form of local government.

The merit principle should be applied throughout the purely administrative public service of the city.

The structural plan of a city government should be simple, centering in a few elected officials responsibility to the people for its conduct.

The successful candidates for elective city office should represent the prevailing local sentiment upon issues of city politics.

When a city is made the agent of the State to enforce and administer general laws within the corporate limits it should never be subjected to the vagaries of arbitrary special legislation, but should always be under the supervision of and responsible to the appropriate central state administrative department.

If a state policy is repugnant to the prevailing sentiment of the citizens of a city, or of a large proportion of them, the State should not attempt to use the city government to administer the policy; for this means the employment of an agent actively hostile to its enforcement.

It is urged by the champions of municipal home rule that the state legislature is unfitted to exercise control over many questions which affect only urban dwellers, because it does not have the requisite time to look into the details of city government or the requisite knowledge of the problems of such government, and does not feel the proper responsibility to urban constituencies. Owing to the constitutional discrimination against cities in favor of the rural districts in the apportionment of representatives, the assemblymen from rural regions are able to impose upon the cities laws and institutions wholly unsuited to their conditions. In the next place, it is contended by the advocates of home rule that there are a number of purely city problems which cannot have any considerable interest for the people of the State at large. They say, for example, that the paving and lighting of the streets, the provision of means of transportation, the establishment of water-works, the maintenance of markets, and many other similar matters should be left entirely to the determination of the municipal voters.

Even if the legislature gave careful attention to the special and local bills before it, the system of absentee law-making would be highly reprehensible. But the legislature does not give proper attention to these local matters. From the nature of the case, it cannot. It must depend upon the judgment of the members from the city to which a particular measure refers, and their judgment is not always a just or honest one. Spoilsmen who have failed with their schemes in a city often find relief in the general confusion that covers the multitudinous labors of the state assembly. Local legislation is used by the party whips to beat members into line on matters that have absolutely no relation to municipal affairs. For instance, a member is expected by his city to get through a special law authorizing the municipality to issue bonds for some needed public work. It looks simple enough. He is to convince the proper committee of the "reasonableness" of the bond issue. In many cases, however, he has to trade his vote on some other matter in order to secure the word of the legislative leaders which will allow his bond issue to go through. The chances are that he may have to vote against a measure of state-wide interest, which he believes to be for the public good, in order to get his local bill through. Without his bond issue, he is politically dead, and to get it he votes "right" on something that is wrong.

The obvious and constantly recurring evils of legislative interference with municipal affairs are everywhere recognized, and they are admitted even by the opponents of home rule. Nevertheless, these opponents urge — there are few, if any, purely municipal functions which have no interest for the State at large, and fundamental matters of economic policy cannot be placed at the mercy of city councils already more notorious than state legislatures. If the city wishes to establish water-works, it is pointed out, it must go sometimes, as New York City has gone, a hundred miles or more into the country, and must, therefore, secure watersheds by a state concession. With the growth of the means of rapid communication, our city populations have spread far beyond the boundaries of municipalities, and the system of municipal transportation accordingly covers far more than the areas under city government. A notable example of this is New York City, which is really the urban center for a vast area extending fifty miles or more in every direction. Owing to the large number of voters in the municipalities, the integrity of the whole state election may depend upon the effectiveness with which the municipal police uphold the election laws and secure an honest count. Finally, the tenements, industries, health, and progress of each city are inextricably woven with larger state and even national problems of the land — taxation, natural resources, labor legislation, and social control. Speaking generally, therefore, the State at large has a fundamental interest in the health and well-being of the city dwellers, and accordingly there is hardly a problem of municipal government that is not vitally connected with the wider problems of state government.

Indeed, Professor Goodnow has shown, by a survey of the historical development of cities, that the whole tendency of modern times is away from that autonomy enjoyed by cities in the Middle Ages. He points out that matters which were once of purely local interest have now become general; that in modern life commerce and industry have become state concerns, and that it is impossible to determine arbitrarily the point at which state interest ends and municipal interest begins. He cites the example of Massachusetts, where the competition of many cities for sources of water-supply became so keen that the State had to interfere and assume general control. He also shows that what may be a municipal function in one city may not be in another, citing, as an example of this, Chicago and New York — in the disposal of sewerage Chicago uses one of the rivers which flows through the State, and thus the sewage question becomes a matter of state concern; while New York is differently situated in this regard, owing to the fact that it can discharge its sewage into the ocean. Professor Goodnow concludes: " Municipal home rule, unless those words are used in a very limited sense, has no just foundation in either history or theory until the conditions of city populations are very different from what they are at present. Municipal home rule without limitation is a shibboleth of days that are past. On account of the reverence in which it is held, it is often used by those who have not the true interests of urban population at heart, or by those who, while possessing good intentions, perhaps are not sufficiently acquainted with the conditions to which they would apply it, and certainly do not consider the problem in the light of the history of Western municipal development."

It is clear, therefore, that the limits of municipal government cannot be fixed for any State or any city by a general rule of law; but it is also clear, in the light of great abuses which cities have suffered at the hands of our state legislatures, that some check must be placed upon the power of the legislature to control municipal affairs. Several plans have been devised to meet this difficult problem.

1. The constitutional convention of Pennsylvania, in 1873, sought to solve the problem by adopting the rule

that the state legislature should not pass any local or special laws regulating the affairs of counties, cities, townships, wards, boroughs, or school districts, but this restriction was found to be entirely too narrow, and when the general assembly sought to legislate for the city of Philadelphia alone by passing a law which should apply to all cities having a population of at least 300,000, the court pronounced this action constitutional. The court held that it could not have been the intention of the framers of the constitution to bolt and rivet down, by fundamental law, the machinery of state government in such a way that it could not perform its necessary functions. "If the classification of cities," said the court, "is in violation of the constitution, it follows of necessity that Philadelphia, as a city of the first class, must be denied the legislation necessary to its present prosperity and future development, or that the small inland cities must be burdened with legislation wholly unsuited to their needs. For if the constitution means what the complainants aver that it does, Philadelphia can have no legislation that is not common to all other cities of the State. . . . We have but to glance at this legislation [relating to quarantine, pilotage, trade, inspection, etc.] to see that most of it is wholly unsuited to small inland cities and that to inflict it upon them would be little short of a calamity. Must the city of Scranton, over a hundred miles from tide-water, with a stream hardly large enough to float a bateau, be subjected to quarantine regulations and have its lazaretto? Must the legislation for a great commercial and manufacturing city with a population of more than a million be regulated by the wants or necessities of an inland city of 10,000 inhabitants?"

2. Recognizing the need for putting some limits to the power of the state legislature to control cities and at the same time recognizing the imperative necessity for special legislation, New York has sought to give the cities a voice in legislating upon the matters especially affecting them. This has been done by a classification of the cities of the State into three groups according to their populations and by providing that special laws — that is, those relating to a single city or less than all the cities of a class — must be passed in conformity to the following principles: When any such special law is passed, it must be transmitted to the mayor of the city affected. In cities of the first class (of over 175,000 inhabitants) it must have the approval of the mayor, and in cities of the other two classes the approval of the mayor and city council, before it can become a law. If the bill is accepted by the proper municipal authority, it is transmitted to the Governor of the State, who may veto it or approve it, as he sees fit. If the bill is not approved by the local authorities, it is transmitted to the branch of the legislature in which it originated, and may become a law if it is repassed (at that session) by the ordinary majority in both branches.

This constitutional provision is further elaborated by a statute which requires that when any such law is transmitted to a city, the authority which has the right of approval or rejection must hold a public hearing on the measure, after having given due notice by publication in newspapers. The design of this is to afford to the friends and opponents of the measure a right to state their reasons for its approval or rejection. This method, while it does not vest the right of final decision in the

city, does guard against hasty legislation, assures publicity, and gives to the authorities of the city some
weight in determining the course of state legislation.
Nevertheless it has not cured the evils of special legislation; and a strong association has been formed to secure the adoption of a constitutional amendment authorizing cities to draft their own charters and conferring
upon them large general powers of self-government.

3. Among the constitutional methods devised for
checking state legislatures and at the same time permitting desirable special legislation for cities, that embodied
in an amendment to the Illinois constitution, adopted in
1904, is important because it has proved more or less
effective, at least in a negative sense. That constitution
has the usual provision against the incorporation or
organization of cities, towns, or villages or changing or
amending their charters by local or special law. To
allow the legislature to give Chicago special treatment
the constitution was amended in 1904 so as to permit
the legislature to pass " all laws which it may deem requisite to effectually provide a complete system of local
municipal government in and for the City of Chicago."
However, it placed a check upon this power of special
legislation for Chicago by providing that no such law
can take effect until approved by a majority of the legal
voters of the city voting thereon at any general, special,
or municipal election. Under this provision the people
of Chicago rejected a special charter passed by the legislature and submitted in 1907. This charter was, in
the main, the work of a commission of Chicago citizens
appointed for that purpose, but it was made obnoxious
when it reached the legislature by the insertion of several

objectionable features. This legislative action caused the rejection of the charter when submitted to the people. So far as one can judge, these constitutional provisions enable the people of Chicago to escape objectionable special legislation while the way is left open for special legislation acceptable to them. They may not be able to get what they want, but they can at least escape improper legislation unless it is embodied in general laws.

4. At least nine States in the Union — Missouri, California, Minnesota, Colorado, Oregon, Oklahoma, Washington, Michigan, and Arizona — have, by constitutional provision, sought to establish home rule for their cities by giving them the right to frame their own charters and by conferring upon them large powers of self-government.

Missouri led in this movement by providing in her constitution (1875) that any city with a population of over 100,000 could frame its own charter, subject, of course, to the constitution and laws of the State. The method prescribed for adopting the charter is as follows: A board of thirteen freeholders is elected by popular vote; this board drafts a charter which is then submitted to the qualified voters, and goes into effect when approved by four-sevenths of them (in St. Louis a simple majority).

California has followed the example of Missouri and enlarged upon her plan in many ways. Any California city having more than 3500 inhabitants may elect by popular vote a board of freeholders to draft its charter. Under an amendment adopted in 1911 fifteen per cent. of the voters may initiate, by petition, proceedings to obtain a new charter so that control over the form of government is vested directly in the citizens. A charter drafted by the board of freeholders must be approved by the voters of the city and by the legislature as well. In addition to the right to draft their own charters, California cities enjoy large powers over local police, education, and municipal elections; and by a constitutional amendment adopted in 1911 they are authorized " to engage in supplying light, water, power, heat, transportation, telephone service, or other means of communication, or to grant any kind of franchise to persons or corporations to perform such services under limitations provided in their charters." Under the home-rule provisions many of California's leading cities — Monterey, Oakland, Berkeley, and Sacramento, for instance —have drafted their own charters; and the repeated extensions of the principle by constitutional amendment show that it has won popular approval.

The other States which have adopted the home-rule plan have also made some variations on the Missouri system. Washington extends home rule only to cities of over 20,000 inhabitants, and requires for approval only a simple majority of the qualified voters of the city voting on the proposition. Under this provision, Tacoma and Spokane adopted commission government.

Minnesota allows any city or village to frame its charter, but provides that the board of freeholders who draft the instrument shall be appointed by the District Court on its own motion or on receiving a petition signed by ten per cent. of the voters; and that the approval of four-sevenths of all those voting at the election shall be necessary to ratify the charter. Although more than forty cities, including St. Paul and Duluth, have adopted frames of government under this constitutional provision, Minneapolis has been unable to secure a home-rule charter owing to the fact that the approval of four-sevenths of those voting at the election is required. For this reason, a constitutional amendment reducing the number to a majority is to be submitted in November, 1912.

Colorado extends home rule to Denver and to cities of the first and second class. It empowers the city council to call a special election to choose twenty-one taxpayers to draft a charter. A majority vote is necessary for the ratification of this charter; and if this vote is not secured a new charter convention must be elected. Colorado also introduces the principle of the initiative by providing that the council must call an election for a charter convention on the petition of five per cent. of the qualified voters.

Oregon forbids the state legislature to enact, amend, or repeal any charter or act of incorporation for any municipality, city, or town, and vests the power to create and amend municipal charters in the legal voters of the respective city or town, subject only to the constitutional and criminal laws of the State.

Oklahoma extends the principle to cities of more than 2000 inhabitants. It allows the city council to call an election to choose a convention of freeholders at any time; and requires the mayor to call such an election upon the petition signed by twenty-five per cent. of the voters. A majority vote is necessary for the ratification of a charter.

The new constitution of Michigan which went into effect in 1909, gives to the legislature of the State the power to provide by general law for the incorporation of cities and villages, and adds that under these general laws the electors of each city and village have the power to adopt and amend their own charter, and through their regularly constituted authorities to pass all laws and ordinances relative to their affairs, subject to the constitution and general laws of the commonwealth. The constitution expressly confers upon each city the power to acquire and to maintain parks, cemeteries, hospitals, alms houses, and all works which involve the public health and safety. It further confers upon each city and village the power to acquire, own, and operate public utilities for supplying water, heat, light, power, and transportation, provided that no municipality of less than 25,000 inhabitants may own transportation facilities.

The Wisconsin Legislature passed in 1911 a home-rule act, and at the same time adopted a joint resolution providing an amendment to the constitution on the subject, which will be submitted to the voters if repassed by a subsequent legislature. In addition to giving the city the power to adopt and amend its own charter, this act reverses the ancient doctrine of the law that the city has only those powers expressly conferred upon it, and lays down the new principle that it is presumed to possess all powers in municipal matters not explicitly denied to it by the constitution and the laws of the State and, of course, the Constitution of the United States. The action of the Wisconsin supreme court in declaring this statute invalid, however, delays the application of the principle until the adoption of the constitutional amendment.

The voters of Ohio, at a special election in September,

1912, approved a proposition establishing home rule in that commonwealth. The provisions of the amendment are thus summarized by Mr. Mayo Fesler who was active in the movement to bring the subject to the attention of the constitutional convention and the State at large:

1. The city or village may determine the form of its government in either of three ways:

(a) A municipality may adopt its own charter by electing a commission of fifteen to frame the charter and submit it to the people for ratification.

(b) The legislature may pass a general or special act which a city or village may adopt by a majority vote.

(c) The legislature shall by general law provide for the government of cities — laws which will automatically take effect in all cities or villages which do not take steps to secure their own charters in the manner indicated above in " a." and " b."

2. Under any form of municipal government " municipalities shall have authority to exercise all powers of local self-government and to adopt and enforce within their limits such local police, sanitary and other regulations as are not in conflict with general laws."

3. Municipalities may acquire, construct, own, lease, operate public utilities and may issue mortgage bonds therefor beyond the general limit of bonded indebtedness prescribed by law, but such mortgage bonds shall be a lien only on the property and revenues of the public utility itself.

4. Municipalities may exercise the right of excess condemnation in appropriating property, provided the bonds issued to pay for such excess shall be a lien only upon the property acquired for the improvement and the excess.

5. The general assembly is given authority to limit the power of municipalities to levy taxes and incur debts for local purposes; to require uniform reports from cities as to their financial condition; and to provide for the examina-

tion of the accounts of all municipalities or of public utilities
operated by the municipality.

Nebraska and Texas will vote on home-rule amendments at the general election of 1912; and the agitation
for the adoption of the principle is well advanced in all
States that are devoting any considerable attention to
municipal affairs.

The experience of the commonwealths which have
tried the home-rule plan has been, in general, highly satisfactory. There is apparently no demand for a return
to the old condition of affairs in which the city lay at
the mercy of the legislature. Indeed, the development
has all been in the direction of extending the doctrine
and making charter-drafting more popular in character.

The substantial powers enjoyed by the city where genuine home rule is established are twofold: the right to
draft its own charter or frame of government, and the
right to perform any function not forbidden to it by
the constitution or general laws of the State. The latter right is, of course, the more important and fundamental of the two; for it confers upon the city the full
authority to perform the new municipal functions rendered imperative by the industrial revolution.

These two rights, however, are not without limitation
for the State must reserve its general legislative power
and this necessity makes the idea of "home rule" far
more complex than it seems at first sight. A constitution must deal in general terms; it cannot enumerate the
matters on which general laws can be made nor minutely
characterize them. Consequently, here is a new field of
law-making for the courts. They must decide when any

general law is really "general," and when it is really "special"—that is designed to defeat the constitutional rights of home rule. Here, as in other fields of law, the attitude of the court on matters of municipal and social economy will be the controlling factors. The way of home rule is beset with thorns — like many other ways that seem smooth at first glance.

Indeed, there is a vast number of necessary limitations upon local autonomy which grow out of the intimate connection between the city and the general political and economic life of the State.

In the first place, the State cannot surrender entirely to the city its control over elections, particularly those at which state officers are chosen. The people of the commonwealth as a whole are vitally interested in the purity of the ballot and in preventing corrupt and fraudulent practices of every kind.

The State can never divest itself of the power to pass laws relative to health, safety, and public welfare — known as police power. Of course the State must share its power so far as local affairs are involved, but state supervision and control can never be wholly surrendered.

Inasmuch as the State derives a large portion of its revenues from franchises and property located within the cities, it cannot surrender the general power of taxation in such a manner as to cripple its own revenues. In connection with this general power of taxation, the State is necessarily concerned as to the amount of indebtedness which its cities may incur; and it must establish positive debt limits for municipalities in order to safeguard its own finances.

The State is also interested in maintaining certain standards of education throughout its jurisdiction; and, although it may leave the city free to provide its own organization and administrative machinery for educational purposes, and allow a great deal of diversity in methods, it must retain the general control.

The State may very well require also uniform standards and methods of accounting throughout all the cities, and maintain administrative supervision over municipal financial officers.

It is clear that in practice the boundary line between legitimate state intervention in municipal affairs is difficult to draw; and that shrewd legislatures, if supported by judicial sanction, may pass a great deal of special legislation under the guise of general acts, in spite of home-rule charters. Nevertheless, it is a decided gain to have written in the fundamental law of the State a provision authorizing cities to draft their own charters and to exercise general powers. It is even a gain to forbid the legislature to pass special city laws fixing wages or salaries of city employees, creating or abolishing city offices, prescribing duties for them, or exempting any person, in part or in whole, from any assessment or tax levied by the municipalities. If these forms of special legislation were excluded, our cities would be at least partially relieved from the irritating charter-tinkering and " ripper " legislation which contributes so much to the chaos existing in American municipal affairs.

CHAPTER III

MUNICIPAL DEMOCRACY

UNLIKE England, the States of the American Union, which enjoy the power to decide who may vote, subject to the limitations of the Federal Constitution, have not made any distinction between the qualifications for voters in general and in local elections. Any person authorized to vote for state officers is also qualified to vote for municipal officers. Two exceptions only bring out the rule: Rhode Island has adopted the principle of manhood suffrage for general purposes but requires every voter in city-council elections to possess real or personal property to the value of $134 — a restriction which reduces the vote about sixty per cent. in Providence; and Kansas admits women to the municipal suffrage while denying them the right to vote in state elections.

Contrary to the popular impression the United States at the beginning of its career as an independent nation, did not recognize the principle of universal manhood suffrage. When the commonwealths framed their new constitutions, during the revolutionary period, they continued, with some modifications, the property qualifications which had prevailed during the colonial period and were based upon old English precedents. In nearly every State the suffrage was limited by the constitution or the laws to property owners or taxpayers. In some States, for instance, Virginia, only the holders of real property could vote. In other States, for example, Massachusetts, the suffrage was extended to the owners of real and personal property of a certain value. In New York only freeholders possessing a stipulated amount of real estate could vote for Governor and senators, while another and lower qualification was placed upon voters for members of the state assembly.

The conservative thinkers of the eighteenth century, who established the independence of the United States, generally agreed in regarding the owners of land as " the best depositaries of political power." Their views were well summed up by Mr. Dickinson in the Federal Convention of 1787, when he declared that the maintenance of the freeholding qualification was a necessary defense " against the dangerous influences of those multitudes without property and without the principles with which our country like all others will in time abound."

The struggle to break down property qualifications imposed upon the suffrage by the early constitutions began almost immediately after their establishment; and during the first quarter of the nineteenth century, it became apparent that the United States was destined to give a full trial to the experiment of universal white manhood suffrage. In 1801 and 1809 Maryland swept away the property qualifications laid down in the constitution of 1776; in 1821 Massachusetts abolished the property test. In the same year New York abandoned the freehold qualification imposed on those voting for Governor and senators, and five years later established the principle of universal white manhood suffrage. By the middle of the century the United States was committed to the doctrine that every adult white male should be entitled to vote in all elections regardless of the amount of property which he held or the religious beliefs which he entertained. And at the close of the Civil War, state action and federal amendments admitted the negroes to the suffrage on the same terms as white men.

Since the Civil War the suffrage has been extended to women in six States: Wyoming, Utah, Colorado, Idaho, Washington, and California. During this period, however, there has been a tendency to impose restrictions of one kind or another upon voters. In about one-third of the commonwealths some kind of an educational test is applied. For example, in Massachusetts, the voter must be able to read the constitution of the State in the English language and write his own name. In some of the Southern States the educational test is employed as an alternative qualification for voters. But there the primary purpose is to exclude the negroes from the suffrage without disfranchising any whites, no matter how low they may be in the social scale. In a few States, as, for example, Tennessee and Arkansas, a poll tax is imposed upon voters. The effect of the various restrictions established since the war in the Southern States has been to disfranchise a very large proportion of the negro population, particularly in the lower seaboard commonwealths.

It can be stated, however, that the recent restrictions upon the suffrage imply no return to the older ideal that property alone should be represented in the Government. In an overwhelming number of the States the principle of universal manhood suffrage is accepted and applied, subject only to limitations of residence and age. Those who would change or reform our municipal government must recognize the fact that the direct rule of the propertied class has disappeared in the United States.

The Boston Finance Commission reported, in 1909, that of the 110,000 registered voters in that city, only 18,500, or 16.5 per cent., paid a property tax, while the remaining 91,500, or 83.5 per cent., were assessed a poll tax, which a large majority of them did not pay. In the neighboring town of Brookline, 58 per cent. of the voters were property owners, but the average percentage of property-owning electors for the entire district of Greater Boston was only 23.

It was suggested to the commission that the payment of the poll tax should be established as a prerequisite for voting, and that an additional vote should be bestowed on those possessing certain property and educational qualifications. It was further proposed that non-resident property owners should be given the municipal suffrage, and that city employees should be disfranchised. The commission, however, refused to recommend any of these changes. It declared that there should be no alteration in the qualification of electors " at least until it is demonstrated that the principle of universal suffrage is unable to secure good results from a form of government suited to the conditions under which it operates."

In the midst of this democratic development, it is surprising to find in some Western States a recognition of the peculiar rights of property in municipal government. The home-rule provisions of several States mentioned above, vest the drafting of charters in the hands

of boards of freeholders. This is based on the Napol-
eonic idea that any one may be permitted with safety
to vote, if the initiation of measures is left to the " proper " authorities. We have, also, another example in the
clause of the Denver charter under which franchise questions can be voted upon only by taxpayers. In the election of May 15, 1906, when certain public-service companies were working for the renewal of franchises, it
was claimed that the concerns interested manufactured
hundreds of voters by deeding vacant lots to their employees.

Broadly speaking, however, there is nothing in recent
American political history to indicate a tendency to narrow the municipal suffrage. On the contrary, it is highly
probable that the next few years will see the wide-spread
enfranchisement of women. Legislators have been directing their attention to devising methods for safeguarding the ballot against fraudulent practices and encouraging the wider participation of the voters in municipal affairs, through direct primaries and the initiative and referendum.

Laws requiring the registration, or enrolment, of persons entitled, and intending, to vote are almost universal;
and in a few of the greater cities, like New York and
San Francisco, special provisions are made for requiring
the personal identification of voters. According to the
New York law, the voter, on registering, in addition to
answering the ordinary questions, must give the number
of the floor or room in which he lives and the name of
the householder or tenant with whom he lives; he is furthermore required to sign his name if he can write, and
when on election day he appears to vote he must again

sign his name opposite the first signature. In case the voter is unable to write, he must answer a long list of questions with regard to his private affairs, residence, and employment; and when he appears on election day he is required to answer the same questions. By a comparison of the signatures or the answers to the questions, the election officials are able to detect frauds and thus prevent from voting a large number of " floaters " and " repeaters. " There is no doubt but that the effect of the law has been most salutary.

The official Australian or secret ballot is now, with some minor and insignificant exceptions, used in all municipal as well as state elections. Before the movement for the secret official ballot began some twenty-five years ago, any party or candidate could furnish ballots in elections, and these ballots were distributed freely among the voters. This system made it possible for those who bought votes to make sure that " the goods were delivered," for they could stand near the polls and watch the venal voter deposit the ballot which had been placed in his hands.

Under the Australian ballot law, ballots are provided at public expense; the names of the candidates of all parties are printed on the same ticket; tickets can be secured only at the official polling place; they must be marked secretly in the polling booth and then deposited, properly folded, in the official ballot box. It is not claimed that the Australian ballot has destroyed entirely corrupt practices in municipal elections, but a comparison between conditions existing to-day in municipal elections and those prevailing fifty years ago reveals decided gains.

Within recent years a remarkable attempt has been

made to secure to the voters of each party a more direct control over the nomination of their candidates. As every one knows, it is the practice of each party to put up its list of candidates for the various municipal offices of mayor, comptroller, councilmen, and so forth. A few years ago it was the well-nigh universal custom for each party to nominate its candidates by "conventions" of delegates chosen by party voters at an election which was called a "primary." When the revelations of corrupt practices, such as the Tweed exposure in New York in 1871, began to stir the public conscience, reformers at once declared that it was the convention system of nominating candidates that enabled the corrupt "bosses" to place their henchmen in office. It was a notorious fact that, generally speaking, only a small proportion of the voters participated in the primaries at which delegates to the conventions were chosen, and it was thus possible for political leaders to secure delegates of their own making by controlling a small coterie of active workers in each precinct.

Under these circumstances many good citizens came to feel that it was a waste of time to bother with voting at the primary when the results had already been determined by the political leaders in advance. Out of the dissatisfaction with the convention method of nominating delegates has grown the "direct" primary movement.

The direct primary is simply an election within the party at which party members are given an opportunity to vote immediately for the candidates whom they wish to represent the party in the coming election. Party members who wish to become candidates for nomination in the primary have their names placed on the ballot, usually by a petition signed by a small number of voters. The direct primary has supplanted the convention method in more than three-fourths of the States of the Union; and it has been applied widely in city as well as in state and county elections. It is trite to say that this nation-wide experiment has not met the high expectations of its promoters, nor fulfilled the dire prophecies of its opponents.

In only a few instances, however, has it been abandoned, and in these instances the convention has not been restored but some new method of nomination has been devised. For example, the direct primary was adopted for the municipal elections in Boston, and in 1909 the Boston Finance Commission, in its report on the condition of the government of that city, presented the following indictment of the institution for municipal elections:

While the present system of nominating the candidates for mayor and city council at primary elections was adopted to correct certain abuses incident to the caucus and delegate convention, it has given rise to new evils more serious still; and it operates to make the nomination and election of representative citizens to the elective offices of the city government more difficult than under the former system.

Whatever force there may be in the argument that party responsibility is a guarantee of good behavior and a desirable check on individual misconduct, this argument presupposes the existence of a true political party with principles, organization, and discipline.

The direct primary system was not intended to abolish partizanship in municipal government; but in its practical working, there is no longer the partizanship of a great organization bound, theoretically at least, by party principles, and having some regard for its political responsibilities in the State at large. It is a partizanship of ward organizations, calling themselves Republican or Democratic as the case may be, but representing no municipal policies capable of formulation.

Under the convention system it is possible for a party to nominate or endorse a candidate from the other party if it so desires. This has frequently been done in the case of the school committee and the county officers, and once in the case of the mayor. Under the present primary system this opportunity disappears entirely. No Republican can be nominated in the Democratic primaries, and no Democrat can be nominated in the Republican primaries. Voters who would like to see their party endorse a strong member of the opposite party for a municipal election rather than put up a weak candidate of their own are powerless to accomplish this result.

Our present electoral machinery is wholly unsuited to the requirements of successful municipal government through popular suffrage. Instead of bringing the choice of candidates nearer to the people it has erected well-nigh insurmountable barriers between the individual voter and the free selection to which he is entitled, and which he must have before he can discharge his duty as a citizen. It has made it artificially difficult to secure good nominations; it has debarred the best and most representative citizens from participation in the government; it has increased the power of money in elections; it has practically handed the city over to the ward politicians. It tends to create bad government, no matter how strongly the people may desire good government; and to discredit the capacity of the people when congregated together in great cities to administer their municipal affairs.

The effect of the present system of nominations upon the mayoralty elections has been particularly unfortunate, and so generally deplored as to require little comment, in this report.

Under the direct primary system a strong, honest, and popular man is theoretically able to secure a nomination against the opposition of the party organization or "machine"; but practically he can do it only by entering into a personal contest with the ward politicians in every district. Desirable men shrink from this sort of a contest. A party nomination for mayor in this city is not so likely to be a choice by the party of its best candidate, as a personal contest between two or more active seekers for the office.

In abandoning the direct primary on the recommendation of the Finance Commission, the voters of Boston did not restore the old party caucus, but provided that nominations for mayor and councilmen in the future should be made by petitions signed by a stipulated number (5000) of voters.

It would be a mistake, however, to conclude that the direct primary has been frequently regarded as a failure in municipal elections. A prominent citizen of St. Paul — Mr. Hugh T. Halbert, president of the Roosevelt Club of that city, and former chairman of the Republican city committee — stated before the New York Joint Committee which investigated the primary election laws in 1910 that the direct primary there was a decided improvement over the convention method of nomination. One witness before the committee had declared that, under the direct primary, any man could get into office by distributing liquor and cigars. To this assertion Mr. Halbert replied:

I differ from that statement very decidedly, as a reflection on the voting public of Minnesota. And if it were true it would be infinitely preferable to the purchase of the support of the politicians, or a boss, so-called. I differ from the statement that the newspapers have a great deal of influence under the primary election law. They do have influence when they represent the wishes of the people. They never have any influence when they misrepresent the wishes of the people. I differ from his statement that there is very little interest, comparatively speaking, in the primaries, or not any more interest than in the party caucuses. I think it might be stated advisedly that under the party caucuses if we had 10 per cent. of the voters at a caucus we were lucky. That at the primaries 50 to 75 per cent. of the voters vote. Comparing the two systems, if you will allow me, under the convention system and under the primary system, there are three parties that have got to be considered, the voter, the aspirant for office, and the public at large. . . . The question is raised, did the voter have more interest in the choice of the candidate for office under the convention system than he has now. If only 10 per cent. attended at a caucus where 50 per cent. of the voters now vote at the primary, it is proof conclusive that he has more interest under the present primary system. There is another reason why he has more interest. Under the old delegate and convention system the voter's wishes were absolutely subordinated to the wishes of the men in control of the party, or so-called boss; and the question becomes one of wise, or unwise leadership, so far as a man running for office is concerned. Under the convention and delegate system, as we had it in this State and in this county, we had the peculiar anomaly of an elective officer and a man who should be elected by the people, who was practically appointed by a coterie of politicians; and as soon as he got the appointment he was assured of his election.

An examination of recent legislation relative to nominations for municipal elections reveals a decided tendency, even in the States which have the direct primary, towards elimination of party designations altogether and the nomination of municipal officers by petition. This newer method is in part the outcome of the standing protest against the injection of national and state politics into municipal elections. Where nomination by petition is employed the idea behind it is the elimination of national politics as well as the abandonment of the direct primary.

An excellent example of non-partizan nominations is found in the primary system of Des Moines, Iowa, where commission government is in operation. No party emblems are allowed on the ballot used at this primary; names are placed upon it by petition; and the two aspirants receiving the highest vote for mayor and the eight aspirants receiving the highest number of votes for councilmen (four to be elected), are put upon the regular ballot as candidates for the offices of mayor and councilmen. The regular ballot is then submitted to the voters at the municipal election. While this system does not prevent members of parties from concentrating their efforts upon their own candidates, it does prevent the politicians from forcing their ready-made " slates " upon the voters. Furthermore, at the regular election it focuses the attention of the public upon only two candidates for each of the five offices.

A further advance has been made upon this method by a few cities in California, notably San Francisco and Los Angeles, where the second election is not held in the case of any person who receives at the primary, an absolute majority of all the votes cast. For example, candidates for the office of mayor of Los Angeles are nominated by petition; and, if, at the primary, any one of the persons nominated receives an absolute majority of the votes cast, he is thereupon declared the elected mayor of the city. If, however, no candidate secures such an absolute majority, the names of the two persons standing highest at the primary are placed upon the official ballot, and the one who polls the higher vote at the election becomes mayor. The same rule is applied in Birmingham, Alabama, under the law of 1911, creating commission government, and in the Idaho commission government law of the same year. This system has a double advantage. It makes unnecessary a second election when it is clear that one of the candidates at the primary is the voters' choice, and it also obviates the danger of election by mere plurality of votes, which is possible when there are three or more candidates who divide the vote fairly equally among themselves.

We have seen above the advances made in the United States in the direction of universal suffrage, and we have noted also the recent efforts of legislators to provide easier ways for the voters to participate directly in the choice of their candidates for office. In an increasing number of cities, the work of the voter does not end at the polling booth where he casts his ballot for city officers. Nearly all of the States have provided a system of initiative and referendum, under varying conditions, for one or more cities within their borders — particularly for commission-governed cities.

The initiative is a device whereby any person or group of persons may draft a charter amendment or ordinance, and, on securing the signatures of a small percentage of the voters, may compel the city officials, with or without the intervention of the council, to submit the same to popular vote. If the required popular approval is secured, the proposal becomes a law. The referendum is a plan whereby a small percentage of the voters may demand that any ordinance passed by the council shall be submitted to the electorate and approved by a stipulated majority before going into effect.

Nearly one-fourth of the States of the Union, including Oregon, Utah, Montana, Nevada, Oklahoma, Maine, Missouri, Arkansas, Colorado, California, South Dakota, and Arizona, have adopted the initiative and referendum in some form for state-wide purposes. Nearly all of these States apply the principle to local and municipal affairs; and many commonwealths, which do not as yet have a state-wide initiative and referendum, have adopted the institution for some or all municipal corporations.

The percentage of voters necessary to initiate any municipal ordinance or resolution varies from State to State. In South Dakota, the right to propose laws, ordinances, and resolutions for the government of any city or town rests with any 5 per cent. of the electors of the political subdivision affected — the percentage in each instance being based upon the number of votes cast at the last preceding general election for the highest executive officer of the municipality. The Ohio law of 1911, on the other hand, provides that municipal ordinances may be proposed only by 30 per cent. of the qualified voters of the municipality.

It is the common practice to submit the measure initiated by petition to the city council first, and if the council passes the initiative measure without change or amendment, it thereupon becomes law unless the referendum is applied to it. If, however, the city council refuses to adopt the initiated ordinance, it is thereupon submitted to popular vote, and goes into effect when approved by the voters at the election.

The number of votes necessary to carry any measure

proposed by the initiative varies. In South Dakota, for example, an ordinance referred to the voters of a city goes into effect if approved by a majority of the votes cast for and against the same. Under the Ohio law, on the other hand, an ordinance does not become operative unless it receives a majority of all the votes cast in the election at which the measure is submitted. As is well known, a considerable proportion of the electors who vote for candidates do not take the trouble to express their opinion on laws referred to them. Under the Ohio system, those who do not vote on the measure referred are thus counted against it.

The percentage of voters necessary to require the submission of any ordinance passed by the town council to popular scrutiny likewise varies from State to State. It is the usual practice to provide that no law, ordinance, or resolution for the government of the city, except such as are for the immediate preservation of public peace, health, or safety, or the expenditure of money in the ordinary course of municipal administration, shall go into effect until the expiration of a stipulated period.

South Dakota provides that 5 per cent. of the electors of any city may file a petition within the period fixed, requiring the submission of any law to the voters of the municipality; and unless the ordinance receives a majority of the votes cast for and against it, it falls to the ground.

According to the Ohio law, any ordinance, resolution, or other measure of a municipal corporation, granting a franchise, creating a right, involving the expenditure of money, or exercising any other power delegated to the municipality by the general assembly, must be submitted to the qualified electors for their approval or rejection, if within thirty days after the passage of the measure by the council, there is filed with the city clerk a petition signed by fifteen per cent. of the qualified electors ordering the submission of the measure to popular vote.

The constitution of Michigan, although it does not provide for a general system of initiative and referendum, does order a popular vote in certain municipal matters. It provides that any city or village can acquire, own, and operate certain public utilities if the proposition has been approved by three-fifths of the electors voting thereon at a regular or special city election. It is interesting to note that at such elections women taxpayers, having the qualifications of male electors, are entitled to vote.

The initiative and referendum have been extensively employed in municipal affairs in the enactment of ordinances and the granting of franchises, and some very careful studies of the operation of the system have been made. For example, in the municipal election of Portland, Oregon, on June 5, 1911, twenty-three distinct legislative proposals were submitted to the voters of the city — thirteen amendments to the city charter submitted by the councilmen, four amendments and four ordinances submitted by initiative, and two ordinances which had been passed by the council, submitted on a referendum. Professor G. H. Haynes in an article published in *The Political Science Quarterly* for September, 1911, makes a careful study of the merits of these several measures and analyzes the vote cast at the election. His figures show a large and discriminating vote on the referenda, averaging 83 per cent. of the total vote cast for the officer standing highest in the election. Some hasty measures proposed by the council and by initiative petition were decisively rejected, and some excellent schemes were approved. Professor Haynes closes his survey by saying: "Unquestionably several of the voters' verdicts were ill-judged. But that city may indeed count itself fortunate whose representative council, during the past year, has shown more intelligent discrimination between the wise and the unwise, the far sighted and the short sighted, the public spirited and the selfish, than the Portland voters exhibited in the election of last June."

The latest instrument of public control, put in the hands of the voter, is the recall — a device whereby, on petition of a certain percentage of the electors, a public officer may be required to submit his policy and official conduct to a review at the polls. Like all other general principles, the recall is subject to a large number of variations, which ought to be taken into consideration by those who have occasion to pass upon the merits or demerits of the system.

It may be applied on petition of 10 per cent. of the voters as in San Francisco, of 15 per cent. as in Oakland, Cal., 20 per cent. as in Fort Worth, Texas, 25 per cent. as in a majority of the commission-governed cities, 35 per cent. as in Dallas, Texas, and even 75 per cent. as in the commission cities of Illinois, under the law of 1910 — a percentage which was found excessive and reduced to 55 per cent. in the following year.

The period which an official shall be allowed to serve before the recall is applicable is an important element to be considered. He may be removed at any time, as under the Iowa commission government law of 1907; or he may be allowed to hold his office at least six months before the recall can be brought into operation, as under the Oregon constitutional amendment of 1908. The New Jersey commission government law of 1911 stipulates that no recall petition shall be filed against an officer until he has served at least twelve months. Again, as in Boston, he may be allowed to retain his position for two years before he is brought to book at the polls.

Another element to be considered in connection with the recall is whether a continuous bombardment of an officer by recall petitions shall be allowed. The New Jersey statute of 1911 specifically forbids this by stating that not more than one recall petition shall be filed against the same officer during his term of office. The Oregon constitutional amendment of 1908, however, permits a continuous performance, by providing that after one petition and a special election, further recall petitions may be filed against the same officer during the term for which he was elected, if the petitioners first pay into the public treasury an amount sufficient to cover the election expenses for the preceding special election.

A fourth element, which should be overlooked under no circumstances, is the vote at the special election which may be required to displace an officer against whom a petition for recall has been filed. The recall petition may be divided into two parts. The question, " Shall the officer against whom the petition has been filed be recalled? " may be submitted separately, and it may be provided that the officer shall not be deemed recalled unless there is cast against him an absolute majority of all the votes cast in the special election or a vote equivalent to a majority of all the votes cast at the election at which he was at first chosen. If an officer may be recalled by a mere majority of those voting at the special election, he may be thrown out of office by a small minority of the electors of the city in case a light vote is polled. In most cities having the recall, however, the proposition, " Shall the officer against whom the petition is filed be recalled? " is not separately submitted to popular vote, but, after the filing of the petition against him, the officer in question is simply allowed to stand as a candidate for reëlection and to retain his office only in case he polls the highest vote at the special election.

After these generalities, we may now consider some types of recall systems in force in the United States. In Des Moines, Iowa, the holder of any elective office may be removed at any time. The petition for removal must be signed by electors equal in number to at least 25 per cent. of the entire vote for candidates for the office of mayor at the last preceding general election. The petition for recall thus signed must be filed with the city clerk, and contain a general statement of the grounds for which the removal is sought. If the clerk finds the petition to be sufficient he submits it to the council and the council must fix the date for an election to be held not less than thirty days nor more than forty days after the date of the clerk's certificate. The officer who is thus attacked may be a candidate to succeed himself, and unless he requests otherwise in writing the clerk places his name on the official ballot without nomination. Other candidates for the office are placed on the ballot by petition. At the recall election, therefore, the voter is simply given an opportunity to choose from among a number of candidates, including the officer against whom the recall petition is filed, in case the latter sees fit to make a fight for his office. If at the election some person other than the incumbent receives the highest number of votes the officer is deemed removed, upon the qualification of his successor.

A second type of recall is offered by the commission-government charter of Sacramento, California, adopted by popular vote on November 7, 1911, subject to ratification by the legislature. According to this charter any elective officer may be removed after he has held his office for at least six months. The petition for recall must be signed by at least ten per cent. of the total number of voters registered at the last municipal election. The petition for recall is filed with the city clerk and, if he finds it to be sufficient and the officer sought to be removed does not resign, the city commission, if the petition requests a special election, shall cause the same to be held within not less than fifty nor more than sixty days after the filing of the petition. Before any petition is circulated for signatures an affidavit in triplicate must be filed with the city clerk by or on behalf of the persons proposing the recall; and the affidavit must contain a declaration of the intention to circulate a petition for the recall of the said officer, a statement (not more than 200 words) giving the grounds for such recall, and the address of the party making the affidavit. The officer sought to be recalled is given five days in which to formulate a statement of not more than 200 words, justifying his course in office. These reasons for and against the recall of the officer must be printed on each individual certificate forming a part of the petition. At the recall election, the reasons for and against the recall are set. forth on the ballot; and the question submitted to the voters is simply, " Shall the officer (naming the officer) be recalled? Yes, or No." If the majority of the voters voting in the election vote in favor of the recall, the officer is deemed removed and the city commission appoints his successor to hold office until the next general municipal election at which the office is filled in the ordinary manner.   In case the whole commission of the city is removed by recall a special election is held.

A third type of recall is that established in Boston, for the mayor of the city.   There the mayor is elected for a term of four years.   However, at the state election in the second year of the mayor's term, the secretary of the commonwealth causes to be printed on the official ballot to be used in the city of Boston, the question, " Shall there be an election for mayor at the next municipal election? " with the words " yes " and " no " and squares in which the voter may designate his answer by a cross.   If a majority of the qualified voters registered in the city for the state election vote in the affirmative, there must be an election for mayor at the municipal election held in January immediately following the state election.   At the Boston election of 1911 the question of the recall of the mayor was duly submitted, and a vote of 37,692 was cast for the recall and 32,144 against it, a majority of a little over 5000 for the recall.   However, the total registered vote of the city at that election was 110,000, and although a majority of the voters at the election favored the recall of the mayor, that vote was about 18,000 short of a majority of the total registered vote in the city.   Hence, the mayor was allowed to retain his office to the end of the term of four years, without being compelled to go before the voters in an election.

The recall has been widely adopted and is indeed commonly regarded, though not rightly, as an essential part of commission government; but its application has been very limited. It was used for the first time in Los Angeles in 1904, against a councilman, Mr. Davenport, who was ousted, his opponent receiving 63 per cent. of the votes cast. Five years later, the recall was invoked against A. C. Harper, the mayor of Los Angeles, who was charged with treating public appointments as private spoils, and non-enforcement of the laws against vice; and in the spring election of 1909, Harper was unseated by popular vote. On another occasion, in Los Angeles, the city council voted away a valuable franchise in the face of a storm of popular protest; and on finding that the petitions for recall were being signed by a surprisingly large number of voters, the councilmen revoked the franchise.

In 1911, the mayor of Seattle, Hiram C. Gill, was recalled on the charge that he was unduly favoring local public-service corporations and particularly encouraging gambling and other forms of vice by careful police protection. An investigation into the conduct of the mayor's administration by the city council revealed a number of specific instances of maladministration. A "Public Welfare League" was formed, which conducted a campaign against Mayor Gill, and at the election in February, 1911, he was ousted by the choice of a successor. About the same time the recall was put into operation in Tacoma, and resulted in the removal of the mayor.

On the workings of the recall in general, a careful student of the system, Mr. H. S. Gilbertson, says:

Those prophets who have predicted that the people with this new political ax in easy reach would be swinging it at frequent intervals have been disappointed. Mob rule, so often the subject of earnest warnings, has failed to raise its head as yet. The recall, to date, has been invoked successfully only where a clear case has been established, showing that an officer has violated, wilfully and flagrantly, what will generally be understood as better public sentiment in the community. In the case of the mayors in Los Angeles, Seattle, and Tacoma, the issues took on a distinctly moral aspect on account of the questions of police administration involved. In San Diego the councilman openly defied the charter. In Los Angeles, Councilman Davenport was convicted as a too-friendly friend of " special interests." In Dallas, the demand was for fair play to certain individuals. On the other hand, in Huron, where the question was one purely of financial policy, the recall was unsuccessful. Thus the available evidence, in the infancy of this new institution, ought to be sufficient to allay the fears of those who profess a horror of popular control.

In respect to the publicity which accompanies recall proceedings, the officials indicted by popular opinion have had a hearing, whose thoroughness is unique in American city politics. Through the simplicity of the situation, attention is directed to one, or a very small group of persons, and a single set of issues. Ideal " short ballot " conditions prevail, and there is no confusing the voter as to what is going on; no outside assistance is needed. The verdict of the election, for good or evil, is the people's verdict. Recall campaigns, too, have been the source of intense popular interest. Newspaper space was used up in great abundance in the mayoralty campaigns, and every available public auditorium was employed. The most accurate index of public interest, however, was the large vote, which, in

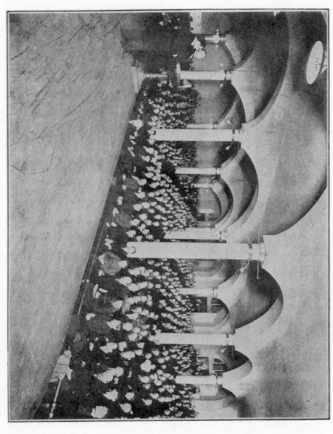

Courtesy of The People's Institute.

Audience at free lecture, Great Hall of Cooper Institute, New York City.

some cases, has exceeded that cast in a presidential year. Popular interest in the processes of a recall is not always impartial and judicial, to be sure. Personalities naturally come prominently to the fore through the very simplicity of the situation.

No survey of municipal democracy which is confined to a description of primaries and elections is complete; for the citizen influences his government not only at the polls but also through membership in private associations, performing services which are quasi-governmental in character. Indeed, a study of the origin and development of some of the most interesting and important recent municipal enterprises, in nearly every case, leads us back to the work of a private organization of citizens who, seeing an aspect of social work neglected, have set about to remedy the situation.

The desirability and practicability of many municipal reforms have been first demonstrated by private effort and then taken over by the municipality. For example, the appalling death rate among children in New York City, due in part, to a defective milk supply, first attracted the attention of some public-spirited citizens who formed a milk committee and began to maintain during the summer and winter milk stations at which pure milk could be secured at a low price. The efficacy of this work was soon discovered, and in the budget prepared in October, 1911, provision was made for the maintenance of fifty-two milk stations at the expense of the city under the control of the health department. A number of the milk stations originally established by the milk committee were taken over by the city.

A survey of the innumerable and varied committees

and associations which are quasi-governmental in character — in that they are participating directly in government or perhaps in governmental action — shows that there are four general types.

In the first place, there are associations which are more or less political in character, although they claim to be non-partizan. Such an association is the Municipal Voters' League of Chicago, established in 1896. This League is composed of voters scattered throughout the city, who express their approval of its purposes and methods by signing cards. The purpose of the League is not the establishment of a new party, but the concentration of public opinion and public scrutiny upon the candidates nominated by other parties. It is, in a word, a publicity committee. Previous to each election it maintains headquarters into which pour suggestions for nominations and criticisms of city officials. As soon as candidates are announced or nominated the League sends letters of inquiry to them, in order to ascertain what stand they intend to take if elected; and throughout the campaign it labors to secure the widest publicity in regard to the character and policies of the various candidates.

A second type of quasi-political organization is the United Improvement Association of Boston, which is a federation of local improvement societies throughout the city. The Association has a secretary and an executive committee; it publishes a monthly bulletin, dealing with various questions arising from time to time in the city. It holds periodical conferences of delegates from the local organizations; and at these conferences resolutions involving changes in the city government and administration are adopted. The Association maintains various committees for the study of particular questions: parks, playgrounds, and public buildings, legal and legislative affairs, streets, schools, transportation, fire hazard, and other matters. These committees report from time to time the results of their investigations and these reports are made public in many forms. Thus the citizens are encouraged to take part in their government, and are helped to understand its problems, its shortcomings, and its mysteries.

The number of associations and city clubs in the United States is steadily growing and it is now a backward city that does not possess some kind of a civic society. Through these organizations the citizen is able to voice continually his views on municipal administration and to bring pressure to bear upon public authorities in many ways. Such associations may study the city budget and recommend increases or decreases in appropriations, advise the undertaking of new functions or the revision or discontinuance of old functions; they may impress upon a public officer the fact that any remissness in the discharge of his duties, or any neglect of a public function bearing upon the welfare of the inhabitants of the city, will be visited by publicity, and, if opportunity offers, legal proceedings.

A third type of private association, verging upon the borders of government, is afforded by those organizations dealing with special city problems, such as children's societies, committees for the prevention of infant mortality, milk committees, child-welfare associations, charitable organizations, societies for the improvement of the condition of the poor, and committees for the prevention of blindness. These societies, usually started as purely private organizations, very soon find that their activities lead them into direct contact with municipal functions, and indeed with government activity in its broadest sense. For example, a society for the prevention of blindness discovers that a great deal of eye trouble is due to the improper care of children at birth, and to neglect during the school years. This society, finding its work necessarily limited by a lack of funds and authority, sooner or later turns to the municipality. It calls for increased powers for the board of health in supervising the licensing of midwives, the inspection of the eyes of children at school, and perhaps the furnishing of free glasses by the public-school authorities.

A fourth type of private association, coöperating in local governments, is to be found in the bureaus of municipal research which are now established in a number of the leading cities of the country, including New York, Philadelphia, Cincinnati, Memphis, Chicago, St. Paul, and Minneapolis; — in Boston, and Milwaukee (until 1912), in direct official connection with the city authorities. The purpose of the bureau of municipal research, as set forth in the publications of the New York institution (established in 1906), is to advance efficient and economical government, to promote the adoption of scientific methods of accounting and of reporting the details of municipal business with a view to facilitating the work of public officials, to secure constructive publicity in matters pertaining to municipal problems, and to collect, classify, correlate, interpret, and publish facts as to the administration of the municipal government.

These bureaus, wherever possible, work in close rela-

tion with the heads of municipal departments in a coöperative spirit, whenever the municipal officer shows a
sincere desire to improve the efficiency of his branch of
administration. On their advice, methods of accounting have been placed upon a more scientific basis, and
intelligent interest has been developed in budget reform
and publicity. Public-service corporations have been
compelled to fulfil more exactly the terms of their franchises; abuses in the assessment and collection of taxes
have been reformed; new departments of social-welfare
work have been undertaken by municipal authorities;
city debts have been analyzed; wasteful methods in purchasing supplies have been checked; and the public has
been brought to see more clearly than ever the necessity
of standardizing municipal activities and keeping up a
sustained interest in city administration between election
times.

Along with the growth of these activities on the part
of private associations, has gone a steady increase in
the number of methods employed in educating the public
in municipal science. When the citizens come to learn
that good municipal government cannot be secured
merely by stirring up a fever heat at each election, but
rather by maintaining a constant and discriminating
scrutiny over public authorities all the year round, newspapers and other journals will increase the space devoted
to the less spectacular but more important questions of
city administration. The efficient administration of a
health department which decidedly reduces infant mortality in a hot and trying summer, becomes a more interesting " story " than a squabble between political leaders
over municipal spoils.

The work of the daily newspaper in giving publicity to the interesting facts of city government is now being supplemented by official city papers and municipal journals published by civic organizations. Denver, for example, publishes a weekly paper entitled *Denver Municipal Facts*. This publication gives an official roster of the city government, a review of the proceedings of the council and short articles on topics of interest to the inhabitants of the city. San Francisco also issues a paper called *The Municipal Record*, which puts in the hands of the citizens a weekly survey of the official activities of the city. New York issues a daily, *The City Record*, which is devoted entirely to a dry statement of the city's activities, which, however useful it may be to the student, is so forbidding in its aspect as not to invite perusal by the ordinary citizen.

The most interesting of all these municipal publications is the journal which the electors of Los Angeles voted to establish at the election in December, 1911. The Los Angeles paper is a veritable city weekly, publishing news of the world at large, as well as articles bearing directly upon the government of the municipality. Its columns are open to the citizens for the discussion of every kind of problem that may interest the voter.

All these enterprises, of course, are in danger of falling into the hands of partizan organizations and becoming mere tools for the advantage of the administration in power. However, Los Angeles has sought to guard against this by giving all political parties and organizations the right to publish articles under reasonable restrictions.

A new factor has recently entered into the politics of American cities, which has proved most disconcerting to the old-party organizations. This new factor is the Socialist party, which now has possession of several hundred offices in cities scattered throughout the North. Its most important victories have been in Milwaukee, Berkeley, Schenectady, Akron, Columbus, Dayton, and Lima.

It must not be assumed, however, that these victories have been due entirely to the complete acceptance of the Socialist program by the voters of the cities which have elected Socialist officers. A detailed analysis of Socialist gains by Dr. Robert F. Hoxie, published in the *Journal of Political Economy* for October, 1911, shows that only in a small proportion of the cities, which have elected representatives of this new and revolutionary party, has the electorate been converted to all the articles in its program. In some instances, local labor troubles, strikes, and lockouts have contributed largely to the Socialist gains; in other cases the victory may be attributed to long-continued Socialist agitation, education, and organization; but frequently it is the deplorable state of municipal politics and administration that is accountable for the triumph of the new party. As Professor Hoxie remarks, " It is in the boss-rule, corporation-ridden, tax-burdened city, with its poorly paved, ill-lighted, dirty streets, its insufficient water supply and air-filled mains, its industrial fire traps, its graft-protected vice districts, its fat politicians, untaxed wealth, crooked contracts and wasteful resources, that Socialism finds its best object-lessons, and has won some of its most significant if not most of its numerous successes."

In no city where Socialists have been victorious, have
they undertaken to carry out impossible programs. Indeed, shortly after his election in 1910, Mayor Seidel
of Milwaukee said, " There will be no Utopia, no mil-
lennium, none of the wild antics that our opponents have
charged to us. . . . We are not planning to do anything
to injure the best interests of the city. It is true that
we have many plans for the improvement of conditions:
we shall make the corporations pay their share of the
taxes and shall improve the condition of the laboring
men of the city, but we will not do anything revolutionary. That would turn sentiment so strongly against us
that we would not even accomplish the good that we can
by being conservative."

The municipal program of " immediate demands " put
forward by the Socialist party, in general, embraces the
following features:

(1) Complete home rule in municipal matters, with
    the initiative, referendum and recall.
(2) The municipal ownership and administration of
    public-service corporations.
(3) The erection of municipal abattoirs, markets, and
    cold-storage plants.
(4) The abolition of the contract system for public
    works. Direct employment of labor by the mu-
    nicipality in all public enterprises.
(5) An eight-hour day in city works.
(6) The relief of the unemployed by opening public
    works.
(7) The strict enforcement of sanitary conditions in
    factories and tenement houses.

(8) The establishment of free employment agencies.
(9) Adequate provisions for the education of children, including medical service, free text-books, and free midday meals.

In Milwaukee and Schenectady the Socialist officials announced their determination to make efficiency an official part of their program by entering into relations at once with bureaus of municipal research. In Milwaukee the Socialists immediately organized a bureau of economy and efficiency, which combined the functions of the New York bureau of municipal research with those of the New York official commissioners of accounts. The Milwaukee bureau, however, has not limited its activities to investigating problems of economy and efficiency. It has undertaken a social survey or inquiry into the conditions of living in the city, into health and sanitary problems, housing conditions, industrial accidents, and standards of living. According to the authorities of the New York Bureau of Municipal Research, no library of municipal progress is complete which does not contain the reports of the Milwaukee institution, illustrating the municipal research methods at work.

Judging from the limited experience we have thus far had with Socialist municipal administrations, it seems that they are endeavoring to combine efficient administration and practical ideas with large and generous notions of public policy. Their gains have also had a salutary effect upon the older party organizations, in showing them that old-fashioned "politics," consisting of the distribution of spoils and the exploitation of the

municipality through public-service corporations is bound
to come to a certain end in the United States.   Whether
the old party organizations in municipalities will be able
to go on at all without enjoying the spoils of office and
retaining "the cohesive power of public plunder," remains to be seen.   In Los Angeles in 1911 old party
lines disappeared altogether before the rising tide of
Socialism, and the program of the good-government
party which was victorious at the polls embraced nearly
all of the "immediate demands" of the Socialists.

The Socialists are well aware that these victories are
small gains toward the realization of their ideal, but they
differ among themselves as to their significance.   All
agree that municipalities under the control of state
courts and legislatures and the federal courts cannot go
very far in Socialist experiments, but some contend that
their achievements in cities give them the preparatory
training for their larger undertakings and at the same
time demonstrate the excellence of the Socialist ideal.
Other Socialists, however, hold that a taste of the spoils
of office tends to transform ardent revolutionaries into
mere reformers content with petty changes which really
afford small relief to the working class and, in fact,
strengthen the hold of the capitalist system on the country by making it somewhat more palatable.   Certainly,
it is largely a waste of time for the Socialists to concentrate their attention on municipal elections when the
real seats of power over property are in the state and
national governments.

Any fair valuation of popular movements in cities
to-day must take into account the remarkable activ-

ities of women as private citizens, electors, and public officers.

In six commonwealths, of course, women possess the municipal as well as the general franchise, and in Kansas they are allowed to vote in city elections. In a large number of States the peculiar interest of women in educational affairs is recognized by acts conferring upon them the right to vote for school authorities.

There is also an increasing number of women in municipal offices, in various parts of the Union. Since 1889, Kansas has had at least twenty women mayors. Recently, the auditor of Pueblo, the treasurer of Leadville, the city clerk of Colorado Springs and one of the aldermen in Durango, all in Colorado, were women. The director of playgrounds in San Diego, California, is a woman. As superintendent of schools of Chicago, Mrs. Ella Flagg Young has won a national reputation. Women are serving as members of school boards, tenement-house inspectors, city health officers, food inspectors, police officers, bacteriologists, juvenile-court officers, civil-service commissioners, as well as members of city and state legislatures. That they are rendering as efficient and commendable service as their male colleagues in office is quite commonly admitted; and in many instances they have made marked improvements on their accession to office.

While steadily increasing their political activities, woman's share in municipal government up to the present time has been principally in the organization and management of private civic associations of every type. Women are among the leaders in all beneficent and humane enterprises designed to make our cities more beautiful places in which to live and to improve the common lot of those who do the world's work. The importance of woman's place in the scheme of municipal affairs is so fully recognized that it has been made the subject of a volume entitled, " Woman's Part in Government, Whether She Votes or Not," by Dr. William H. Allen, director of the New York Bureau of Municipal Research. In this stimulating and suggestive volume, the manifold branches of municipal government in which women may do effective service are laid out; a clear and unmistakable guidance is offered to women who wish to make their influence count in public betterment.

Following the example of the men, the recently enfranchised women of several leading California cities have formed civic associations for the discussion and investigation of public questions of every nature. In the cities of other States, where women are not enfranchised, they demonstrate their capacity for the suffrage by a wide and intelligent range of activities. A recent report of a woman's municipal league for one of our large municipalities embraces the following program of achievements:

Campaign for pure milk, including rigid inspection. The league was one of the first civic organizations to appreciate the need of this.

Encouragement of men in the street-cleaning service by the offering of medals and money prizes.

Revival of juvenile citizens' leagues, formed in the public schools to promote interest in civic affairs.

Erection of twenty free ice-water fountains in congested portions of the city.

Women voters in line at one of the schoolhouse polling places in Los Angeles.

Courtesy of The American City.

A campaign of education among housekeepers with a view to improving sanitary conditions.

An investigation of moving-picture shows and cheap amusement places, resulting in the establishment of a censorship.

Financial aid and committee service for the investigation of summer amusements of young girls not reached by the settlements and churches.

Establishment and maintenance of playgrounds for children of the congested districts.

CHAPTER IV

MUNICIPAL GOVERNMENT AND ADMINISTRATION

In the beginning of our history, the town council was the most interesting and important branch of city government. It was, after the old English example, a single-chambered body at first, but early in the nineteenth century the older and simpler system was generally abandoned in favor of the bicameral idea, borrowed from the state governments. In New England the growth of population in the cities at length made the open town meeting too unwieldy. For example, the qualified voters of Boston numbered more than 7000 in 1821, and mass meetings, at which the business of a city with a population of over 40,000 had to be transacted in an orderly and reasonable fashion, were obviously impossible. Accordingly, a charter was adopted the following year, vesting the government in a mayor, eight aldermen, elected at large, and a council of forty-eight members, four from each ward of the city. Nearly all the large cities of the United States have experimented with the bicameral system, and most of them have now abandoned it. Toward the close of the nineteenth century at least seven of the twelve cities having a population of over 300,000 — New York, Philadelphia, St. Louis, Boston, Baltimore, Buffalo, and Pittsburgh — still clung to the old system; but three of these — New York, Boston, and Pittsburgh — have gone back to the simpler form of one house. A recent Baltimore charter commission proposed a single-branch council, and its recommendations will doubtless be accepted soon. The drift is all toward the single, small chamber.

Up until May 31, 1911, Pittsburgh had a bicameral council composed of a select council, comprising one member from each ward elected for a term of four years, and a common council, whose members were elected for two years from the various wards, each of which was entitled to representation on the basis of its number of taxables. Under this law councilors were paid no salaries — at least by the city. By an act of May 31, 1911, applicable to Pittsburgh and Scranton, the old system was swept away and a single-chamber council was provided, composed of not less than five members and one additional member for every 75,000 inhabitants above 200,000 up to 500,000. The members are to be paid not less than $2000 and not more than $6500 a year and are to be fined for each failure to attend council meetings. The councilmen are to be elected at large for terms of four years, but a portion go out every two years, so that the municipal chamber is a continuous body.

Boston abandoned the bicameral system in 1910 in favor of the single chamber, in a form approaching commission government. Under the new Boston charter, the city council consists of nine members, elected at large. At the first election all of the nine members were chosen, and thereafter, according to the provisions of the charter, three members of the council are to be elected at each annual municipal election. Thus the new Boston council, like the Pittsburgh council, is a continuous body, one-third of the members going out every year. The members of the council are paid an annual salary of $1500, but are not allowed any additional sum from the city treasury on account of any personal expenses directly or indirectly incurred.

This revolution in the Boston system was largely the outgrowth of an investigation conducted in 1909 by the Finance Commission, which reported that the bicameral and representative form of government had failed to give the city decent government. In speaking of the double-chamber council, existing at that time, the Commission said:

The possession of concurrent power over appropriations and loans aggregating $25,000,000 a year and over the municipal ordinances for a population of 600,000 people would seem to furnish sufficient honor to make a seat in the city council an object of legitimate ambition, and to cause whatever sacrifice of time may be involved to be looked upon as a civic duty. Membership in the city council, however, is quite generally regarded as a discredit rather than an honor; and it is difficult to induce representative men to become candidates for either branch. . . . The reasons for the disrepute into which the city council has fallen and for the consequent disinclination of competent and representative citizens to serve in it, are to be found in the conduct of that body and its members.

The city council as a body gives no serious consideration to its duties. In 1907 twenty-eight of the forty-two joint standing committees had no papers referred to them, and held no meetings. In the common council of the year four hundred and seventy orders were introduced and referred to the mayor without discussion or vote. Its work on the annual appropriations bill consists generally of attempting to raise the mayor's estimates to the maximum amount allowed by law, with a preference for those departments

where the patronage is largest. Loan bills are log-rolled
through with more regard for the demands of interested
constituents and the possibility of jobs than for the needs
of the city as a whole. The annual borrowing capacity of
the city within the debt limit is treated as affording so much
more money to be spent; and every occasion is seized to
petition the legislature for leave to borrow additional millions outside the debt limit. This phrase, the "debt limit,"
has lost its meaning, and each additional authorization to
borrow in excess of it is regarded as a "gift" of money
by the State to be spent as soon as the act can be accepted.
Notwithstanding the small amount of legitimate business
transacted, weekly meetings of both branches are held
throughout the year, except in summer, and a small army
of high-salaried clerks, stenographers, messengers, and assistants is maintained. At least $50,000 a year is wasted
upon superfluous employees, generally politicians, retained
to aid the city council in the non-discharge of its duties.

The theory of the bicameral system is that an upper
chamber will serve as a check upon hasty and ill-consid-
ered action on the part of the lower house. But the
theory certainly has not been realized in practice, either
in state legislatures or in city councils. It is true that
the mistakes of one chamber are sometimes corrected
by the other. The Boston Finance Commission, mentioned above, calls attention to the fact that not infrequently in the history of that city an unwise exercise
of the borrowing power by one branch had been blocked
by the other, but adds, "Much more frequently improvi-
dent loans desired by one branch have been added to
similar loans offered by the other and incorporated in a
single bill."

Under the charter enacted by the legislature in 1830,
New York City established a bicameral council, but it

was abandoned in the charter of 1873, in favor of a single chamber, supplemented by a board of estimate and apportionment, which, in a way, may be regarded as a sort of an upper house. However, in the charter for Greater New York, which went into effect in 1898, an effort was made to rehabilitate the city council and provision was made for a double-chamber legislature with large and important powers. This attempt at rehabilitation proved to be a miserable failure, and after four years' experience, a single-chamber board of aldermen was reëstablished, and its powers have been gradually shorn away either by positive limitation or transfer to the board of estimate and apportionment, until the ancient and honorable assembly of city fathers is a poor and mean apology for a legislature.

Among the cities which have employed the single-chamber system for some time, or have recently adopted it, two types of council may be observed: the large and the small. Chicago and New York fall into the first class. The city council of Chicago is composed of seventy members, two from each of the thirty-five wards into which the city is divided. The board of aldermen of New York consists of seventy-three members, each of whom is elected in a single aldermanic district. Among the cities with the smaller councils, may be included Boston, whose system has been described above, San Francisco, with a small council of eighteen members, and New Orleans, with seventeen.

The present drift is all in the direction of the single-chamber council, composed of a few members. This tendency has taken its most radical form in what is known as "commission government." The movement for commission government may be dated from the re-construction of the municipality of Galveston, Texas, after the great storm of 1900, which destroyed a large portion of that unhappy city and sacrificed some 6000 lives. For a time, the local government was paralyzed, because the great problems connected with the reparation of the ruin were too much for the old political machine which had control. Accordingly, a committee of citizens was chosen to formulate a new charter, and they drafted an instrument which vested the entire government in the hands of five commissioners, three appointed by the governor and two elected by the people of the city without regard to ward lines. This charter was adopted, but its appointive feature was declared unconstitutional.

A revision soon followed and the government of Galveston was vested in a mayor and four commissioners elected at large by the voters of the city and invested with all the rights, powers, and duties of the mayor and board of aldermen. The administration of the city is divided into four departments: police and fire, streets and public property, water-works and sewage, and finance and revenue; and the mayor and the four commissioners are required by the charter to designate from their own number a commissioner for each of the four great departments. The mayor president is merely one of the commissioners, although no city department is assigned to him, and exercises a " general coördinating influence over all." The board meets at stated times for the transaction of public business very much as the board of directors of a great corporation would meet to discharge their functions.

This commission form of government with modifications has now been set up in over two hundred cities scattered from Massachusetts to California; and a number of States, including Iowa, Kansas, North Dakota, Mississippi, Minnesota, Wisconsin, and Oklahoma, have passed laws authorizing their municipalities, under certain conditions, to adopt the new plan. Among the larger cities which have adopted it are Birmingham, Alabama, with 132,685 inhabitants; Oakland, 150,174; Springfield, Illinois, 51,678; Des Moines, 86,368; Kansas City, Kansas, 82,331; Lowell, Massachusetts, 106,294; St. Paul, 214,744; Omaha, 124,096; Trenton, 96,815; Memphis, 131,105; Dallas, 92,105; and Spokane, 104,402.

Commission government is not a simple and uniform type, as its advocates have sometimes imagined. A number of variations are possible. The members of the commission may be all equal and share alike the appointing and legislative powers. On the other hand, there may be, as in the Houston (Texas) plan, a centralization of power in the hands of the mayor, who appoints and removes city officers, vetoes legislative acts of the commission and thus assumes large responsibility for the proper conduct of city affairs.

However, there are certain fairly constant elements in the commission system which are summed up as follows by Dr. E. S. Bradford, in his valuable work on commission government:

The first and most striking feature is the centralization of power in the hands of a small body of men, usually five, but in some instances three, and in one instance (High Point, N. C.) nine. The idea behind the reduction of the number of councilors is that embodied

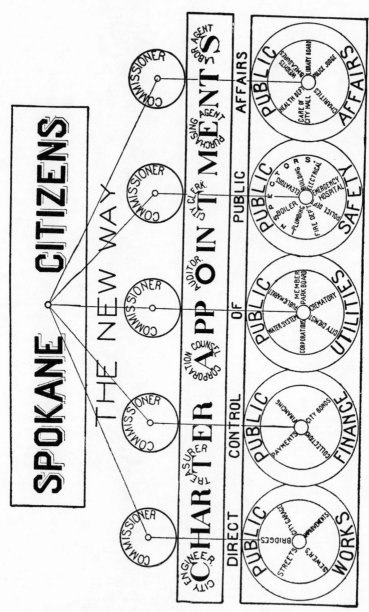

The new way.

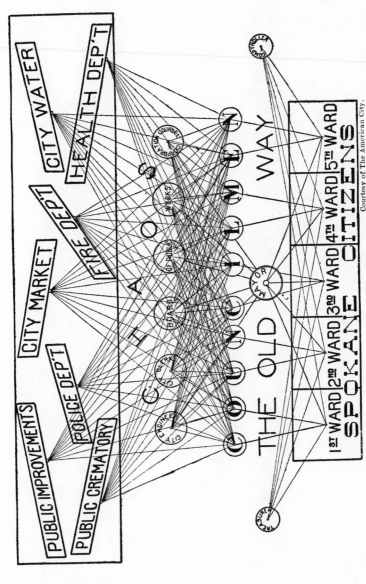

THE OLD WAY

Courtesy of The American City.

Illustrating the simplicity of the present charter as compared with the complexity and confusion of the old way in Spokane.

in the short-ballot principle: first, that only those offices should be elective which are important enough to attract and deserve attention, and, second, that very few offices should be filled by election at one time, so as to permit adequate and unconfused public examination of the candidates.

The second feature in commission government is the abandonment of the old representative idea of electing councilmen from wards or districts and the adoption of election at large on a general ticket.

The third feature is the concentration of legislative and executive powers in the hands of the same body, for as a general rule the commission as a whole acts as the city council and is at the same time responsible for the administration and execution of the law.

The fourth principle is the distribution of municipal administration among the members of the commission by making each commissioner the head of a definite department, for the administration of which he is directly responsible.

A fifth, but not indispensable feature, is a system of initiative, referendum, and recall. These newer devices were not included in the original Galveston plan but they have been adopted either singly or in combination in a large majority of the cities possessing commission government.

Commission government, as Professor Goodnow points out, is a return to the original type of city government in the United States in so far as it concentrates all powers, administrative and legislative, in one authority. It differs, however, from the original council system in that its members do not represent single districts, but are elected at large by the voters of the entire city — a practice which, of course, substantially excludes minority representation, and is so highly undesirable as to constitute a serious objection to the adoption of the scheme in large cities.

From the standpoint of pure business administration, the commission form of government has many features to commend it. It centralizes power and responsibility in a small group of men constantly before the public and subjected to the scrutiny of public criticism; it coördinates the taxing and spending powers, thus overcoming the maladjustment so common to American public finance; and it throws down that multiplicity of barriers behind which some of the worst interests in American municipal politics have screened their antisocial operations.

On the other hand, it destroys the deliberative and representative element in municipal government, and may readily tend to reduce its administration to a mere routine business, based largely upon principles of economy, to the exclusion of civic ideals. Election at large prevents the representation of minorities; and nonpartizan elections, in addition to being impossible, are based upon the erroneous notion that there can be no real party divisions on municipal policies. Furthermore, it is possible to secure greater responsibility by concentrating administrative power in the hands of the mayor than by dividing it among five commissioners.

Another serious criticism of the commission system is based on the contention that, in the light of our municipal experience, it concentrates too great a power in the hands of a few men and makes it easier for those who wish to buy a city government to carry out their design. Iowa, however, has sought to meet this objection by establishing the system of recall noted above. Under this system twenty-five per cent. of the voters, who disapprove of the policy of any commissioner or believe that he is not discharging his functions honestly and efficiently, may petition for his removal and compel a new election. The whole question is then submitted to the electorate at large, and if the commissioner is upheld, assuming that he stands for reëlection, he retains his office, but if defeated is supplanted by the popular choice.

Under the Iowa scheme all important franchises must be submitted to popular vote before going into effect; municipal ordinances may be initiated by the voters, and ordinances passed by the commission must be referred to the electorate on a petition properly signed and filed.

The danger of concentrating the power in the hands of such a small body is further offset in the Iowa law by the abolition of the party convention as a means of nominating candidates for the offices of mayors and councilmen and the substitution of nomination by direct primary described above in the chapter on " Municipal Democracy."

Along with the revolt against the bicameral council and the large " representative " council elected from wards, which has made such a revolution in municipal government, there has gone an increase in the power of the mayor, in those cities which have not adopted the commission plan. Originally, the mayor of the city was more or less of a figurehead; his position was very much like that of the Governor of the State under the first constitutions. Generally speaking, he was elected by the council, possessed no veto power and appointed no administrative officers.   Under the Boston charter of 1822, for example, the English practice was adopted of conducting the city's administration through committees of the council, who either acted as administrative officers themselves, or selected the heads of the several departments which they supervised.   The mayor presided over the board of aldermen, but he did not enjoy the veto power; neither did he have the right to appoint the municipal officers, over whom he was the titular executive head.

The development of the executive branch of city government in general followed the lines of the state government.   The principle of separation of powers was introduced; the mayor was made elective by popular vote (in New York in 1833); and he was given the veto power. During the middle period in our municipal evolution the experiment of elective administrative officers was tried. Heads of departments and boards and commissions charged with administrative duties were elected by popular vote.

More recently, however, we have entered upon a third stage in the evolution of the office of the mayor, which reaches a high point in the governments of New York and Boston as now constituted.   In New York City, the heads of all the departments are appointed by the mayor and removed at will, without a hearing or the assignment of cause.   The mayor enjoys the veto power over all ordinances and resolutions passed by the board of aldermen.   He is the head of the board of estimate and apportionment, which prepares the city budget, and he possesses three out of sixteen votes cast by the members of that board. The responsibility for the efficient administration of the city government is centered in him, and he possesses powers, at least so far as the law is concerned, commensurate with this responsibility.

The New York idea has found acceptance in the Boston charter of 1910. There the mayor is elected by popular vote. He submits to the council the annual budget for the current expenses of the city and county, and the council can only omit or reduce the items which he presents — it cannot increase them. The heads of all departments and members of municipal boards (except the school committee and officers appointed by the governor) are chosen by the mayor without the confirmation of the city council — but subject in most cases to the approval of the state civil-service commission. The mayor may submit to the city council any ordinance or loan bill which he may deem to be for the welfare of the city and the council must consider it and adopt or reject it within sixty days.

It would be a mistake, however, to assume that the tendency toward the concentration of executive power in the hands of the mayor in some of the large cities is a characteristic of municipal administration universally in the United States. On the contrary, a great number of the cities still retain the old form of municipal government, in which executive, legislative, and judicial powers are separated and the executive branch is split up into innumerable departments — some composed of boards and the others headed by single officers appointed or elected. The condition of affairs existing in Boston twenty years ago is very nearly typical of the smaller cities which have not adopted commission government.

At that time the mayor of Boston had directly under his control thirty-nine separate departments, including ninety-two separate heads and one hundred or more sub-heads, and assistants, to say nothing of about twenty-five hundred minor offices filled by him, subject to confirmation by the board of aldermen. The entire municipal government was elected annually, so that there was constant shifting about in the several branches of administration and the affairs of the city were always in a state of chaos. It is small wonder that the Finance Commission in 1909 found the government of the city inefficient and the prey of the spoilsmen.

This is not merely a bit of ancient history. Under the law as it stood in 1911, the voters in a typical Ohio city selected by ballot twenty-one municipal officers, including mayor, president of the city council, auditor, treasurer, solicitor, three councilmen at large, ward councilmen, three justices of the peace, three constables, five members of the board of education and one assessor. If we include the state officers in this list, we find that the voters of the larger Ohio cities were confronted every two years by the task of expressing their choice of men to fill fifty-one offices ranging from governor of the commonwealth down to the constable. On Nov. 7, 1911, the voter of Cleveland had placed in his hands on entering the booth seven separate ballots, one containing seventy-four candidates for city offices, another twelve candidates for the board of education and a third fourteen candidates for municipal court judges, to say nothing of the ballot containing candidates for the constitutional convention of that year and those containing referenda submitted to popular approval.

Under the Minneapolis Charter of 1900 "the mayor had the power to appoint practically all the heads of departments, but not the power of removal. To prevent a new mayor from raiding the departments and appointing his henchmen, the departments were placed in charge of boards. For example, police, fire, water, parks, and workhouse, were under the control of five boards of five members each, serving for five years, one member retiring each year. The board of public works and control had three members each; the school board, seven; the library, nine (appointed by the district court); and equalization, eleven. The mayor could appoint only one new member each year and since the mayor's term was two years he could not secure a favorable majority on any of these boards, unless he secured a reëlection, excepting only public works and control, of which he could gain the majority in his second year. Having no power of removal the mayor had little power of controlling the departments, beyond calling the presidents of the boards to a monthly conference, asking for reports and giving advice and admonition. The departments were also independent of the council, excepting that the maximum sum appropriated each year was fixed by that body. Since the charter stated exactly the maximum sum which could be spent by each board annually, the council could do little more than appropriate that sum." But under the new charter proposed in 1912 a decided change is to be made in the direction of the concentration of power in the hands of the mayor.

If we go further west, we find in the city of Denver (in 1911) two groups of administrative officers, who are elected: mayor, clerk, auditor, treasurer, the election commission, sheriff, assessor, county clerk, recorder, coroner, county superintendent of schools, and county judges. The council is bicameral. It includes a board of supervisors, composed of seven members nominated in districts but elected at large, so as to give the majority party in the city control of the upper house, and a board of sixteen aldermen, one for each of the several wards of the city. It is fair to say that the home-rule charter convention of Denver in 1903 drafted a city charter providing for a simpler form of city government. But the spoilsmen and the public service corporations, that had long regarded the city as their private possession, were able to bring about the defeat of this simpler system and secure the adoption of a complicated charter, which they hoped would serve as an ambush for their operations. Another movement for revision, however, is now under way.

A general survey of the recent municipal tendencies in the United States seems to show that, in so far as the smaller cities are abandoning complicated and irresponsible forms of government, they favor the commission plan rather than the mayor-and-council plan. In view of the positive demand for orderliness in the larger cities and the growth of commission government generally, one is warranted in saying that the outlook for simpler and more direct municipal government was never so encouraging as at the present time.

Although the interest of the student and citizen usually centers in the mayor and council, the branch of municipal government which maintains the most intimate contact with life and property is the group of administrative officers charged with carrying out the great functions

which the city undertakes. These subordinate officers
afford little of the spectacular in the regular discharge
of their duties, but upon them really depends the excellence of a city's government. The making of laws is
a relatively simple matter. The execution of them
against all and sundry, the application of them to thousands or millions of people and enormous property
interests — that is the function which throws the greatest strain on the machinery of government. Moreover,
it is constant. The lawmakers speak their will and their
task is done; the executive officer's labors and responsibilities continue day and night without cessation.

These somewhat obvious truths are often overlooked
by those who would reform municipal government by
the introduction of popular lawmaking through the initiative and referendum. The making of wise laws is
of course fundamental; but the construction, management, standardization, and efficiency of the administrative departments are likewise fundamental, and they
must receive the attention which is devoted to the larger
and more interesting branches of city government.

The first problem in the organization of the administrative departments is the grouping of functions to be
assigned to each. This depends of course largely upon
the size of the city and the number and magnitude of
duties assumed. With the growth of commission government there has been a tendency to consolidate departments and group them all under a few heads, so that
each one of the commissioners may be responsible for
a separate executive department. Des Moines, Iowa,
for example, has five departments: public affairs, accounts and finances, public safety, streets and public im-

provements, and parks and public property. Under each of these are ordered the allied minor branches of administration. In a larger city there will be found additional subdivisions: police, fire, water supply, street cleaning, taxes and assessments, tenement-house, health, and the like — each constituting a separate department.

The crossing of the interests of the several functions makes an entirely satisfactory subdivision difficult. The relation of street cleaning and pavement repairing is obvious; but these matters are often under entirely separate heads. The department in charge of public buildings will naturally seek to control the lighting of the buildings, but the head of the department of gas and electricity will also want to have a word to say on these points. Each department, under an energetic officer, will endeavor to enlarge its jurisdiction and the scope of its control. Consequently we have a great deal of pulling at cross purposes in city governments and this is augmented when vitally related matters are placed under the management of distinct departments. Efficient government therefore demands that careful attention be given to the interrelation of administrative subdivisions.

Professor W. A. Schaper, of the Minneapolis charter commission, has proposed the following classification of administrative functions for that city, and it is full of suggestions for cities of any considerable size:

1. Department of city records
2. Department of law
3. Department of health and hospitals
    Under this department should be placed all the health

and hospital work of the city, organized into proper branches with a subordinate officer in charge

(*a*) The city hospital
(*b*) Hopewell hospital
(*c*) Quarantine hospital
(*d*) The care of the poor
(*e*) Garbage collection (may be transferred to public works)
(*f*) Inspection services
(*g*) City bacteriologist and all other health activities of the city

4. Department of public works (or the city engineer)
This department should have charge of all the engineering work of the city, embracing under proper subdivisions:

(*a*) Streets, sidewalks, and bridges (abolishing the thirteen street commissioners)
(*b*) The city sewers
(*c*) The city water-works

5. Department of Finance (or city comptroller)
Under this department should come three subdivisions:

(*a*) Office of city accountant
(*b*) Office of city treasurer
(*c*) Office of city assessor

6. Department of public safety
This should embrace:

(*a*) The city police
(*b*) The city firemen
(*c*) The city building inspector
(*d*) License inspector, etc.
(*e*) Workhouse

7. Department of parks and public grounds.
Here should be grouped all the activities of the present park board.

In order to unify the work of the several departments, Dr. Schaper also recommends the creation of a special conference committee — consisting of the mayor, the city attorney as legal adviser, and the heads of four other leading departments — to be entrusted with the general conduct of the city's business, including letting contracts, acquiring lands (except for schools), proposing the budget, suggesting ordinances to the council, and making appointments under the civil-service rules.

When the functions of a department have been decided upon there remains the knotty problem of how the personnel shall be made up. Shall the department have one head or three? Shall the bi-partizan element be introduced — two men of one party and a third of a second party to " balance " each other? Shall the heads be appointed by the mayor or elected? By whom and under what conditions shall the heads be removed?

Experiments without number enable us to answer some of these questions with a reasonable degree of certainty. The multiple-headed department is now discredited because it has been discovered that when three men are responsible, nobody is really responsible. Hence, cities are now moving rapidly in the direction of the single-headed administrative department, in order to concentrate power and responsibility. The bi-partizan board is generally discredited because it has been found that instead of checking each other the party representatives quite often unite to divide the spoils.

There is also a general tendency to have the department head appointed rather than elected for two reasons. It is absurd to elect a mayor on a pledge to carry out certain policies and then not give him the power to appoint the chief officers who are to help him in executing his promises. Otherwise, the heads of the executive departments might be pulling at cross purposes, if representatives of different factions and parties filled the several branches of the government. A second reason is the importance of having unity in an administration in order to concentrate responsibility somewhere. When the mayor appoints, he is responsible for the doings of all his chief officers and the conduct of the business of each department under him.

Along with the tendency to vest the appointment of the department heads in the mayor has gone a corresponding tendency to give him the removing power also, for it would seem illogical to permit him to appoint his adjutants and not allow him to remove one whom he thinks unworthy.

This system of single-headed and appointive offices, which is coming into favor generally where the commission form of government has not been adopted, is not, however, without its defects. The terms of the officers are short and no one can look for a career as the head of a great branch of municipal administration. Consequently inefficiency is all too common, because able men are not willing to leave high-grade private employments for uncertain public offices. If long terms are introduced the bureaucratic or martinet spirit may develop in the officer who is for years out of touch with the common life. Hence it is sometimes suggested that a combination of lay boards, composed of citizens exercising general supervision, with expert permanent official heads should be tried. Thus both expertness and touch with common affairs might be secured.

Under the several department heads, there is an army of employees of all grades and capacities — from the expert engineer who plans and directs large public undertakings down to the humblest laborer who sweeps the streets. To secure skilled and efficient service throughout the hierarchy of municipal employees is one of the obvious and pressing problems of our time, and it is just beginning to receive the attention which its importance deserves. We are now experimenting with new methods of appointment, promotion, and supervision, and the next decade will doubtless see some decided advances over the political methods which have been in vogue so long.

The practice of distributing municipal offices, high and low, as rewards for party services had nothing to commend it when our cities were small and their administration simple; and it becomes little short of criminal when the health, safety, and comfort of millions depend upon the ability and efficiency of public servants. The number of city employees is steadily increasing as new administrative duties are undertaken; and the public sentiment, which is demanding the enlargement of municipal functions, will not be indifferent to the requirements of efficient service.

Taxpayers, of course, have long protested against wastefulness; but "our leading citizens" have often profited so largely from inefficient city government that their voice of protest has sometimes not risen above a whisper. Now, however, we are having an awakened citizenship. The thousands who hang on straps in street cars and subways, drink badly filtered water, work in unsanitary factories, suffer from overcrowding, and haunt the streets for work in times of unemployment, are developing a "consciousness of kind," a solidarity of interest, which will make effective the demand for expertness and efficiency in municipal administration.

The first step in the direction of increased efficiency is the separation of politics from administration — the recognition of the place and function of parties in the election of city authorities and the determination of city policies and a corresponding recognition of the fact that expert technical service cannot be secured by distributing offices, involving a high degree of expertness, among party workers, as rewards for " keeping the rank and file in line." It is the function of politics to determine what the city should do and to control and supervise the execution of the policy decided upon. It is the function of administration to perform the countless technical, scientific, clerical, and manual tasks which the policy determined upon necessarily involves.

No doubt the line between politics and administration is difficult to draw. In an ever-increasing number of cities the attempt is made to draw it a few grades below the heads of administrative departments by putting the entire service below the commissioner and his immediate aids on a civil-service or merit basis. This system has many theoretical advantages which are not always realized in practice. It places at the head of each department a man appointed by the mayor and responsible to him. Thus the general direction of the department is under an officer immediately controlled by the chief executive of the city — the mayor.

The theory of this arrangement has little against it, but it overlooks the fact that, in practice, the mayor is not an altogether free agent in the selection of his immediate subordinates; for he must constantly reckon with the party leaders who placed him in nomination and fought for his election. Thus a power behind the mayor often forces him to select as heads of the branches of the administration committed to his care, men who are not fitted by training or character for the technical work involved. He is responsible to the public for the proper discharge of his executive functions, but the subordinates who do the work for him are not always of his choosing, in spite of the charter provisions.

Boston has sought to meet this problem by a new scheme. The recent charter provides that the heads of departments and members of municipal boards shall be appointed by the mayor without the consent of the council. It requires, however, that such officers shall be " recognized experts in such work as may devolve upon the incumbents of said offices, or persons specially fitted by education, training, and experience to perform the same and . . . shall be appointed without regard to party affiliation or to residence at the time of appointment." In order to fulfil the terms of this requirement, the mayor must certify each of his appointments to the state civil-service commission for its approval. This commission is expected to make a careful inquiry into the qualifications of the candidate nominated by the mayor, and if it is found that he is fitted by education, training, and experience for the office his appointment is confirmed. Without such confirmation no appointment is valid. The removal power of the mayor is substantially absolute, for the only check upon him is the requirement that he must file a statement of his reasons for any removal.

There is some politics about this system, for ordinarily the State is in Republican control while the city of Boston is frequently under a Democratic mayor. The principle behind the provisions, however, is the elimination of petty politics from appointments to the chief offices of the city. According to a report of the Boston Finance Commission (also a state authority), on August 17, 1910, the objects of the charter stipulation on this point were threefold: to strengthen the mayor's hands by requiring appointments to be made without regard to political affiliations or geographical limitations, both of which seriously restrict the range of selection; to prevent coercion of the mayor by the board of aldermen which formerly enjoyed the power of confirming appointments and practically dictated them by threats of withholding appropriations; and, finally, to prevent the appointment of incompetents to office by giving a supervisory power to a state commission independent of the mayor and having no means of coercing him by threats of holding up money bills and ordinances.

Up to August 17, 1910, the mayor had made thirty-seven appointments to paid positions and of these fourteen were rejected by the civil-service commission. Of the twenty-five appointments to unpaid positions made up to that date three were not approved by the commission and one was pending. The pressure of the politicians for paid offices seems to be greater than that for the unpaid posts.

A single example will illustrate the working of the system. On August 10, 1910, the Finance Commission complained that, in spite of the rejection of one appointee to the position of health commissioner, the mayor had appointed another person " who was not a physician or a sanitary engineer, or one who had had experience in public health administration, or whose education, training, or experience otherwise fitted him for the office," and recommended that thereafter the mayor should consult physicians and sanitary engineers of high standing and familiar with the problems of public health administration for the purpose of obtaining the names of persons competent to serve as health commissioner. That the relations of the mayor and the civil-service commission are not altogether amicable goes without saying, but whatever demerits the system may have, it certainly affords the public an opportunity of knowing something about the appointments to important public offices.

Another method of eliminating politics and securing experts for high positions in municipal service was inaugurated in Kansas City, Missouri, in 1910, under the administration of Mayor D. A. Brown.   In that year a new civil-service commission was appointed and it devised the following plan: Whenever a high post in the city government is vacant, a board of citizen experts is chosen to coöperate with the commission in formulating examination questions, conducting the oral examinations, and grading the written papers.   An example or two will show how this system works.   In July, 1910, the post of city engineer was vacant, and three expert examiners were chosen to select the proper candidate: Major E. H. Schultz, of the United States Army Engineers located in Kansas City for river protection work, E. I. Farnsworth, for several years a member of the board of public works and at the time a member of the fire and water board, and J. L. Harrington, member of a firm of leading bridge contractors and construction engineers.

Shortly afterward when it became necessary to select a municipal librarian a committee composed of the city librarian, the Dean of the Graduate School of the University of Kansas, the secretary of the City Club, and a lawyer and expert in municipal legislation were called in to conduct the examination. The ideal of this system has been to summon to the aid of the city in selecting its experts, prominent men who have had experience in choosing for private positions employees with qualifications similar to those required in the several more or less technical public posts.

The method of securing experts and civil servants generally, which is now gaining most rapidly in favor in the United States, is the merit or competitive system under which city employees are appointed on the basis of examinations designed to test the abilities of the candidates to discharge the duties of the offices which they are seeking. Where this system is adopted for any municipal offices the tendency is to extend it to ever larger numbers of employees. On the one hand it is being widened so as to cover more highly paid and technical positions, as well as those denominated purely clerical; and on the other hand it is being extended to include mechanics and unskilled laborers. The United States Civil-Service Commission, in its Twenty-seventh Report (1911) printed a list showing the extension of the merit system to some or all branches of administration in 217 municipalities, including New York, Massachusetts, Ohio and Wisconsin cities. California has recently applied the merit system to San Francisco; Chicago has made a wide extension of the principle, including the park employees; Los Angeles has used it in the selection of employees for the great aqueduct; and Kansas City, Missouri, has adopted it with marked improvements in efficiency and economy.

The administration of the merit system of selecting city employees is generally placed in the hands of a municipal civil-service commission, composed of three members.[1] Appointment by the mayor is the most approved method of selection. This commission makes rules governing all the employees placed under its jurisdiction by law. It classifies them according to their duties, and plans examination papers and tests designed to discover the fitness of the candidates for the positions for which they are severally applicants. It conducts examinations, grades the papers, and arranges them in order of merit on the lists so that the names of those who stand highest may be certified to the proper appointing officers whenever vacancies occur. For example, take any single class of employees, such as the bookkeepers; the commission prepares questions designed to test the fitness of the candidates for such clerical positions; examinations are held on these papers at stated intervals; and those passing an examination are arranged in order of rank on " eligible lists." When a bookkeeping position is open in any city department, the appropriate appointing officer calls upon the commission for a list containing three of the eligibles standing highest, and from this list he may select any one. The remaining two are returned to the commission for certification on another occasion.

The examinations for the different groups of city employees vary, of course, according to the requirements

[1] In Massachusetts a state commission controls the civil service in cities.

of the several positions. A policeman's test includes knowledge of the city's geography, and laws, and physical tests, in addition to the common branches. A civil engineer's examination is prepared by an expert on the basis of the knowledge which experience has shown to be necessary in this branch of municipal work, and so on throughout the list.

The rule to the effect that the appointing officer may select from among three standing highest on the list is designed to give him an opportunity to consider the personal qualities of the candidates as well as their rankings. It may be that the man standing highest in the examinations lacks certain qualities of character and experience which are possessed by the man standing lower. This " rule of three," however, has its disadvantages, for it enables " politics " to creep in. The appointing officer, by subtle and mysterious means, generally learns something about the party affiliations of the three eligibles, and often favors his party man as against the other two who may be better qualified. This abuse has led some civil-service reformers to declare that the examining commission should apply all the legitimate tests in the examination and require the appointing officer to take the men absolutely in order of rating.

This proposition has an intimate connection with another problem of civil service; that is, the removal of employees. It is the common practice to place candidates just appointed on a " probation " for a few months, previous to final confirmation. During this period removal is easy and simple; but when the employee is at length placed on the regular rolls of the city, it commonly takes some extraordinary process to get him off. If the chief officer has a free hand in making removals and then has also a choice from among three candidates for every vacancy, he can very readily clear out employees whose politics he does not approve and put in men of his own party. This has led most cities, which have advanced civil-service laws, to place close restrictions on the removal power — particularly the restriction requiring every officer on removing an employee to show neglect of duty and inefficiency, and above all to show that there is no " politics " in the case. If the officer fails to make good his complaint the court, or some higher authority, will reinstate the man in spite of his chief.

This works badly. It checks the officer who would use his removal power for political purposes, but it also prevents the discharge of large numbers who are really inefficient. That is, the capable officer who cares only for the proper administration of his department may find under him any number of incompetent employees of whose inefficiency he is fully aware, and if he cannot prove each case to the satisfaction of a court, however, he is compelled to retain employees who do not do their duty.

Many officers would rather permit their departmental work to remain unsatisfactory than face the ordeal of wrangling in court or before a board over the petty details which constitute an employee's inefficiency. And if the decision goes against the chief, he is compelled to have under him a disgruntled subordinate with whom his personal relations will hardly be pleasant, to say the least.

These circumstances have lead some civil-service reformers to demand the abolition of the "rule of three," and the loosening of the restrictions on the removal power. If the officer knows that he must take the candidate for a vacancy who stands highest on the eligible list, he will hesitate a long time about removing an efficient employee merely for political reasons. The risks are too great. This seems to be a promising method of meeting the problem.

Another question which has risen in connection with civil service is that of pensions. Permanency is one of the features of employment under the merit system. Promotions are possible through the same methods as appointment, so that a person may look forward to a career in municipal service. But old age comes on, and the chief officer, not being under the stress of competition which marks the business world, has not the heart to throw the old civil servant out on account of his inefficiency. Yet his retention means poor work and the blocking of the way of younger and more capable employees much to their dissatisfaction.

Accordingly it is proposed that pension systems should be established in municipalities in order to make it easy to retire those employees who have passed beyond the line of efficiency on account of age. Beginnings of this system are to be seen everywhere. It is quite common in connection with fire departments, the public schools, and some other special branches of civil service, and is extending rapidly to include other divisions.

In the choice of departmental heads and technical experts, American cities may doubtless learn something from the practice in England. There such officers are appointed by the town council on the basis of the applications and recommendations filed in behalf of the experts seeking the vacant place. It is customary for the committee of the council in charge of any particular post to advertise in newspapers for applicants and to call to the vacancy some person from another city who has had experience in a similar line of work. Local politics seldom enter into such appointments, and the principle of residence being entirely disregarded, the council has practically the whole Empire as a field for the selection of officials. Of course promotions are frequently made from lower ranges of the service, but even in such cases applicants from competitors are invited. Thus technical municipal service offers a career to ambitious men and women.

There is no doubt but that this question of securing expert servants will receive serious attention in the United States in the near future. Our practice of calling men from private life for short terms and restricting the range of their advancement to a single city or State is essentially unsound and is beginning to be abandoned. Furthermore, cities are coming to recognize the importance of the expert; and the politicians, even though they are not celebrated for their devotion to ideals of economy, are awakening to the fact that their continuance in power depends upon their establishing at least a reasonable degree of efficiency in municipal administration.

A significant response to this new demand is to be found in the establishment of a Training School of Public Service in connection with the Bureau of Municipal Research in the city of New York. The purposes of this new school are, in part, as follows: To train men for the study and administration of public business, to qualify men to meet the growing need for students and administrators, to test and to improve methods and results of municipal service, to publish text-books on the science of practical administration, to furnish a connecting link between schools and colleges and municipal and other public departments for practical field work, and to secure an open discussion of public business which will emphasize the need for training on the part of officials and employees alike.

For the improvement of our expert municipal service certain conditions are imperative:

Recognition on the part of the public that expert municipal administration cannot be realized by calling butchers, bakers, and candlestick makers from private life for short terms in public offices with which they are not familiar.

The establishment of educational facilities for training men and women in public service.

The selection of experts without regard to local residence.

The adoption of the practice of selecting public servants of the higher rank by competition among qualified persons from all over the country.

The recognition of expert municipal service as a career worthy of the ambition of the best minds and characters.

Payment of adequate salaries.

In undertaking its several administrative functions the city is in the position of a large manufacturer and contractor. It must purchase materials, fashion them for particular ends, employ workmen, and carry out engineering projects. In this branch of municipal administration two methods, broadly speaking, may be employed by the municipal authorities. The various functions may be transferred to private contractors who purchase the materials, employ the workmen, and assume the responsibility for executing the enterprises according to specifications. A second method is for the city itself to assume the particular functions and discharge them by the direct employment of the foremen and laborers and the manufacture or purchase of materials.

The chief branches of municipal service in which large numbers of workmen are now employed are: street cleaning, street extension, paving, and repair, laying and extending water-works mains and sewer pipes, maintenance of parks, construction and superintendence of public buildings.

In these several branches of administration, the methods of employment and construction vary greatly from city to city and department to department, but it may be said that, generally speaking, there is a tendency in the United States to avoid direct employment in favor of the contract system, although there are many noteworthy exceptions. A recent investigation of the methods of sewer extensions in ninety-seven leading cities, including New York, Chicago, Philadelphia, and San Francisco, made by the Boston Finance Commission, shows that sixty-one cities employ the contract method, thirty-two the day-labor system, and four both methods.

Street cleaning, garbage collection, and the removal of snow are commonly done by direct employment of day labor.

The merits of the two systems have been made the subject of an extensive investigation by the Boston Finance Commission, and may be summed up as follows in the language of its report.

It is argued in favor of direct employment that it enables the city to employ local workmen and thus helps to relieve the amount of unemployment which is always more or less acute in a large municipality. This particular objection to contract work may, of course, be obviated by requiring contractors to employ at least a certain number of local workmen on the jobs entrusted to them.

A most serious objection to the contract system is to be found in the collusion among contractors in bidding and in the relation of contractors to political " deals." Speaking of the condition in Boston previous to 1909, the Finance Commission of that city says:

In the matter of contracts under $2000 there was seldom any pretense of competition; the work was " handed out " to selected contractors, often members of the city council in disguise, always friendly to the administration. These were called " gift " contracts, and, as they were obtained by favor, the inspection was lax, the performance often poor, and the cost always excessive. . . . Reputable business houses, including some of the largest corporations in the country, conspired to defraud the city, descending in some instances to the acceptance of such petty sums as $300, $200, and $150 as their share of the plunder. The treasurer of one of these large corporations, who had been a member of the governor's council, justified his company's share in these dealings as a part of its regular business methods, and as an " entirely proper business transaction." The treasurer of another company testified that his concern had done much business with the city, that on several occasions he had paid money to competitors for putting in apparently genuine bids which by preconcerted agreement were higher than his, and that his company had paid out a part of its profits for this accommodation. He admitted also that he had destroyed the books of the company which would disclose these transactions. Two fireproofing concerns doing an extensive business in this city combined for the purpose of parceling out the work. Contract for contract was generally conceded, although in some cases money was paid as the price of abstaining from competition. Both concerns, by keeping up the appearance of an active and real competition, with the attendant circumstances of figuring and bidding, gave the city officials to understand that there was no collusion. Even charity secured no exemption, and the profits obtained from a hospital, a home for crippled children, and the city of Boston, were united in one check which represented the cost of collusion on these jobs.

About the year 1900 a carefully planned combination was created embracing practically all the firms and corporations engaged in structural steel work in New England. This was sometimes called the " Boston Agreement." Meetings of the members interested in a particular work were held at which it would be determined whether an arrangement for collusive bidding should be entered into. If this was decided on, an agreement was made as to who should get the job, as to the price at which it should be taken, and as to the consideration which was to be received by the others. In order to preserve the appearance of competition and to insure the success of the scheme, the parties to the agreement would arrange the bids to be submitted on a progressive scale above the prearranged bid of the concern to which the work had been allotted. The consideration to be paid by the selected bidder to the other parties to the combination was sometimes a cash payment, but more frequently an understanding that the service rendered by these " complimentary bids " should be returned when other work was to be figured. A code was established to conceal the identity of the members of the combination who were designated at one time by the names of various countries and at other times by numbers. It would be impossible to estimate the cost to the city through the operation of the " Boston Agreement," because the consideration generally paid for an award of a contract by the bidders to one of their number was the return of the same favor on other occasions. . . . In the case of the Brookline-street bridge two of the competitors testified that eleven of the bids, submitted by the largest corporations in the country were prearranged and collusive, the parties not only submitting bids as if they were independent and competing bidders, but signing statements that their bids were made in good faith, without fraud, collusion, or connection with any other persons bidding for the same work.

Collusion in the matter of contracts is not confined by any means to the private companies themselves. Arrangements are frequently made between municipal authorities and contractors for the division of the huge profits derived from public works. Business concerns sometimes agree to employ a certain number of party " heelers " as a condition of receiving contracts for public undertakings. Campaign funds are frequently swollen by builders and construction companies who expect large rewards in the form of contracts. In short the public can never know when there has been genuine competition in bidding and there seems to be no way of preventing " gentlemen's agreements."

Another serious objection to the contract system is to be found in the incentive which it offers to " scamp " the work and use materials of a lower grade than those required in the specifications. When competition is genuine and the winner receives the contract at a figure which leaves a narrow margin, he is under a strong temptation to recoup his losses by slighting his work. To avoid this result, the city must have capable and honest inspectors who can withstand the pressure which the fraudulent contractor may bring to bear upon them. Effective inspection on a large undertaking requires a staff of competent men, and the cost of this to the city is often enormous. In comparing the efficiency and economy of the two methods this additional charge should always be taken into consideration.

Another objection to contract work is to be found in the difficulty of making the plans and specifications of the contract with absolute definiteness so that the contractor cannot bring in a huge bill for changes in the original plan. When changes appear to be desirable, they may be easily accomplished under the direct employment system, for all that is necessary is to direct the foremen to alter their operations to suit the new conditions. Under the contract methods, the contractor takes advantage of every change to impose new and onerous terms upon the city.

A final objection is that the city must pay large profits to contractors which might be saved by direct employment. This objection is based, however, on the assumption, which is by no means always warranted, that the city can perform its own undertakings with a reasonable degree of efficiency.

Over against these disadvantages connected with the contract system should be set the difficulties connected with direct municipal employment and chief among these is the difficulty of securing capable experts, foremen, and laborers. And granting that this problem may be solved satisfactorily, direct employment involves many questions of public policy which are not raised at all by contract labor system.

We have seen how collusions among competing contractors are often made at public expense; but we should not overlook the fact that where the city employs directly large numbers of workmen collusions between "labor leaders" and politicians are just about as common. Labor leaders enter into alliances with municipal authorities, agree to deliver a certain number of votes on election day in return for payments made outright or in return for office, and then fortify themselves by courting the favor of union labor. In other words labor leaders by distributing a large number of "soft jobs" on public works to their immediate followers may bribe workmen into accepting corrupt and inefficient public service and supporting corrupt parties that are sworn foes to any enlightened labor policy. This is not a matter of speculation. We have had plenty of revelations on this score also.

Other problems than those of corruption in labor politics are raised by direct employment. Where the city becomes a permanent employer of labor on a large scale it is confronted by the question of how best to select municipal workmen and how to treat them as they approach old age. Competition in private business compels employers to weed out the older employees as quickly as their services fall below the efficiency line, but public officials can and do listen to dictates of humanity. Old men cannot be turned out to die simply because

they have ceased to be able bodied, but if they are retained the public suffers from impaired service. Thus
arises the demand for a complete system of civil-service
pensions for city employees, and the justice of this demand is meeting an ever wider recognition. Granting
this, however, the question arises whether the burden of
pensioning its employees should fall upon the city alone,
or should form a part of a general system of old-age
pensions to be sustained by the State and nation at large.

In short, direct employment raises issues of social
policy which are not purely municipal in character. It
is related to the question of unemployment, poverty, and
industry at large; and it is certain that not much can be
done to meet these larger social issues by a system of
direct employment.

Nevertheless, some immediate gains may be made for
labor by adopting a system of direct employment under
a wise administration of public works. High standards
of hours and wages may be prescribed, although these
may also be secured by stipulations in contracts. Some
relief may be given in critical times of wide-spread unemployment by a proper distribution of labor on public
works. A higher grade of local labor may be developed
in place of the casual, low standard labor brought in by
employing contractors.

All this presupposes, however, a more profound study
and application of the principles of efficiency management and cost units than has yet been made in American
cities generally. Speaking on this lack of efficiency
management (one cannot correctly speak of " business "
management, for private business is also notoriously lax
in its physical records), Dr. E. C. Meyer, expert in the

statistics of cities in the Bureau of the Census at Washington, says:

In what confused condition the physical records of most of our cities still are was revealed by the recent investigation of the Bureau of the Census. Numerous cities with a population of 30,000 and over were wholly unable to provide statistics of even approximate accuracy concerning such fundamental things as the areas of paving of different kinds in existence or laid during a specific year, or the area of streets subject to cleaning, or of the amounts of street sweepings removed, or of the area subject to sprinkling, or of the amount of refuse collected, or of the capacity of refuse disposal plants, or of the cost of paving, or of the number of men employed in various city services. In some cities nothing less than wild guesses were obtainable as to many of these significant items. Men carried on a pay-roll for highway employees and paid from appropriations for highways were found employed on refuse disposal or sewers or some other branch of city administration. In fact the conditions revealed by this investigation were so appalling that were the details to be set forth, they would seem almost incredible.

In many cities much attention is given to the installation of excellent systems of accounting, whereas the physical records of the city remain in confusion, being both incomplete and inaccurate. To install a good accounting system under such conditions is like planting a tree in barren soil. Fruit can be garnered only after a productive soil has been provided in the form of accurate and complete physical records. Of what value in the measurement of administrative efficiency is it to know in great detail the cost of labor of a given type when the work performed by that labor as expressed in the things accomplished is not known? Of what value is information as to the cost of machine sweeping when no accurate record has been kept of the areas cleaned, the character and conditions of pavements cleaned, or other vital factors which enter into the cost of such public services? The city which expends large sums for the improvement of its financial records and neglects its physical records acts in deplorable ignorance of the real ends to be attained by such improved accounts.

It is obvious that cities at present undertaking direct employment on a considerable scale must revolutionize their physical-records system. It is incumbent upon them to do this, and when they have established the proper standards, they may eliminate contract work, save the enormous tribute paid to contractors, set up better labor conditions, and get rid of a large part of the inevitable corruption connected with contract methods. Los Angeles, California, operates a successful cement mill, turning out a high-grade product at a price with which private mills cannot compete, and that city is now working on a consolidation of municipal enterprises and the establishment of direct employment on a large scale. The Borough of Brooklyn has demonstrated the economies of the public manufacture of paving materials. The bureaus of municipal research throughout the country are giving special attention to the problem of standardization and record keeping; and there is no doubt that within a short time our cities will have raised their efficiency to a point that will enable them to assume with safety the responsibilities which direct employment involves and at the same time reap the possible advantages which the system affords.

CHAPTER V

RAISING AND SPENDING THE CITY'S MONEY

THE very mention of the word "finance" brings up in the mind of the reader a vision of dreary volumes filled with columns of figures; but rightly viewed, the financial tables of a city are not dull. They are not merely a record of the income and outgo of dollars and cents; they are in a large measure the barometer of city welfare. The change of a few figures in the budget of a city may mean that the lives of thousands of children are to be saved by some extension in the activities of the health department; that prostitution is to be routed out of the tenement-house districts; that the people's children are to have more efficient education; that the public-service corporations are to be compelled to discharge their full duties to the community.

Such changes in figures are, however, by no means fortuitous. They express the interest or the apathy of those citizens and associations having power in public councils. They represent the ballots on election day. No citizen, church, trade union, civic organization, or political party can escape responsibility for them. The rise of the city in well-being and business efficiency is recorded in them. Forbidding as they are, they are vital. The city's budget is the central problem of the city's administration.

In 1905 the total revenues from general property taxes of the cities of the United States having over 30,000 inhabitants was $309,441,271. In 1909 the budget of New York City alone was four times the combined state budgets of Alabama, Arkansas, California, Colorado, Connecticut, Delaware, Florida, Idaho, Illinois, and Georgia. The tax rates of cities are steadily rising, and the valuation of city real estate is more and more approximating its true worth. Municipal debts are on the up grade. Boston, in 1905, owed $166.60 for every inhabitant within its gates and New York City owed $161.94.

The city, however, cannot tax its inhabitants and increase its debts at will, for it is subject in its financial matters to certain fundamental limitations laid down in the state constitution. These restrictions in general are as follows:

The rate of taxation which a city can impose is limited to a certain percentage of the assessed value of the real and personal property within its borders.

Cities are compelled to derive most of their revenues from a tax imposed equally on real and personal property.

The city is often forbidden to loan its credit to private corporations. This limitation is the result of grave abuses on the part of municipalities in floating bonds to aid in the construction of railways, the location of factories, and the establishment of other private enterprises.

It is also the common practice to limit the indebtedness of the city. The municipality is not allowed to become indebted for any purpose or in any manner to an amount exceeding a certain per cent. of the assessed valuation of the real estate as it appears on the assessment rolls. Exceptions to this limit are sometimes made by excluding from the regular indebtedness amounts invested in certain public improvements owned by the city, which yield a current net revenue, after due allowance is made for repairs, depreciation, and the provision necessary for the ultimate discharge of the debts incurred in the construction of such improvements.

The great source of municipal revenue is the general property tax; that is, a tax imposed at a certain rate upon real estate and stocks, bonds, mortgages, household goods, and other personal property. It is the practice to have this real and personal property evaluated by local assessors and the State usually imposes a certain rate in addition to that levied by the city.

The real and personal property tax is held to be so equitable that in a majority of States it is made the chief source of revenue by constitutional provision. The theory behind it is that there should be no discrimination among the different forms of property and that all should be taxed alike. However excellent the theory may be in itself, it is becoming increasingly difficult to apply it in practice. In the small cities where there is no great amount of wealth and intangible property consists largely of recorded mortgages, it is relatively easy to discover most of the personal property. But, as joint-stock concerns and corporations come into existence, citizens invest their wealth in the stocks and bonds of companies in other States and even in foreign countries, and by locking their papers up in strong-boxes and keeping the matter secret, they can avoid the assessment.

In the older Eastern commonwealths the proportion

of personal property which can be discovered by the assessors shows a tendency to decrease. A special tax commission in New York in 1907 declared that the real estate was assessed at very nearly its full valuation, while only approximately eight hundred millions out of the estimated twenty-five billions of dollars in personal property owned by citizens of the State had been listed for taxation. Even in a Western State like Minnesota, it was reported in 1905 that the per capita assessment of personal property was no larger than it was in 1880. A Minnesota tax commission called attention in that year to the fact that the money reported by all the citizens to the assessors amounted to less than four per cent. of the known bank deposits in the State. This is certainly an evidence of the defects in the personal-property tax, and the methods of assessments. In 1912 in New York City the total assessed valuation of real estate was $7,861,898,890, while the assessed valuation of personal property was only $342,963,540.

Experts in taxation all over the country including such an eminent authority as Mr. Lawson Purdy, of the New York department of taxes and assessments, are coming to view the personal-property tax as a flat failure. State after State has sought to prevent evasion by drastic and inquisitory laws. They have tried assessment under oath, tax inquisitors, and tax " ferrets." They have threatened to visit with imprisonment and fine every person who failed to make a full and true statement of the amount of his personal property. As a Massachusetts tax commission declared in 1907, human ingenuity has been exhausted in the United States in inventing drastic measures in securing the true declaration of personal property. The only means they seem to have overlooked is the use of torture employed in the Roman Empire to force reluctant taxpayers to disclose their personal property. A few years ago Ohio made a desperate attempt to unearth personal property for taxation, but in 1905 the amount of personal property including the property of railways and some other corporations was relatively lower than it was thirty-five years before.

The failure of drastic inquisitorial methods has led many leading authorities on municipal taxation to favor the abandonment of the personal-property tax. A New York City commission of 1906 declared, " The personal-property tax is a farce. It falls inequitably upon the comparatively few who are caught. The burden it imposes upon production is all out of proportion to the revenue it produces. Year after year, state and local assessing boards have denounced it as impracticable in its workings and unjust in its results. . . . It is time the situation was faced squarely and the tax in its present form abolished. . . . So far as the personal-property tax attempts to reach intangible forms of wealth, its administration is so comical as to have become a by-word. In practice it has come to be merely a requisition by the board of assessors upon leading citizens for such donations as assessors think should be made, and is paid as assessed or reduced according as the citizen agrees with the estimate of the assessor. Such a method of collecting revenue would be a serious menace to democratic institutions were it not recognized as a howling farce."

With the failure of the personal-property tax has come a demand for its abolition, and for the transference of the burden principally to real estate. The practical argument in favor of this is that a real-estate tax is simple, easily assessed, and readily collected. It is not inquisitorial in its nature and it is not expensive in its operation.

The advocates of the real-property tax do not, however, confine their arguments to these practical aspects of the question. They favor the real-property tax on ethical and humanitarian grounds. Following out more or less logically the doctrines of Henry George, they would materially reduce, if not entirely abandon, the tax upon buildings and personal property, and shift the burden to the land by taxing what is called the " unearned increment" in ground values. This unearned increment is the result of a steady increase in the value of land in cities which is not due to the efforts of the landowners or any single individual, but to the growth of industry and population in general. At the present time, this unearned increment goes into the hands of the landlord, who may not own the improvements upon the land or do anything at all to advance the industry or prosperity of the city. It is a tribute paid by those who labor to those who are fortunate enough to have possession of land in a growing community.

Mr. Frederick C. Howe gives the following interesting example of the growth of unearned increment in a great city, New York:

The whole of Manhattan Island was first sold to the Dutch by the Indians for $28.00. In 1904 the land values of Greater New York were appraised for taxation at $3,057,-161,290. By 1906 the land had increased in value to $3,391,711,526. In two years' time $334,550,236 had been added to the fortunes of those already enriched through the city's growth. They had done nothing to create this value. They had given no labor, no thought to the development of the city. Many of the owners lived in distant parts of the world. The growth continued just the same. By 1907 the appraised value of the land underlying the city had advanced to $3,557,591,504, or an increase over the year before of $165,879,978. In 1908 the valuation had still further increased to $3,843,165,597, or an increase of $284,-271,643. (From Annual Reports of Commissioners of Taxes and Assessments of New York.)

The human imagination cannot comprehend such stupendous figures. The total area of the city is but 190,000 acres. The land is worth $213,400 per acre. One acre of the metropolis would buy an average farm of 5000 acres in extent. The land values of Greater New York exceed the total value of all the buildings and improvements in the city, on which generations of labor have been expended, by over $700,000,000.

In 1900 the value of all the farm property in the nine States of New York, New Jersey, Pennsylvania, Massachusetts, Connecticut, Maine, New Hampshire, Vermont, and Rhode Island was but $2,950,532,628, or $607,058,876 less than the value of the naked land in New York City in 1907. This value exceeded by nearly $1,000,000,000 all of the capital in the United States invested in machinery, tools, and implements in 1900. It was almost equal to the value of all the farm buildings in the United States.

This narrow point of land which forms the gateway of the nation, and which can scarcely be discerned upon the map, exceeds in value the census appraisal of all of the farming land with the improvements thereon lying to the east of the Alleghany Mountains. It is equal to one-sixth of the total value of the 841,201,346 acres of improved land in the United States. Into these farms have gone three centuries of struggle. They represent the sacrifices of the pioneer, of the log cabin, and the prairie schooner, the drought and the scourge of the Western prairie. In this making of a nation are all the sacrifices and the isolations, the struggles and the disappointments, the lack of opportunities for education, and the unceasing toil of those who have converted the plains of America into fields of golden corn and grain. Yet a few thousand landlords, who have possessed themselves of a spot of land but little larger than a Western township, have come into possession of wealth half as valuable as all the farm products produced in a single year in the United States.

No thrift of the owners created this value; but the coming of population, the development of commerce and industry, the perfection of the arts and sciences, all these agencies have brought into existence unearned incomes more princely than that which enabled Crassus to unite with Cæsar and Pompey in the control of the Roman republic.

In order to impress upon the citizens of Chicago the enormous growth in unearned increment in that city, three former members of the school board gave out, in 1909, the following statement:

In 1818 the United States Government gave the square mile between State, Madison, Halsted and Twelfth Streets to the State of Illinois, to be held in trust for the support of the public schools and the education of the children of Chicago. Except for one block, between Madison, Dearborn, State, and Monroe Streets, nearly all of this square mile was sold about seventy years ago for less than $40,000. Within fifteen years after it was sold this square mile was worth six million dollars. To-day its value is hundreds of millions of dollars (without improvements). The rent from this square mile of land would be sufficient to support for all time the entire school system of the State of Illinois without an additional dollar of taxation.

Even the representatives of real-estate interests are being forced to recognize the injustice of compelling the

Some Instances of Increase

In Real Estate Prices at Pittsburgh.

The Property at 311-4th Av. 4800 sq. ft. 40x120.	Schmidt-Hamilton Bldg. Dimensions 60 x 240 ft.
	WORTH PER FRONT FOOT

Worth in 1908	$400,000.00	1908	$15,000 A Front Foot
Sold in 1896	$185,000.00		
Sold in 1888	$55,000.00	1884	$3,500 A Front Foot
Sold in 1887	$52,000.00		
Sold in 1884	$30,000.00		

public to pay an enormous annual tribute to those who render no service to the community. Recently Mr. Allan Robinson, president of the Allied Real Estate Interests of New York, declared: "I hold no brief for the man who owns land he will not improve. Worse than the miser who hoards his gold and thus keeps it from circulation, more culpable than the capitalist who spends his wealth for his own pleasure is the landowner who for distant profit, withholds from use land that the exigencies of the community require. The corroding cares, ill health, stunted growth, and inequality of opportunity which haunt the habitations of the poor in our cities may well be laid at his door, and I shall make no effort to relieve him of responsibility which his ownership has entailed upon him and which he has been unwilling to assume. Ownership of land carries with it corresponding burdens. The welfare of the race may be jeopardized through the selfish policy of landowners. The voters of the future are the children of to-day. Take from them what they now need for normal growth and development and when they reach man's estate they will take from you or your children all that land which you are now withholding from them."

The taxation of land values is now passing out of the realm of economic theory into actual practice. The Commission on Congestion of Population in New York City reported in 1911 in favor of the transfer of a considerable portion of the burden of taxation on improvements to the land. In a measure known as the Sullivan-Brooks Bill, introduced into the New York legislature in that year, it was provided that the rate of taxation on the buildings and improvements in New York City should be gradually reduced to one-half of the rate on the land. The text of the measure reads as follows:

The board of aldermen shall, for the year nineteen hundred and thirteen, in fixing the rate of taxation on real estate in the city of New York, exclusive of special franchises, so apportion the rate that the rate on the difference between the value of such real estate with its improvements, and the value of such real estate wholly unimproved, assessed as provided for in section eight hundred and eighty-nine of this act, shall be ninety per centum of the rate on the value of such real estate wholly unimproved. Every year subsequent to nineteen hundred and thirteen the rate on the difference between the value of such real estate with its improvements, and the value of such real estate wholly unimproved, shall be still further reduced ten per centum of the rate on the value of such real estate wholly unimproved, until the rate on the difference between the value of such real estate with its improvements, and the value of such real estate wholly unimproved, shall be fifty per centum of the rate on the value of such real estate wholly unimproved; and thereafter the board of aldermen shall so apportion the rate of taxation that the rate on the difference between the value of such real estate with its improvements and the value of such real estate wholly unimproved, shall be fifty per centum of the rate on the value of such real estate wholly unimproved.

This measure, although it was twice defeated, elicited warm support, and there seems to be no doubt that the principle which it embodies will steadily gain adherents until it will become in one form or another a part of the law of New York City.

On March 5th, 1912, the electors of Seattle, Washington, defeated a measure more drastic in character than the New York provision; but the large vote in favor of the proposition shows that such measures can no longer be treated as academic. The Seattle amendment provided that

from and after the first day of July, 1912, no tax for corporate or municipal purposes in the city of Seattle shall be levied or imposed on any improvements on, in or under any lands in the city of Seattle, nor on any form of personal property except leasehold interests in land; but, from and after the first day of July, 1912, all taxes within said city for corporate or municipal purposes shall be levied on and collected from the assessed value of leasehold interests in land, public service corporation franchises, and on and from the assessed values of all lands and all other natural resources in said city, except such lands as are used only for municipal, educational, literary, scientific, religious, or charitable purposes already exempt from taxation by law; provided, that nothing herein shall be construed to prevent the imposing of licenses on certain occupations within the city of Seattle in the exercise of the police power or affect any charter provision or ordinance regulating the sale of intoxicating liquors.

Sec. 2. No tax or fee for corporate or municipal purposes shall be imposed in the city of Seattle upon any trade, labor, business, person, industry, or profession under the pretext of a license or the exercise of the police power except where the imposition of such tax or fee is for the avowed purpose of limiting and discouraging the pursuit or object so taxed; and all ordinances imposing such taxes shall state clearly that the purpose is to limit and discourage the pursuit or object so taxed.

In 1911, Pennsylvania abolished for Scranton and Pittsburgh the obsolete practice of classifying unimproved city real estate as agricultural land chargeable at only one-half the regular city rate of taxation. " In Pittsburgh this system had resulted in gross abuses, land being kept as pasture near the heart of the city and profiting by this low tax-rate as well as under-assessment; while the added burden fell upon the owners of improved property assessed at full city rate and especially upon small home owners." The new commission charter of Everett, Washington, provides for the single tax in the following language:

The assessment, levy and collection of taxes on real and personal property for all corporate or municipal purposes of the city of Everett, and to provide for the payment of the debts and expenses thereof, shall be uniform in respect to persons and property therein: Provided, that for the years 1912 and 1913 there shall be exempt from such taxation 25 per cent., and for the year 1915, 50 per cent., and for the year 1916, 75 per cent., and thereafter 100 per cent., of the value of all buildings, structures and improvements, and other fixtures of whatsoever kind upon land within said city. Nothing herein shall affect property in said city exempt from taxation under the laws of the State of Washington.

The chief of the tenement-house division of the bureau of health of Philadelphia in his report of January 1, 1910, calls attention to the " social " character of the whole housing problem, and emphasizes the element of the land by saying: " No one can go far astray in the study of housing and living conditions without being continually reminded of the fact that the land is at the base of all these problems. . . . The settled and proper respect which all Americans have for private property and for the protection of every citizen in the enjoyment of the products of his labor does not entail any veneration for the protection of private land values which the holder has done nothing to create. Without subscribing to the

' single tax ' theory or any other general philosophy, it must be obvious to every one that land values in a city are mainly created by society itself. It is inevitable that society will grow more and more to demand for all the people an increasing share of these values which the people have produced."

A second important source of municipal revenues is the franchises of public-service corporations. This tax rests upon no very clearly formulated principles at present. Sometimes it is collected in a lump sum by the sale of the franchise or special privilege to the highest bidder. Frequently it is imposed in the form of a percentage tax on the gross or net receipts of the corporations. Occasionally it is employed by exasperated citizens as a method for "getting even" with municipal monopolies that have made enormous gains at public expense either by taking advantage of loosely drawn franchises or by watering stocks and rendering poor service to customers. More recently the tendency has been to tax franchises as real estate, and the experience of New York City in this form of taxation has commended it to other cities. The taxation of franchises as real estate is based upon the theory that a franchise is "a right to the use of land" and should be strictly classed along with landed property.

The owners of franchises however have very strenuously fought this form of taxation on the ground that inasmuch as their franchises were exempt from taxation at the time of granting the imposition of a tax is simply confiscation. For example, a street-railway company holds a franchise. It invests $100,000 in its plant, tracks and rolling stock, but by virtue of the monopoly which it enjoys is able to pay a dividend of five per cent.

upon $200,000. Under such circumstances, the franchise alone would be treated as worth $100,000, although in fact efficiency in operation might be partly responsible for the large dividend. Under the old law, the corporation would pay a tax on only $100,000 — the value of its tangible property; but if the franchise is taxed as real estate at two per cent. the corporation must pay on $200,000 valuation. Thus by taxation two-fifths of the capital value of the franchise, that is $40,000, is cut away. The dividend paid by the corporation is thus reduced on account of the necessity of paying that rate into the treasury of the city.

The expediency of taxing the franchises of public-service corporations is the subject of no little debate. The taxpayers of cities usually favor putting a portion of the burden upon the public-service corporations on the ground that it reduces the tax rate. On the other hand, the customers of the public-service corporations prefer to see charges for gas, electricity, and the like reduced rather than any relief afforded to the taxpayer. The franchise tax is at bottom, as Dr. Wilcox remarks, " a consumption tax on the common necessities of life which appears as a special burden upon the poor and is therefore unjust and undemocratic. On this theory, then, democracy will necessitate that franchises for the supply of the common necessities of urban life must have their value regulated .in the interest of cheaper and better service."

A third source of municipal revenue is derived from fees, licenses, and poll taxes. The original practice of paying municipal and county officers under the fee system has been generally abandoned in favor of a fixed salary. The most lucrative licenses for municipalities are those granted to saloons. In 1901 the large cities of the United States having more than 100,000, derived twenty million dollars from liquor licenses. It is customary to license push-cart peddlers, omnibus, carriage, and taxicab operators, and theaters. The poll tax is not commonly employed as a strictly municipal tax, but it is levied in Boston at the rate of $2.00 per capita. Inasmuch as citizens are not deprived of the suffrage on account of their failure to pay the tax, a large proportion of the amount remains uncollected every year.

A fourth source of municipal revenue is the business tax, which is commonly employed in Southern cities; and was recently proposed in New York by the mayor's commission on new sources of revenues in the form of a tax on hotels, theaters, restaurants, and other concerns which cannot be driven away but depend upon the city for their profits. In the South this form of tax is applied not merely to saloon keepers, but is frequently imposed upon bankers, tradesmen, and staple business concerns. In some Southern cities as much as one-fourth of the municipal revenue is derived from business taxes, other than liquor licenses.

Finally, there are the municipal revenues derived from the operation of public utilities such as gas plants, electric-light plants, and water-works.

The determination of the amount of money to be raised by taxation is vested in the budget-making authority of the city. The budget is the list of annual appropriations made for the various city needs. The distribution of the total amount appropriated among the several branches of municipal administration is the central element to be considered in budget-making, for this is the point at which the demands for efficiency and social services collide with the claims of the politicians to the spoils of office and with the protests of those who would reduce government activities to the minimum.

In the old-fashioned city charters budget-making was vested in the common council, and the annual appropriation represented a collection of items which the several members of the council were able to secure by "log-rolling." The American science of log-rolling is simple. One member of the city legislature says to another, "Your constituents and party organization demand certain appropriations for local benefits, and so do mine. You vote for my lot of little 'jobs' and I will vote for yours. That's fair, ain't it?" Thus the larger interests of the city are subordinated to petty local interests — a "respectable" method of getting money from the city treasury.

Speaking of the city council under the old régime, the Boston Finance Commission said: "Its work on the annual appropriation bill consists generally of attempting to raise the mayor's estimates to the maximum amount allowed by law, with a preference for those departments where the patronage is largest. Loan bills are log-rolled through with more regard for the demands of interested constituents and the possibility of jobs than for the needs of the city as a whole." This condition of affairs is common throughout the United States where "representative" councils make the budget, and each member is allowed to introduce and press through items of appropriation by the log-rolling process.

Under this system large measures of public policy are often swept aside by councilmen in their frantic efforts to secure from the city funds " jobs " for their constituents, which generally means jobs for the " boys " who stand by the political machine. Those civic organizations which demand enlightened municipal legislation of a general character — more appropriations for schools, health bureaus, tenement inspection, milk stations — have under the log-rolling system no central point of attack. No councilman is responsible for anything; and the association supporting some particular measure can go to no important city officer for a hearing, can secure no adequate publicity, no fair discussion of the merits of its demands. It must beg from one councilman's door to another and the councilman, however good his intentions, is so overwhelmed by the importunities of " the boys " that he can give little heed to anything which appeals to the people at large and to no job hunter in particular.

Of course, the theory of the system of budget-making by " representative councils " is that by adding together the special local interests the interest of the whole is secured. But in practice this is not true. If the people of a city were asked directly whether they would favor appropriating $100,000 for ice and milk stations in the summer, or the same amount for paid jobs for party workers, they would not hesitate long in making their decision in favor of the former. But when a civic association demands such an important appropriation from a council built on ward politics, it generally finds that the necessity of meeting the local demands overrules the councilors' good will.

In some cities responsibility in budget-making is even more widely diffused than in the ordinary council government. In Milwaukee, for example, under the law as it stood in 1911, the budget in part originated with the board of estimates, consisting of the mayor, president of the common council, comptroller, city attorney, president of the board of public works and the city treasurer; but the common council could treat the recommendations of this board as mere pious wishes and revise them at will. Other sections of the Milwaukee budget were prepared by separate boards — the school board, the park board, the library board, the museum board, and the city civil-service board — within certain limits as to amounts, but not subject to the council's approval. Such a system invites confusion, waste, and extravagance, and can be worked reasonably well only with great friction and loss of civic energy.

It is the recognition of this evil, which is apparently inherent in the budget-making by ward politicians, that has led a number of cities to take this important financial activity out of the hands of the council and vest it in some authority representing the larger municipal interests. In New York City, the budget is made by the board of estimate and apportionment, composed of the mayor, comptroller, president of the board of aldermen, and the presidents of the five boroughs — all elected by popular vote. The board of aldermen may increase* or omit items, but it cannot increase those presented by the board of estimate and apportionment or add new items. The budget of Boston, under the recent law, is originated by the mayor; the council may reduce but cannot increase items; and city finances are to be scrutinized

*PUBLISHER'S NOTE: This should read "decrease." (It has been reproduced here exactly from original edition.)

by a commission appointed by the governor. In several
other cities, budget-making is also vested in the hands
of some special authority. In Ohio cities, the mayor
makes up the budget from estimates furnished by the departments; the council may omit or decrease items, but
cannot increase the total of the budget. In Denver, the
mayor prepares the estimates and a two-thirds vote is
required in the council to change them. In Detroit, the
budget is prepared by the comptroller; and in San Francisco, by the auditor after public hearings.

It must not be cheerfully assumed that ward politics in
budget-making is entirely eliminated by wresting the
power to originate the budget from the council. As
Mr. Dooley once remarked, " A stone wall is often a
triumphal arch to the eye of the experienced." Heads
of departments annually require certain appropriations
and increases for the efficient discharge of the duties
entrusted to them. These appropriations and increases
are granted by the budget-originating authority, but they
may be *reduced* by the council. The ward politicians
put their heads together and threaten departmental chiefs
with reductions unless some " jobs " are granted in the
way of patronage and contracts for local interests.
Again, in New York City, heads of departments are frequently compelled to ask the board of aldermen to vote
special revenue bonds to meet extraordinary needs, and
it has been the practice of the board to refuse many of
these demands at first — and then yield later. While
it is not true that the power of refusal is always used
as a club to compel the departmental heads to grant
favors in return — such operations on the part of the
board of aldermen may justly be viewed with suspicion.

Nevertheless, the newer plan of vesting the budget-originating power in the hands of some authority representing the city as a whole, is shown by experience to be a decided improvement over the old methods. It centers the attention of those interested in appropriations upon a single officer or a small body of men who can be reached by publicity and are more sensitive to the demands of large policies. It materially reduces the power of the local ward-worker over city funds and patronage, and it tends to dignify the trying task of budget-making. It encourages publicity and helps to educate the citizens in one of the central issues of municipal politics.

Budget-making embraces many distinct and important processes. At the outset, estimates must be secured from the heads of the several departments who are in charge of the disbursement of city funds. The preparation of these estimates is not the simple matter which it might appear to be at a glance. It is important that uniform methods should be employed by the departmental heads in formulating their demands upon the treasury —" so that the dates talked about, the salary changes, and cost of supplies and repairs, etc., will mean the same thing in all estimates for each department and for each main division of work."

Whatever additional details and classes of expenditure ought to be included in departmental estimates, the following features should never be neglected. Estimates, on being analyzed, ought to show:

I. Proposed expenditures for current purposes. (1) Salaries and wages — title of office — rate per unit: day, week, month or year; classes of laborers and units of payment; proposed new positions and jobs; increases in payments per unit of present employees. (2) Maintenance of buildings and plants — former expenses; increases; new enterprises. (3) Supplies and materials — standardized; increases in amount and in cost per unit.

II. Permanent Improvements. Detailed analyses of the nature and cost of each. For example a square yard of asphalt should mean the same for one street as for another, or differences should be noted. Estimate of the degree of permanency. The city ought not to be selling fifty-year bonds to buy fire hose or dump carts.

III. Interest on debt and appropriations to sinking fund.

IV. Estimates for contingency funds — for it is unwise economy to overlook the possibilities of contingencies which experience has demonstrated.

V. Income-receiving departments — such as the waterworks department — should prepare special balanced budgets in addition to the estimates regularly laid before the budget-originating authority.

When the estimates from the several departments are prepared they should be printed and distributed so that adequate popular scrutiny may be secured. In addition to the detailed estimates available for experts, a special statement should be prepared for the general public, arranged with a view to attracting interest and discussion. For smaller cities it has been suggested that the estimates should be classified under the following social services and a brief elementary description given of the proposed work of each branch:

General Administration
Protection of Persons and Property
Health
Sanitation
Highways
Charities
Corrections
Education
Recreation
Public Utilities

The most unique and effective method of presenting the essential features of the budget to the people was inaugurated in 1910 by New York City (on the initiative of the Bureau of Municipal Research), in the establishment of an official budget exhibit, representing in graphic form the past and proposed expenditures of the municipality. In the spring of that year the officers charged with submitting estimates for the next budget were instructed to submit " in addition to the information prescribed by the comptroller such charts, diagrams, photographs, plans or representations as would serve the purpose of appropriate illustration of budget requests, as well as their relation to permanent city improvements, either in progress or projected." During the month of October, 1910, these charts, diagrams, and illustrative materials, effectively arranged, were thrown open to the public and each day addresses were given by public officers on aspects of city finances. The records show that over 800,000 visits were made to the exhibit.

The experiment of the first year was so successful that it was repeated in 1911 with more effect. On this occasion the finance department displayed the cost of operating the city departments by gilded cubes, and the increases asked for the 1912 budget by purple cubes. The work of the commissioner of accounts in unearthing crooked finance in several branches of city government was shown by a large ledger of placards turned by an attendant and lighted by a searchlight. By charts, placards, photographs, and models the problems of street-paving, sewerage, and water supply were graphically represented. Plans of the metropolitan sewerage commission for a general sewerage system for the whole city were shown; and the high-pressure bureau was represented by ingenious models showing the difference in the height and quantity of water thrown by ordinary hydrant pressure, by fire engines, and by the high-pressure service. By these and other devices the manifold activities of the city administration were made clear to the citizen and the budget brought out into the light of publicity.

Another, and perhaps the most important, aspect of budget publicity is an intelligent discussion in the press while the budget is in process of formation. Newspapers are beginning to see that, by the use of a little imagination, striking " news " elements may be found in the appropriations which touch in a most intimate way the daily comfort and convenience of their readers. Of course young and inexperienced reporters may find only reams of printed sheets containing statistics, but it is good journalism for newspapers to assign their keenest men to the task of keeping track of the budget process from day to day until the final word is said.

Coupled with publicity, and essential to its efficacy, are

the open hearings afforded by the budget-making authorities. These hearings should be held on the estimates
before they have been acted on at all by the budget-
originating authorities. Hearings should be held — as
in New York City — on the tentative budget as it will
be put through by the authorities, unless strong enough
forces are brought to bear. Finally the authorities
should be required to publish the requests for appropriations definitely refused. Under such a system, it is the
fault of the citizens and civic associations — providing
they have done their duty at the polls — if they do not
secure a budget which corresponds to the public needs.

When the budget is made and the purposes for which
the funds of the city are to be spent are finally determined, the interest of the citizens in finance should not
cease, for the proper expenditure of the moneys granted
requires not only expertness on the part of the spending
authorities and those who supervise but also watchfulness on behalf of the public. Otherwise wastefulness
will result through the inefficiency of officials, their
ignorance of improved methods, faulty accounting, or
plain malfeasance and corruption.

It is a common practice, for instance, in some cities
to transfer the unexpended balance of one department
to another with an "understanding" as to the beneficiaries. A benevolent despot in Pittsburgh is reported
to have secured money for street repairs, which the public was willing to approve, and then used it to buy parks
which the public was not intelligent enough to demand.
But such despotism is seldom benevolent. Hence there
should be a rule to the effect that every item in the budget

should go for the specific purpose for which it is appropriated and no other.

Another happy practice of careless municipal finance is for the head of the department to spend in short order the sum set aside for his purposes and then rely upon revenue bonds or special grants to piece out the year. Often these grants cannot be withheld because the needs of a department that has spent its money are imperative. Hence there should be a rule to the effect that the regular pay-roll of any department should not exceed one-twelfth of the annual appropriation. This rule will help stop the practice of loading the city pay-roll at election times for party purposes.

Money wisely appropriated may be foolishly spent by haphazard methods of purchasing supplies. For example, it was discovered some time ago in New York that ordinary coat-hooks worth five cents apiece cost the city $2.21 apiece when placed in position, including labor, materials, etc. Frequently one department is paying twice as much for the same kind of soap or nails as another department. This evil should be remedied by establishing central purchasing bureaus and by standardizing units of supplies so that the advantages of large purchases may be realized and the lowest price uniformly paid, the conditions of production being taken into account.

Standardizing purchases and expenditures generally implies uniform and scientific accounting that will show accurately where the money has gone and what the respective units of work and materials have cost. The absence of uniform accounting makes city finances a jungle wherein petty pilfering and grand larceny may go on undiscovered.

The Bureau of Municipal Research of New York, determined to find out the exact status of affairs, "has examined the financial reports of seventy-five American cities on the hunt for an intelligible balance sheet. . . . Of the seventy-five cities, sixty-eight do not show, with respect to current expenses and revenues, how much they have spent, including bills not paid and revenues due but not yet received. There is thus no proper income account. Assets are not shown by forty-eight of the cities, which thus have no balance sheet, twenty-nine do not show the balance of appropriations unexpended, and twenty-one do not state their bonded debt. If the books of large private corporations were kept with the looseness displayed by the municipalities no expert accountant would or could certify to their correctness."

In 1902, Ohio came to the conclusion that this form of tangled finance would have to stop, and accordingly the legislature passed a law creating a state bureau of inspection and supervision for the accounts of cities, counties, townships, and villages. This bureau has developed a system of accounts that is designed to make plain the income and outgo of the city. Massachusetts passed, in 1906, a law requiring the financial officers of cities and towns to report to the state bureau of statistics upon a uniform schedule supplied by the bureau. Indiana, Iowa, Wisconsin, and other States have uniform accounting laws for municipalities, and within a few years it will be possible to know something definite about the business side of city governments. Units of cost may be compared then, whereas now one cannot be certain that a yard of asphalt means the same thing in the report of any two officers in charge of paving repairs.

In order to make effective the newer devices for standardization and public control, it has been found necessary to create special authorities to supervise expenditures. Boston has recently been trying a new and interesting experiment with its finance commission. This commission consists of five members, voters in Boston, appointed by the governor of the State and his council for terms of five years, one going out every year. This commission is empowered to " investigate any and all matters relating to appropriations, loans, expenditures, accounts, and methods of administration affecting the city of Boston or the county of Suffolk or any department thereof that may appear to the commission to require investigation and to report from time to time to the mayor, the city council, the governor, or general court." The mayor may refer to the commission any claim, pay-roll or bill against the city for investigation, if he questions its validity or thinks it excessive; and, pending the report of the investigators, payment is withheld. The commission on its own account may also investigate any financial question relative to the city which, in its opinion, requires looking into. Moreover, a bureau of municipal research has been established in connection with the commission to throw a constant light on municipal finances.

In its report for January 20, 1911, the commission states that it had held seventy-nine meetings, concluded eighty-eight hearings on various subjects, examined over two hundred witnesses, and issued twenty-five reports. Much of its time was spent in hearing contractors who claimed to have made the lowest bids on city work and failed to receive the awards, in discussing with heads of departments and other contractors the claims of unsuccessful bidders, in examining appropriations, loans, pay-rolls, overtime charges, and the purchase of lands and supplies by the city. The commission also employed many experts to examine closely into the management of several departments.

New York City has a special scrutinizing authority known as the commissioners of accounts or, popularly, as "the mayor's eye." This commission of two members is appointed by the mayor. It examines receipts and disbursements in the office of comptroller and chamberlain in connection with all departments. It may make special examinations of the accounts of city officers, on its own initiative or at the suggestion of the mayor; and it has full power to compel the attendance of witnesses. "Complaints, rumors, suspicions, criticisms by the press, disputes over contracts, public work in progress, delays, violations of specifications, comparison of equipment with that of other cities, chemical analyses of coal, reports on tests of materials, and so on, come under the jurisdiction of the commission." It pries about everywhere, and recently it has become a wonderful check on the financial vagaries of municipal officers. It found out that fireworks for the celebration of the Fourth of July were purchased at enormous prices and that aldermen received their reward for their generosity with the city's money. Little thieves and big are liable at any time to find their peculations exposed. For the benefit of the public the commission has established a bureau of information where the citizen may find out anything he wants to know about the city government, and also a bureau of complaint at which the citizen may lodge his grievances against the doings of any officer or department.

With segregated budgets, made after full hearing and public discussion, uniform accounting, special scrutinizing officers, ample opportunity for the private citizen to complain against the conduct of any city officer, there is no reason why the finances of an American city should not reach the standards set in the best-managed business concerns.

CHAPTER VI

GUARDING THE CITY AGAINST CRIME AND VICE

It is the principal business of the police force of a city to prevent crime by constantly keeping watch and ward, and to arrest those who commit offenses in spite of its vigilance. This appears to be an easy matter until it is remembered that the crime that they are to guard against is not a simple list of offenses which the whole community is agreed should be visited with punishment. There are, of course, the greater crimes — such as murder, burglary, arson, and highway robbery — on which there is common agreement; although there is no little diversity of opinion as to the degree of punishment that should be meted out. But there is a fundamental difference between this type of crime and the vices declared by law to be crimes — such as gambling, conducting immoral shows, prostitution, and evasion of the liquor laws.

The greater offenses may be committed in a city in spite of the vigilance of the police force, honestly administered; but penalized vice conducted on a revenue basis cannot thrive there without either active support from the police or, at all events, their indifference. It is the vesting of the moral guardianship of the city in the police force, composed of ordinary men, not clergymen or experts in ethics, that makes police administration perhaps the most difficult branch of city government.

Vice conducted on a revenue basis is always ready to corrupt every member of the police force from the roundsmen on their beats to the commissioner in his central office.

There are everywhere opportunities for discrimination and persecution; saloon-keepers are willing to compensate the police for overlooking violations of the liquor laws; gamblers and keepers of houses of ill-fame are glad to pay handsomely for " immunity "; in short, all of the lawless elements of the city which derive profit from plying their respective trades are ready to share their gains for " protection."

The ordinary sources of police corruption are augmented by the attempts of rural communities to force upon the cities moral standards which the latter do not accept. Furthermore, there is in the United States a marked tendency to penalize every action which the religious elements regard as sinful. Moral enthusiasts unite in pushing through legislation which they are not willing to uphold by concentrated and persistent action. When the police are called upon to enforce country-made laws in communities that do not believe in the wisdom or morality of such laws, it is small wonder that the granting of " immunity " becomes easy. Even when the moral laws which are enacted into criminal statutes are adequately supported in the conscience of the community, the burden of enforcing them is a heavy strain upon the police.

The lines of connection between vice and politics and administration are so varied and tangled that only an expert can hope to unravel all of them. The first link is, of course, the cash nexus; that is, the direct payment

of money to police authorities for immunity. This
varies in amount from the paltry dollars which a roundsman takes from a prostitute in return for allowing her
to escape arrest up to the thousands of dollars paid by
organized vice for general immunity; for it must be remembered that vice is organized. Speaking of pool-
selling and gambling in New York City, former commissioner of police, William McAdoo, now chief magistrate,
said:

The reader must forever get out of his mind the idea that,
in New York, pool-selling and gambling are sorts of sporadic
vices conducted here and there by shady characters, dangerous, disreputable, and criminal men. It is indeed true that
the admitted agents who run some of the low order of these
places are ex-convicts and men with bad or criminal records, and in a few instances they are desperate and dangerous men. But, taking the thing as a whole, it is simply
a vast business run on business principles, backed by men
of influence and power, capitalized liberally and on a strictly
cash basis; there is no watered stock or over-issuing of bonds
on the part of these syndicates; everything is down to actual
money.

This great business has its alliance with other business
interests. It helps the sale of luxuries, dress, jewels, wines;
it asks no questions about rents, it pays the highest; it employs an army of shrewd men with "pulls" in politics, and
has friends among the press men; it is a liberal contributor
to campaign funds; and, to tell the truth about it, there is
no more generous giver to charity. Indeed, some of them
are most exemplary church-members, and when the police
administration is honest and persistent, some of them are
great agitators for reform of other abuses. They hire the
best talent at the bar when it is needed. On the big cases,
when they go up on appeal, they are represented by the most
distinguished and able counsel. They control the pen of

able writers. The Louisiana lottery, just before it was
exiled, hired a clever and studious writer in Chicago, whom
I knew personally, to write a book on gambling from the
historical, philosophical, ethical, and moral point of view.
It was an intensely interesting history of gambling from the
earliest times, with ethical and philosophical deductions favorable to the business. The book was freely distributed
to legislators and congressmen and wherever it was thought
it would do the most good.

The gambling fraternity in New York have their clearing-
houses and exchanges just as well known and just as prominent as those of the business institutions in the lower part
of the town. The little fellows in this business, just as in
the other big speculative concerns, hang on the words of
the top man. A hint that there will be a change in the
Police Commissioner's office, or that matters had better be
kept quiet for a month or so, is just the same as a tip given
by some master of finance in Wall Street.

During the investigation conducted by the Lexow
Committee of the New York legislature, into police
methods in New York City in 1894, the business relations between vice and the police were fully disclosed.
Police Captain Schmittberger, in testifying, explained
how he levied tribute on the policy shops and liquor dealers in the precinct over which he had command. He
had a confidential man under him whose duty it was to
make the collections in the several precincts. It was
definitely understood with the gamblers that each policy
shop should pay $20 a month, and a liquor dealers' or-
ganization $80 a month. This money was collected
by the confidential agent and delivered to Captain
Schmittberger, who handed about twenty per cent. of
the amount to the inspector of the general inspection district, in which the precinct in question was located.

Schmittberger was forced to make this tribute to the
"man higher up," because it was within the power of
the inspector to raid the policy shops over his head, in
case the tribute was not shared.

The witness explained how in another precinct he collected about $800 a month as tribute from the poolrooms
and policy shops. In this precinct, he made no collections from the liquor dealers on the understanding that
they had made their peace with Tammany Hall, thus
purchasing their immunity by dealing directly with the
chief authorities of the city government.

A second way in which gambling secures immunity
from police interference is through political control.
Former Police Commissioner McAdoo declared that
gambling was generally permitted in Greater New York
because the leaders of all parties, particularly the party
that happened to be in power, wanted to use the pool-
rooms for party advantage. Whenever a gambler
wished to open an establishment, he would seek out the
political leader in the assembly district and gain his
friendship by agreeing to allow him to appoint a number
of employees at the poolroom, at an average salary of
$5 a day. Of course, these five or ten employees of a
poolroom had no duties. It was a polite way for the
gamblers to secure immunity; and the political leader
was thus able to "take care of" a few "boys" who had
rendered patriotic services in saving the country on election days.

Even more lucrative than organized gambling is organized prostitution, and the white-slave traffic. The
recent Commission on the Social Evil in Chicago, made
an estimate that the gains in Chicago from that source,

now organized on a business basis, are over $15,000,000 a year and that "the traffic is conducted by men principally, on purely commercial lines — as a profit-making concern." This commission laid bare the business ramifications of the traffic and showed how the managers had built up a system of securing girls and disposing of them on a percentage basis. The system maintained a small army of men as panders, cadets, and managers of the traffic, whose annual revenue totaled into the millions. The power of such a system in politics and in the administration of the police force can hardly be estimated.

When the police commissioner of a city is at open war with organized vice he often finds himself handicapped by innumerable tricks of the trade. One of the tricks formerly employed by poolroom gamblers in New York is described by Mr. McAdoo in his interesting book entitled "Guarding a Great City." It was the practice of a poolroom manager who wanted to open up a place of business to rent a room as a doctor's office, and install in the office some degenerate doctor, who was "kept sufficiently sober to be exhibited at the place for an hour or so every day." When the doctor was duly established and started in his "practice," the proprietor of the establishment would arrange with a dishonest police captain for a raid on the doctor's office. At the appointed hour the police battered in the doors only to find the doctor surrounded by his patients, apparently engaged in the legitimate practice of medicine. The doctor was promptly outraged at this raid by appointment, and with his patients and the proprietor of the establishment, ably seconded by a well-known firm of lawyers, went over to a judge in Brooklyn and secured a writ of injunction, forbidding the police to interfere with "an honorable citizen engaged in the legitimate practice of medicine." Armed with this injunction, the doctor's office then begins the business for which it was originally intended.

The administration of the police force may be placed in the hands of a board or a single commissioner elected by popular vote or appointed by the mayor, with or without the consent of one or both branches of the city council. During the middle period of our municipal development the supervision of the police force was often entrusted to a board of three men, frequently composed of representatives of both political parties, on the theory that a system of checks and balances would thus be instituted within the administration itself. It was soon found by experience, however, that in bi-partizan boards, the representatives of the two parties, instead of watching one another like hawks, generally combined to distribute the spoils of office. The board system, moreover, does not fix responsibility in any single person and when charges of corruption and inefficiency are preferred, each member is likely to plead "not guilty." The difficulty of placing responsibility has led our large cities to abandon the board system and concentrate police supervision in the hands of a single officer appointed by the mayor, and responsible to him.

The single-headed department is a highly centralized system, but if the police force is corrupt and the enforcement of the law is lax, the citizens know who is responsible — at least directly — although the head of the department and the mayor who appoints him cannot be

independent of the political organization which they both
ultimately represent. Where the police administration
is vested in a single officer, he is charged with the supervision of the entire force; he appoints his deputies and
his detectives and he can direct the operations of the
force all down through the hierarchy — at least theoretically.

In the selection of the police commissioner some important questions are to be considered. If a professional
chief is placed in charge of a professional force, a
bureaucratic spirit is likely to pervade the entire administration. A man taken directly from military service
or from any service in the police force naturally has
more interest in discipline and prompt discharge of
duty than in what are loosely termed, " the rights of
the citizen." It is obvious that men engaged in the same
business develop a code of ethics of their own, and are
likely not to be in sympathy with persons outside the
range of their particular work. A police officer who
has had occasion to use his stick on an obstreperous citizen and perhaps has been more or less beaten up himself in the discharge of his duties, if he rises from the
ranks to the office of police commissioner, is quite likely
to sympathize with the patrolman as against a citizen
who complains of petty interference or a sound clubbing.
Partially on this ground, it has been a common practice
in the United States to put non-professional men at the
head of police departments.

Safeguarding personal liberty against bureaucratic
police is not, however, the sole reason for choosing lay-
men to head this important branch of municipal administration; for, as Dr. Fuld points out, the non-profes-

sional head of the police department is often a professional politician, and he is appointed to the office for the express purpose of using the department as a source of revenue. It frequently happens that an efficient and somewhat bureaucratic police commissioner who attempts to execute the letter and spirit of the law is responsible for a reaction, which drives out of power the administration which he represents, and brings about the appointment of a politician who will favor, if not the positive criminals, at least that large element of the city who believe in "taking the lid off." The opportunities for revenue offered by "proper police administration" are so great that the professional politician cannot refrain very long at a time from interfering with the enforcement of the laws.

Even if the non-professional head of the police department is an honest man and desirous of conducting his department efficiently, he is greatly handicapped by his lack of practical experience with the operations of criminals and the habits of policemen. His term of office is short and before he learns the rules of the game which he is to play he is likely to be retired to private life.

A shortness or indefiniteness of term militates against the professional chief as well as against the non-professional man. As General Theodore Bingham, former police commissioner of New York City, has pointed out, the policemen know that the head of a department may be removed at any time, that the mayor who appoints the chief will be out of office after a few years at most, and that the permanent element to be considered is the party organization back of both of them.

"As the policeman is in office for life," says General Bingham, "he very logically looked past both the mayor and me and made his allegiance and took his orders from the only permanent influence concerned — the politician. I could not at that time even choose the leading officers of the department whom I wanted to carry out my orders. I was in command of a body of men who, by the logic of their position, were forced to take their final orders from some one else."

The almost insuperable objection to the non-professional police commissioner is his lack of knowledge of the ways of criminals, and the habits of thought and standards of conduct of the men under him. The policemen on the force come into direct contact with the people against whom the laws are to be enforced. Many of them have been in service for ten, twenty, or even thirty years. They know the police courts; they know the life in all parts of the city; they know the laws through actual experience; they know just about how far they can go in forcing saloon-keepers, gamblers, and the vicious elements to obey the letter of the law. They have seen police commissioners come and go; they suspect that much of the high talk at police headquarters about "putting the lid on," is directed to the tender-hearted public rather than to those who have to adjust it. They are liable to have small respect for a layman at headquarters.

The unit for police administration in the municipality is generally the precinct which is in command of a captain. This officer is responsible for the maintenance of order, enforcement of the law, and the protection of life and property in the area subject to his jurisdiction. In order to discharge his duties effectively he must make periodical inspection of the workings of the force under him, and in times of serious difficulty he is the commanding officer who assumes personal responsibility. On the one hand, he is in direct touch with the police commissioner, and, on the other hand, he knows the roundsmen and patrolmen under him. More than any one else he is responsible for the actual execution of the general policies formulated in the central office. It is true there are inspectors over him, and there may be detectives working alongside him without his knowledge; nevertheless, for the police work day by day the captain is the responsible officer.

Under the captain are the several platoons of patrolmen, each under an officer who assembles them at the station house, marches them to their posts and maintains a sort of inspection over them, while they are on their beats. As he tramps from post to post in the region kept by his platoon, the roundsman can discover how effectively the law is being enforced and how attentive are the men under his jurisdiction.

As a rule, the roundsman rises from the ranks. It has been found by experience impossible to secure the best service from the patrolmen unless the opportunity for promotion is open, and it has been found unwise to appoint to subordinate offices in the police department men who have not received the early training in practical patrol work. We do not have in the police service a system analogous to that offered by West Point for men desiring to become officers in the Army.

Although the practical experience of the roundsman as an ordinary policeman serves him well in some respects when he is promoted, his former comrades do not forget that he was yesterday a private in the ranks. If he begins by showing his authority and maintaining a high standard of discipline, he is apt to be reminded by some of them that he himself, as a patrolman, often grumbled at a strict enforcement of the rules. As former Police Commissioner McAdoo says: " The new roundsman is not apt to demand the respect due his rank, and is likely to be too familiar with the men under him, and they with him. This lack of distinction is often more marked under civil-service rules than under the old system. Under the old system it required men of nerve and dominating personality to fight their way up and then pay to get in. As a general rule, the officers commanding the police do not exact proper respect from their subordinates, and do not insist as they should upon the recognition due their rank and authority. They forget to drop good-fellowship and friendly acquaintance when they put on their uniform to perform official duty."

The patrolmen in the ranks in the leading cities of the United States are now selected under the civil-service rules. The old method of selection, commonly in vogue until a generation ago, was appointment by the head of the department or the mayor, which placed the service on a spoils basis. Whenever there was a change in the city administration the police force was revolutionized by the discharge of the old men and the selection of a new staff from among the political workers.

Beginning with the passage of the law in New York in 1883, civil-service reform, as applied to the police force as well as to other branches of city administration, has been gaining steadily. Under the New York civil-service rules, candidates must be citizens and endorsed by four persons of good character who are not saloon-keepers. They must, furthermore, submit to examinations, physical and mental. The physical tests are designed to discover whether the applicant has a sound body and the proper physique for the police service. A minimum height of five feet and eight inches is prescribed. There is a story told of a candidate who was a little short of this minimum and ingeniously added a half-an-inch bump to his height by having a friend hit him on the head with a shovel the day previous to the examination. The mental tests embrace some knowledge of the government and geography of the city, arithmetic and memory. Men who pass the examinations are placed on the " eligible " list from which appointments are made for the force.

It must not be thought, however, that the establishment of civil-service rules entirely eliminates politics. Party leaders maintain civil-service " training schools," and they bring pressure to bear upon the appointing officer to secure the selection of their candidates as soon as they are placed among the eligibles. Moreover, after a candidate is appointed he is required to serve a probationary period before his position is made permanent; and the men who stand high with their party run little risk of being dropped at the end of the preliminary trial.

Neither does the civil service afford a complete protection to men against political interference after their appointment. It is true that, under the merit-system rules, a patrolman cannot be dismissed without a hearing on the charges preferred against him, but he may be persecuted by being frequently transferred from one part of the city to another and compelled to move his family about, until his spirit is broken or he is driven from the force.

The difficulties of securing an efficient police force, either under civil service or the spoils system, are enormous; and in nearly every city there is constant clamoring against police administration. There are at the present time, a number of schemes for the improvement of this administration. There is, of course, always a demand for a large numerical increase in the force, and whenever there is a crime wave the administration can escape part of the responsibility by declaring that the department is undermanned. The basis upon which the number of patrolmen should be determined is not easy to establish, and no one can say positively when a city is adequately patrolled. It is easy to prepare tables showing that our American cities have fewer policemen per thousand of population than do European cities, and politicians anxious to secure positions for their henchmen, make much of our inadequate forces.

A second method of improving the police service, suggested by Mr. McAdoo, is to make some officer directly responsible for what happens in the district under his jurisdiction. Much can be said in defense of this doctrine at least theoretically, but it can only be fairly applied on the assumption that the responsible officer has under him enough men and the right kind of men.

Another method which has sometimes been used in American cities in their attempt to hold patrolmen to the faithful discharge of their duties is the use of plain-clothes detectives or " shooflies," as they are called. Although the immediate effect of the use of the " shoofly " may be the elimination of some unfit patrolmen, experience seems to show that reliance upon him tends to demoralize the force. As Mr. McAdoo points out: " The work of the spy is detestable, and the class of men who are willing to degrade themselves by performing these duties is such that but little credence can be placed upon their testimony. It injures the morale of the force when favored patrolmen are sent out in citizens' clothes to spy upon other policemen of the force. It is doubtful whether it is good policy to allow superior officers to spy upon the force. It is undoubtedly bad policy to encourage citizens to spy upon them."

A fourth proposition for the improvement of police administration is the establishment of stricter state supervision. The spirit of local autonomy is strong in the United States and attempts at establishing state control over police administration are regarded as bureaucratic and out of harmony with the spirit of American institutions. Nevertheless, many of our large cities have, at one time or another, been subjected in police matters to the control of state-appointed officers.

Generally speaking, however, police administration by state officers is regarded as anomalous and temporary, while almost complete local autonomy is held to be the natural and desirable condition. The police administration of Baltimore, St. Louis, and Kansas City, has been in the hands of state authorities, and it can hardly be said that by reason of this fact these cities stand at the head of American municipalities in the efficiency and integrity of their police forces.

According to a careful student of state supervision, Professor A. R. Hatton, the quality of police administration has risen and declined in conformity with the quality of the state government. " In general, the average result has been no higher than in cities with forces entirely independent of state influences. This conclusion is also valid for other cities, which after a season of state control, have been restored to independence. On the whole, it can hardly be claimed that the destruction of all local autonomy in the matter of police has justified itself in the quality of service which has resulted therefrom. . . . The temptation of the state administration to use the police forces for political purposes seems at times almost irresistible. When that occurs the effect upon local government is bad in the extreme. The city is practically helpless. Moreover, the evil conditions do not act as a spur to local spirit, because the power to eliminate them does not belong to the city voter." Although the experiment with the state commission has been fairly successful in Boston, it may be attributed largely to other circumstances than mere state influence.

There are certain advantages to be derived from a central supervision of police administration; and it is suggested by Professor Hatton that the governor should be given the power to remove municipal police commissioners for cause and should be assisted by a state inspection and detective force, charged with the duty of aiding him in securing information as to the conditions of law enforcement in the municipalities.

The criminal courts are an integral part of the police system, not separate judicial institutions to be treated under the head of the judiciary. The spirit and method of the magistrates determine in a large measure the effectiveness of police control. Magistrates with an academic knowledge of the law and without an intimate acquaintance with the habits of criminals and the difficulties which the policemen encounter in securing absolute legal proof in all cases, may destroy the zeal of a force by allowing notorious criminals to escape on technical grounds.

Mr. McAdoo in his book on the police system of New York City gives an example which illustrates the danger that arises from a lack of sympathetic coöperation between the courts and the police. An officer brings a prisoner into the court, and says to the magistrate, " This man is a pickpocket; he is a vagrant; his picture is in the Rogues' Gallery. This is the seventh time that I have personally arrested him; I caught him on a Thirty-fourth Street crowded car with two or three other pickpockets who escaped. A great many citizens are having their pockets picked every day. He has no honest means of support. Down at the Detective Bureau all know him as a professed crook all his life. He is a dangerous man to be at large." The magistrate then demands from the officer legal proof that the prisoner has no means of support. This, of course, the officer cannot produce and he is confounded when the prisoner " hauls $500 bills out of every pocket, shows a large diamond and calls up an accomplice, who swears that he keeps a small tailor shop and that the prisoner works for him." The magistrate, ignorant of the tricks of the trade, discharges the prisoner and roundly abuses the officer with interference of " personal liberty." The spirit of the officer is thus broken; and when he discovers another branch of the thieving fraternity in operation, shrugs his shoulders and thinks, " What 's the use? "

There is, however, another side to the case. A magistrate too closely in sympathy with the police force and incapable of taking a more or less detached view may err on the side of bureaucracy, and help to cultivate in the force a spirit of contempt for the rights of the citizen, particularly when the citizen happens to be a poor man. This aspect of judicial tyranny has been illustrated many times recently in the case of strikes, when peaceful picketers have been arrested on charges of " disorderly conduct " and railroaded to the workhouse by intolerant judges.

Employers who find that they are losing a strike frequently bring pressure to bear upon the police authorities and secure the indiscriminate arrest of leaders on slight charges, and with the aid of judges obsessed by a class bias send them to jail. An instance illustrating the spirit that exists all too commonly in American life, occurred in one of our great cities two or three years ago, during a strike. The police were rounding up a number of strikers engaged in picketing, and they arrested with the working girls a rich young woman who, through her sympathy with the cause, was helping to persuade strike breakers to walk out. When her identity was revealed to the police magistrate, he apologized and told her that she had no business to be there, and that he was sorry she was arrested. Her poorer accomplices, however, were promptly despatched to the workhouse.

In view of the twofold relation of the magistrates' courts — to the morale of the police force on the one hand, and to the rights of the citizens on the other — the selection of police judges is a serious matter. It is important that they should be in close and sympathetic touch with the social and economic conditions under which the people brought before them are compelled to live. A kind word, a gentle rebuke, or a helping hand at the right moment, may stay a new offender on his downward course, or may save from despair some poor person, whose chief offense is his ignorance, or who may have been arrested without warrant by an ignorant policeman. On the other hand, brutality and indifference in a police magistrate may fill the prisons with people who have no business there; may embitter a large portion of the population against what purports to be a system of justice; and this may stir up a feeling of hatred for the government among people who only see it in the person of a policeman or a magistrate.

The desirability of having magistrates in sympathy with the people over whom they have such large powers, has been used as a strong argument in favor of electing police judges. It has been found, however, that popular election does not often mean popular selection, but rather the choice of magistrates by political bosses and organizations supported by the elements which pay for immunity against the enforcement of the criminal laws. Thus it frequently happens that police magistrates are nominated by criminal elements operating through party organization and the names of the nominees appear on the ticket along with two or three hundred other candidates for twenty-five or thirty offices, so that no adequate scrutiny of their merits is possible. Thus a group of thoroughly corrupt and inefficient police magistrates may be swept into office at the tail of a ticket headed by "distinguished and honorable citizens."

Flagrant cases of machine control over police magistrates have been revealed by various investigations in the United States and have led reformers to advocate the abandonment of popular election in favor of appointment by the mayor. This does not necessarily mean, however, that politics is eliminated, and there have been plenty of cases of corruption among appointed magistrates to set over against the "horrible examples" discovered under the elective system. Speaking theoretically, one may say that where the mayor enjoys the appointing power and the public at large knows that he is responsible for the character of the courts, there is a greater probability of securing a high-grade magistracy.

Neither method of selection in itself is perfect. The essential thing is that the public should understand and be interested in the functions of the police courts. When it is remembered that the police magistrates for the Boroughs of Manhattan and the Bronx have before them every year about 125,000 cases (in 1910, 108,102 males and 20,191 females) charged with every crime from disorderly conduct to perjury and homicide, the importance of the magistrates in protecting life and property and helping to determine the quality of our citizenship is apparent.

It is a mistake to suppose that it is only the lower courts that have a direct relation to police administration in the maintenance of good order in the cities. The criminal elements look beyond the police magistrates, and stay proceedings against themselves by appeals to higher tribunals. Thus the efficiency of police administration is seriously impaired. And it is the worst offenders — the biggest criminals — who expect relief in this way, for the petty and minor offenders, in their poverty and ignorance, usually abide by the decision of the police magistrate. This is particularly true of the organized criminals, defended by astute lawyers who make a system out of appeals to higher courts. A big criminal is caught; the lower court sentences him; he appeals and gives bail; his shrewd counsel secures a continuance of the case on some technical grounds when the first hearing comes up; other cases crowd the docket and the prosecuting attorney finally gives up in despair so that a second continuance of a case generally means that the accused goes free.

Here, too, the system of bailing out offenders may be grossly abused. The poor man arrested for intoxication, disorderly conduct, or some petty misdemeanor, who appeals from the decision of the police magistrate, generally has to wait in jail until the day of his trial in the higher court. It is otherwise with a real criminal connected with some organization, for he can always obtain friends or professional bondsmen to release him until his case comes up for final trial.

Of course, there can be no doubt that wrongs done in the lower courts are often righted in the higher tribunals, but constant reversal on appeal has a demoralizing effect upon the police courts and the force. If the magistrates make wrong decisions in a large number of cases it is evident that they are hopelessly inefficient; and if they are frequently reversed on purely technical grounds they become disgruntled and lax in the administration of justice. Whoever, therefore, undertakes a reform in the police magistracy, must of necessity go into the question of appeals — a subject which is now receiving more attention than ever from students of criminal law and administration.

The consensus of the best opinion on this matter seems to be that the dignity and salary attached to the position of police magistrate should be greatly increased and the freedom of appeals more narrowly restricted. The initial cost of securing high-grade men by assuring adequate salaries and higher standing would be overbalanced in the long run by the saving in preventing the law's delays. Moreover, such a reform would have a wholesome effect upon the administration of justice generally.

Very decided improvements in the police magistracy are being made by the creation of separate courts for special classes of offenders. Long ago the attention of reformers was drawn to the anomaly of arraigning little children charged with petty offenses alongside hardened criminals at the bar of justice. It took many years of agitation, however, to secure the establishment of separate courts for the trial of juvenile offenders. The first children's court in the United States, according to official investigation of the Bureau of the Census, was established at Rochester, on August 23, 1895. Albany followed in 1897, Woonsocket (R. I.) in 1898, and Denver in 1899. At the present time all of the large cities have juvenile courts: Chicago (1899), New York (1902), Philadelphia (1903), St. Louis (1903), Cincinnati (1904), Seattle (1905).

The offenses triable in juvenile courts vary from city to city. In New York crimes of all kinds are included, except capital offenses. In St. Paul all violations of state laws and city ordinances by children are triable in the juvenile court. In Chicago, dependents and delinquents, and in Pittsburgh incorrigible delinquents are brought before the children's court. The maximum age of offenders triable in juvenile courts is about sixteen years. In Chicago it is seventeen years for boys and eighteen years for girls; in New York it is sixteen years for boys and girls alike; in Detroit it is sixteen years for boys and eighteen years for girls.

The New York law provides that whenever a child is taken into custody it shall be the duty of the officer making the arrest to proceed with all convenient speed to the children's court if in session and if not in session, to the rooms of a duly incorporated society (the Gerry Society) for the prevention of cruelty to children. It was at first specifically declared to be unlawful for a police officer to take a juvenile offender to a police station; but this requirement was omitted in an amendment of 1911.

Experience shows that the judge in the children's court should be a man peculiarly qualified for the work, and should devote his entire attention to trying juvenile offenders. The law of 1910 reorganizing the lower courts of New York City, however, did not create a special children's magistracy, but provided that justices of the court of special sessions should be assigned from time to time by the chief justice to hear and dispose of cases involving the trial of children.

The newer legislation on children's courts enjoins upon the magistrate in charge the duty of considering the accused " not upon trial for the commission of a

Judge Stubbs and the Indianapolis Juvenile Court.
The room does not suggest a court. The Judge can study the children closely.

crime, but as a child in need of the care and protection
of the State." In New York, the justice may, on request of the child or a guardian, suspend the trial at any
stage, and inquire into the facts and the collateral elements of the case. If he finds that circumstances warrant, he may stop the proceedings, and treat the child
under the provisions of the law for children not having
proper guardianship. He may, if he sees fit, place a
child convicted of an offense on probation for such time
as he deems proper. The New York law limits the probationary term to three years; provides that the period
may extend beyond the time such child attains the age
of sixteen years; and stipulates that, whenever practicable, a child placed on probation shall be put in charge
of a supervising officer of the same religious faith as
that of the parents.

A number of magistrates have won national reputa-
tions as children's justices. Among these are Judge
Lindsey of Denver, Judge Stubbs of Indianapolis, and
Judge Addams of Cleveland, Ohio. A recent student
of children's courts at first hand, Mrs. Reta Childe Dorr,
described in *Hampton's Magazine* for November, 1911,
the operation of the Cleveland Children's Court, as
follows:

I sat beside Judge Addams through a day in his court.
The first case he considered was of a boy of eleven charged
with robbing a slot machine.
"Well, James," said the judge kindly, "what have you
to say about this business?" The boy, too frightened for
speech, simply nodded his head.
"You did take the money, then?"
Another nod, accompanied by a choking, "Yes, sir."

The judge looked around. " Miss Bardau," he remarked, " this is your case, I believe. What do you know about it? "

A young woman probation officer came forward, and said:

" Jimmie lives in a wretched shack over on East Twenty-fifth Street, near old Broadway."

She was naming a neighborhood which is a worse slum than you will find in crowded New York. The street is a culvert where, all day long, switch engines haul trains to and fro, belching clouds upon clouds of black, malodorous smoke into the houses. To the south the towering chimneys of the Standard Oil works send up more columns of smoke. The neighborhood breathes smoke. The people are wretchedly poor or they would not live there. To give Jimmie's home address practically presents his life history.

The probation officer, however, continued. " Jimmie's mother is a widow. She works at office-cleaning. There are three other children to share with Jimmie the seven dollars a week she is able to earn. Jimmie has a fair school record. He attends pretty regularly, but he is two grades behind the one he is supposed at his age to occupy. He has never been in court before."

In a case like Jimmie's, clearly the thing to do is to remove Jimmie from the environment which in time may mean his moral ruin. Jimmie needs an entire change. He needs a farm and the healthy atmosphere of field and barnyard. Fortunately, the city of Cleveland provides such a place for its children. Hudson Farm is its name and later I intend to describe it to you in detail. Judge Addams sent Jimmie to this farm to begin the process of rebuilding.

Another type of special tribunal is to be found in the recently established courts for dealing with domestic difficulties. Such a court was created by the New York law of 1910, which transfers to a special magistrate's court, designated as " the domestic relations court," the arraignment, examination, and trial of all persons compelled by law to support poor relatives, and charged with the non-support or abandonment of wives or poor relatives. In connection with each of the domestic relations courts in New York an office of the superintendent of the outdoor poor relief is conveniently established.

A third type of special court is to be found in the night courts, to which offenders arrested after a late hour are taken. Those who are arraigned without proper warrant or on insufficient charges can thus be released at once, without having to spend a night in jail, awaiting trial. In New York there are separate night courts for men and women. When it is remembered that about half of the prisoners brought into the courts are discharged without punishment, the importance of giving a speedy hearing is at once apparent.

Speaking of the men's night court, the chief magistrate of New York says: "A vast number of men, young and old, arrested for trivial offenses, which, in court would merit nothing more severe than a reprimand, or who had been unjustly or unwisely arrested, have been quickly discharged, so that they could go to their work in the morning and would not be obliged to seek bondsmen or remain in prison over night. And in other cases, by giving quick results, it makes more efficient the police government of the city."

Another hopeful sign in police administration is the development of the principle of probation. Where this system is in force, the police magistrate is empowered to put on their honor adults and children charged with misdemeanors and minor offenses. In connection with each court there is a staff of male and female probation officers; and when an offender is placed on probation, he is assigned to a special officer, who investigates all the details of the case including the economic and social conditions of his charge. It is the duty of the probation officer to keep track of the offenders assigned to him, and to report their progress to the magistrate or justice. If any charge misbehaves the probation may be revoked, and he may be rearrested, arraigned, and sentenced as in an original case.

Probably at no time in the history of criminal-law administration has so much attention been given to the problem of preventing crime — to a study of the social and economic forces which tend to produce crime in cities. It is true that this aspect of police administration does not receive the consideration which it surely deserves; but we are beginning to have a criminology that does not rest entirely upon the doctrine of original sin. A few students are beginning to inquire into the relations between the amount of certain classes of crimes and economic conditions, such as unemployment, low wages, the price of foodstuffs, and congestion.

A study of crime in Berlin, covering the period from 1880 to 1910 shows that the amount of simple stealing per thousand of the population rises and falls with the price of rye, which is the staple breadstuff, particularly of the poor.

Mr. Warren T. Spalding, Secretary of the Massachusetts Prison Association, has recently demonstrated the striking relation between unemployment and criminality. During the panic of 1907, the arrests for drunkenness increased very materially in Massachusetts.

The calendar year of 1907 showed an increase of 4751 over the year 1906. Arrests for burglary during the early months in 1908, while the panic was still felt, were sixty-eight per cent. larger than during the same months of 1907. The number of vagrants arrested during the first six months of 1908 was nearly three times the number arrested during the corresponding months of 1907, while during the first seven months of 1908 miscellaneous offenses increased nearly fifty per cent.

These figures support the general statement made by Professor R. T. Ely: "The losses in a single year of industrial crisis and consequent industrial stagnation amount to hundreds of millions of dollars, and involve untold misery to millions of human beings. Capital is idle; labor is unemployed; production of wealth ceases, want and even starvation come to thousands; separations, divorces, and prostitution increase in alarming proportions."

Although our positive knowledge of the relation of crime to social and economic conditions is at present somewhat limited, we now have enough data to show that the prevention of crime should be one of the first cares of state. Professor Münsterberg of Harvard estimates that the United States spends annually $500,000,-000 more in fighting crime than on all its works of charity, education, and religion. Whether this estimate is exact or not, there is enough material at hand to warrant the conclusion that an enormous amount of crime can be prevented by social amelioration and that it is our duty to concern ourselves at once with this aspect of criminal-law administration. As Professor Münsterberg points out: "All social factors should coöperate in the prevention of crime and no science that might contribute to this tremendous problem should be held back. . . . Above all, a well-behaved mind grows only in a well-treated body; it is true that far-seeing hygiene can prevent more crime than any law. Anything that strengthens family life and works against its dissolution; everything which gives the touch of personal sympathy to the forlorn, helps toward the prevention of crime."

The increase of wages, the diminution of unemployment, the reduction of congestion, the development of recreational facilities, the teaching of sex hygiene, and medical inspection in schools, will contribute more to the prevention of crime than any amount of improvement in the criminal code itself.

If crime is largely due to economic causes — low wages and inadequate vocational training, and there is plenty of evidence to show that it is; if the ranks of the prostitutes are heavily recruited from underpaid working girls, and there is overwhelming evidence to show that this is true; if vice is an organized business built on a profit basis in which landlords, saloon-keepers, hotel proprietors, and a whole range of powerful interests are deeply involved, and report after report demonstrates this to be a fact — then is it not sheer imbecility to waste our time and strength on " exposures " of the police, the " raiding " of resorts, and the whole range of coercive measures which divert " good " people, but do nothing worth while to attack fundamental causes? Mere repressive measures are always and necessarily temporary and ineffectual. Too many ruling persons and their retainers, as the recent Chicago investigation shows, have economic interests in the chief sources of crime and vice.

In addition to attacking the social and economic causes of crime and vice, another aspect of criminology is receiving marked attention in our time — that is, the proper treatment of the criminal during his imprisonment, with a view to making it possible for him to find a place for himself in society at the expiration of his term of servitude. Cleveland, Ohio, under the administration of Mayor Johnson, initiated an experimental farm for the proper treatment of drunkards, vagabonds, and petty offenders. Of this interesting experiment, Dr. Harris R. Cooley, then Director of Charities and Correction, wrote, in 1908, " We have no guards; we have no stockade; there is no one about the place who carries so much as a stick or a revolver. We trust these men, and because we trust them they respect the trust. . . . We used to lock these men up in the workhouse in the city. We put them at pulling brushes, a laborious and confining work. The men were weak enough when they came to us. They were dissipated, unstrung, and for various reasons unable to resist temptation. We kept them in the workhouse until they had worked out their sentence, and then turned them out in the street again. Of course, they drifted into the nearest saloon. Where else could they go? Confinement had weakened their will power and destroyed their physical health, so that their whole nature craved a stimulant. Often they were back to us within twenty-four hours. That was inevitable. They were less fit for work than when they came to us, and they were hardened by the treatment which the city had meted out to them. Instead of punishing these men by exacting tasks for which they are unsuited, we now put them on this beautiful farm. They live out of doors. They are working at something for which they are fitted. We have work here for a generation to come. We have a splendid quarry from which we can build miles of roads, and lay the foundations of our buildings. The prisoner goes back to life again, able to meet the temptations which the city offers. And a very large percentage of these men never come back. But better even than that, we restore their respect and confidence in themselves."

One of the great problems in connection with prisons is that of finding employment for the prisoners on their release. The folly of turning men and women loose upon the streets, often homeless and forlorn, is obvious, and Cleveland has attempted to help by creating in the division of charities and corrections a Brotherhood of Prisoners, whose purpose, according to the official report, "is to find opportunities for employment and furnish to released prisoners a comfortable home until they are able to pay their own way. . . . Under normal conditions of employment, the Brotherhood men themselves nearly pay its current expenses. They form a valuable employment bureau. They are on the lookout for jobs for other members. In seventeen months, during more prosperous times, these men, who by some are regarded as worthless, paid into the Home for board and other expenses, more than ten thousand five hundred dollars which they earned by honest work in the shops and factories of Cleveland."

The attention of the country has also been drawn recently to the management of the police force of Cleveland under the administration of Mr. Fred Kohler who adopted in 1908 stringent rules against indiscriminate arrests. Of the results of this system Chief Kohler reports in 1910: "The total number of arrests for the years 1908 and 1909, which years we were working under the common-sense policy, were 10,085 and 6,018 respectively, as against 30,418 in 1907 while working under the old and general custom of making arrests. It will be noticed the great decrease of 80 per cent. as against the year 1907 was brought about by my new policy of Common Sense, or so-called Golden Rule, of not making arrests where the arrests would do more harm than good, in cases of minor offenders, and being especially careful to make arrests only, when in the judgment of the arresting officers, there was sufficient evidence to secure convictions. . . . We havĕ extended our policy of police repression, believing that the greatest good can be done by preventing the commission of unlawful acts. . . . Arrests are useless unless offenders are properly corrected. It does not cause their reformation and there is nothing gained by disgracing them."

CHAPTER VII

FRANCHISES AND PUBLIC UTILITIES

WHETHER viewed from the standpoint of general welfare, convenience, and comfort, or from that of political and economic power, the administration of the great public utilities — water-works, electric-light plants and transportation systems — takes first rank among the functions of city government. It is not necessary to point out the manifold ways in which efficient services by such concerns affect the daily life of the people of a city; but a few figures are given in order to set in relief their political and economic weight in municipal affairs.

In 1907 there were 4714 central electric-light stations in operation in the United States. The total cost of construction and equipment of these plants was about $1,-100,000,000 and the gross income $176,000,000. The outstanding stocks and bonds totaled the enormous aggregate of $1,342,000,000, and nearly 35,000 workmen were employed in the electric-light, heat and power plants. In that year 221,000 officers and employees were connected with street and electric railways in the United States and their salaries and wages were $151,000,000. The total number of employees in the transportation system of Greater New York was 36,799 on June 30, 1909. On the Brooklyn Rapid Transit 9030 men were employed at an average annual wage of $640 or $12.31 per week — ranging from ticket agents at $437 a year to elevated motormen at $987. The total amount paid out in wages and salaries by the combined systems for the year ending June 30, 1909, was a little over $26,-000,000.

More than ten thousand employees are engaged in the larger gas and electric plants of New York City. Complete figures on the employees of the public utilities in the city and the resident employees of railways having terminals there are not available; but it is safe to place the number at more than 100,000 persons. The wages, salaries, and conditions of life and work for this huge army are more or less immediately involved in the government of the city — in politics, that is. The exact number of voters among these employees is nowhere reported, but 60,000 would certainly be a safe guess; and when it is remembered that the total vote cast for mayor was 595,159 in 1909, the possible weight of public-utility corporations in municipal politics becomes apparent.

And this is only one aspect of the problem. Public-utility corporations, with their enormous capitalization, depend for their very lives upon securing favorable terms in their franchises, in the various regulations issued from time to time by municipal authorities, and in the orders made by the public-service commissioners; and they are bound to be more or less in politics all of the time. The stockholders and directors are among the leading citizens of the municipality. The lawyers employed by them to secure protection of every kind from what they deem unjust interference are keen and shrewd.

Politicians expect at least some of the companies to find places for their unemployed constituents; and managers are drawn through fear or cupidity to make alliances with party leaders. How far employees are coerced or influenced by their employers is a matter for conjecture. The power of coercion exists, and is always a factor even when not used in any gross form.

Obviously, in the relation of public-service corporations to the government we have one of the most vexatious problems of modern city government. The record of proved frauds, corruption, and overcapitalization on the part of utility concerns is long and appalling, and is by no means finished. Property, said Senator Seward more than fifty years ago, " derives its power to oppress from its own nature, the watchfulness of its possessors, and the ease with which they can combine. . . . In every State all the propertied classes sympathize with each other, through the force of common instincts of fear, cupidity, and ambition, and are easily marshaled under the lead of one which becomes dominant and represents the whole." How astutely the forces of private greed and public-service corporations have combined to employ political methods in the exploitation of municipalities is unhappily so well known as to need no demonstration here, but the study of investigations and sworn testimony gathered in cities as far apart as New York and San Francisco reveals certain forms of this exploitation against which municipalities must be on their guard.

Street-railway companies usually find it to their advantage to join with the liquor interests in keeping towns " wide open " for the conduct of pleasure resorts,

because it increases the amount of passenger traffic —
particularly on Sundays when the regular business is
slack. As Dr. Wilcox remarks: "A street railway has
to be operated seven days in the week, and in the larger
cities all night long. The profits of the enterprise depend largely on the stimulation of traffic at odd hours.
A crowd of people in town of a Sunday means profit to
the street railways. A bunch of revelers going home
in the wee, small hours makes the 'owl' cars profitable."

Gas and electric companies also have an interest in
wide-open policies on account of the extra large consumption of gas and electricity in the glaring resorts
which usually run to the latest hours possible.

Gas and electric companies may gain a large political
influence neglecting to compel prominent leaders to pay
their bills. For example, when Mr. Rudolph Spreckels
became a director of a San Francisco gas company, he
discovered that no attempt was made to collect the accounts against certain influential politicians, and only
by making a hard fight in the company was he able to
force an abandonment of the practice.

Public-service corporations have large construction
and repair enterprises under way most of the time, and
party leaders and their friends are frequently rewarded
with contracts and orders for supplies.

Public-service corporations do a large banking business and their deposits are an asset of prime importance
to banks. They may thus bring financial pressure
through the banks on business men who oppose them or
on city officers who may be in debt and silence even
honest criticism.

Corporations whose affairs will not bear daylight often conciliate newspapers by extensive advertising.

Where uncontrolled by commissions or publicity of accounts, utility concerns capitalize their plants on a basis of earning capacity — that is, they capitalize the monopoly elements in their enterprises and make the consumers pay dividends on fictitious values created largely by the public itself. Overcapitalization in the cases where competing concerns are merged is a common practice; and in such instances the anticipated advantages to be secured by the elimination of competition are fully covered by issues of paper. When once the stock is "watered" and unloaded on "innocent" purchasers it is well-nigh impossible to secure relief from the intolerable burden of paying dividends on the inflated values — for the courts are generally tender of private rights as against the public. The advantage derived by the operators from copious stock-watering is twofold: it pays the promoters directly in stocks and bonds, and it checks legislative interference designed to reduce rates and improve services; for the managers can explain, "We are hardly able to pay 4 per cent. on our capital now and regulation means ruin."

On account of the fact that franchises are granted by political leaders and regulative interference comes from political bodies, public-service corporations "go in for politics." It is doubtless true that their political activities are frequently for purposes of defense against blackmailers; but this should not be allowed to obscure the fact that they are engaged in political manipulations. If it is true that corporations are on the defensive, they could allay a good deal of the suspicion that now hangs over them, by showing more readiness to meet the demand for publicity of their financial operations and for the conduct of their business on an efficiency basis, affording reasonable returns on real capital. Corporations, however, in the past at all events, seem to have found that it " pays " better in the long run to gain immunity by yielding to blackmailers and charging the bill to operating expenses.

At all times, it is important for them to get the " right " men nominated for office, and by way of placation they frequently contribute to both political parties. A prominent officer of a large New York City utility concern testified a few years ago that it was the common practice of his company to pay a large sum to the Tammany leader in New York City and make an equally large gift to the chairman of the Republican state committee. The political leaders who are subsidized by corporations look after the proper nominations, and if they are not able to " swing " the primaries without help, the companies will grant some of their employees holidays to assist in rounding up the voters.

Public-service corporations are interested in electing judges as well as executive and legislative officers. The validity of franchises is constantly being attacked by competing concerns and by legislatures, and such matters are ultimately decided by the courts. Rate regulations and orders calling for extensions and improved service can be fought on the ground that they exceed the limits expressed or implied in the franchise or that they are confiscatory in character and are void under the state and federal constitutions. The points to be decided in such cases are not merely questions of law, but they nearly always involve broad principles of public policy. In such cases the training and bias of the judges are the determining elements.

An excellent example of the way in which the courts regard it their duty to protect private rights is afforded by the celebrated case of the People *v.* O'Brien in New York. In 1884 a corporation secured, by the notorious bribery of the common council, the right to lay tracks and run cars over a certain portion of Broadway. The company proceeded to issue bonds, mortgage its property and franchise rights, and make contracts with other companies. Owing to the pressure of the public opinion created by the scandal, the legislature dissolved the concern in accordance with the right specifically reserved in the state constitution, to alter, repeal, and amend charters and laws under which corporations might be organized. The company contended that, notwithstanding its dissolution, all its franchise rights remained intact, and the court of appeals of the State to which the case was finally carried held that while the annulling act of the legislature was valid, its effect was only to take the life of the corporation; that the corporation through its grant from the city had an indefeasible title in the land necessary to enable it to construct and maintain a street railway on Broadway and run cars thereon, which constituted property; that all the said property, including its franchises, contracts, and mortgages, survived its dissolution and went to its trustees as the representatives of its creditors and stockholders; and that the acts of the legislature, providing for the winding up of the affairs of the concern by a public receiver, were null and void.

In the course of its opinion in this case the court said:

The contention that securities representing a large part of the world's wealth are beyond the reach of the protection which the Constitution gives to property and are subject to the arbitrary will of successive legislatures, to sanction and destroy at their pleasure or discretion is a proposition so repugnant to reason and justice as well as the traditions of the Anglo-Saxon race in respect to the security of rights of property that there is little reason to suppose that it will ever receive the sanction of the judiciary, and we desire in unqualified terms to express our disapprobation of such a doctrine. . . . There is little danger to be apprehended in the future from the overgrowth of power or the monopolistic tendencies of such organizations [corporations]; but whatever that danger may be, it is trivial in comparison with the wide-spread loss and destruction which would follow a judicial determination that the property invested in corporate securities was beyond the pale of the protection afforded by the fundamental law.

In view of the valuable rights conveyed by franchises and the tendency of the courts to construe them broadly as against the public, the determination of the body or authority which should be invested with franchise-granting power becomes a consideration of first importance. Unless it is forbidden by the state constitution, the legislature of a commonwealth may itself grant charters to corporations operating wholly within the boundaries of a single municipality as well as to those whose enterprises are state-wide in character. In the early period of our city development, franchises in cities were frequently regarded as the legitimate spoils of the state political organization; and Thurlow Weed, an astute machine politician of Civil War times, frankly acknowledged that his party had used the street-railway privileges of New York City as a source of compaign funds. This perversion of power by the State and the insistence of cities upon more freedom from outside interference soon led to the establishment of limitations on the legislature. These limitations are marvels of ingenuity and variety.

Generally speaking, the state legislature is losing or yielding its former unlimited dominion over city franchises; and the power to grant these special privileges is now being delegated to some municipal authority — the council, commission, or a special body like the board of estimate and apportionment in New York City. The best opinion to-day is that the legislature should be forbidden to grant a franchise of any kind in the form of a local or special law — at least without the approval of the municipality or district concerned.

The local franchise-granting body is not given a free hand, however. In a large number of cities all franchises must be approved by popular vote before going into effect. This is frequently required in connection with commission government, and in some cases is mandatory upon all cities above a certain size. The constitution of Michigan stipulates that "no public utility franchise, not revocable at will, shall be granted by any city or village unless approved by a three-fifths vote of the electors, including women taxpayers." Other States provide for an optional referendum on municipal franchises — that is, reference to popular vote on petition of a certain percentage of electors in the city. The charter of Kansas City, Missouri, adopted in 1908, made obligatory the referendum on all franchises extending for more than thirty years, and stipulated that franchises running for that period or for a shorter term might be referred to the voters at the discretion of the city council, and must be referred on petition of twenty per cent. of the electors.

The obligatory referendum is open to special objections. It is absurd that every petty franchise or extension of a franchise should be submitted to popular vote whether it is of sufficient importance to attract public attention or not. The optional referendum, on the other hand, affords to the inhabitants of a city sufficient safeguards against a corrupt council or commission — for it can be invoked whenever a considerable portion of the voters believe that a particular franchise ought not to go into effect. If five, ten, fifteen, or twenty per cent. of the electors, as the law may provide, are convinced that a special privilege granted by the council is objectionable, they may, by petition, secure its reference to popular vote. This will only happen when the issue at stake is of some importance, and public attention can be directed to the matter. It serves as a check upon the franchise-granting body, and at the same time does not burden the voter with the necessity of passing upon every corporate privilege or extension, whether it involves any large public interest or not.

In some cities, even the initiation of franchises is not entrusted entirely to the franchise-granting authorities. The public opinion law of Illinois, for example, requires a referendum on any question demanded by twenty-five per cent. of the voters, and this system may be applied to secure a vote on a proposal to grant a new franchise or extend an old one. This vote is advisory, however, and may be entirely disregarded by the city council.

In Denver, and Portland, and other cities, the vote upon a franchise initiated by petition decides the matter finally. In the former city the street-railway company and the gas and electric company were able to secure the renewal of important rights by initiating propositions of their own and forcing their adoption, it is charged, by fraudulent means. The dangers of such a system are only too apparent. A public-service corporation may employ the best legal talent to draft a franchise proposition, containing hidden concessions to the company, and yet full of specious promises to the public. It then secures the desired publicity and the requisite number of signatures to an initiative petition by the judicious use of money, and the public votes blindly on the measure. Whenever popular initiation is permitted, it should be safeguarded at least by a provision requiring that " every franchise proposed by petition should be submitted to the city council or to the local-utilities board for report and recommendation before being voted on by the people." Certainly, if any one thinks that the initiative and referendum will automatically drive the interests out of politics he is sadly mistaken.

In addition to the problem of determining by what authorities franchises shall be granted, it is necessary also to come to some sound conclusions on the question of the public policy controlling the stipulations of the charters and concessions. In reviewing the history of American cities, one is struck with the bewildering types of franchises, jokers and all, which have been granted since public-utilities companies began to play an important rôle.

And yet, in the midst of what appears to be chaos, at the outset, certain tendencies in municipal policies are clearly marked, and from these are to be derived some principles of the highest value as guides in the future.

In the early days of franchise granting it was quite common for the state legislature or the city council to grant "perpetual" street-railway franchises, without specifying any conditions as to the length of the term or reserving expressly any power of prescribing publicity, fixing rates, or determining the amount of capital stock; and in fact without making any attempt to defend the public against bribery, stock-watering, or the other evils which could have been foreseen, or were early experienced. Perpetual franchises, says Dr. Wilcox, "assume that the street railway is a private enterprise and that it is appropriate to grant never-ending special privileges to maintain structures in the streets to be used primarily for private profit. This theory has found expression more extensively in the Eastern States than elsewhere in the country. Nevertheless, there are cities in the South, in the West, and in the North which have made grants that are specifically perpetual or at least unlimited. Substantially all the important surface street-railway franchises of Greater New York are perpetual. . . . Perpetual franchises have been the rule in Maine, Connecticut, Pennsylvania, Delaware, and, until recently, in New Jersey. The earlier grants in Baltimore and most of the Rhode Island franchises are also perpetual."

It is one of the encouraging signs of our generation that this policy of granting perpetual and substantially unlimited franchises, subjected to no regulation, has

been almost abandoned. The unfortunate consequences
of the earlier folly, however, remain in a large part as
sins of the fathers visited upon their sons and daughters.

From this older type of franchise, based upon the
doctrine that all social values are the legitimate spoils
of private property, up to the latest form of a detailed
franchise safeguarded in every respect against the evils
which history has revealed, there are many gradations.
A common type is afforded by the Indianapolis street-
railway franchise, which fixes the fares which the company can charge, provides the methods by which extensions are to be secured, and stipulates for the proper
paving of the streets along the tracks; but institutes no
limitation and supervision of stock issues and secures no
adequate publicity of accounts. Under this franchise
settlement of 1899, one specific gain was made. The old
company contended that its franchises were perpetual,
while the city claimed that they would expire in 1901;
and in the settlement of the dispute the city was able
to secure, as a definite consideration in the new grant,
a specific stipulation that all the rights of the company
should come to an end in 1933. The exact agreement of
the company runs as follows: " It will peacefully yield
possession (in 1933) of every part of every street, avenue, alley, and public place in said city then occupied by
any of its lines of street railway and cease the operation
of its said street-railway plant or system and every part
thereof and from thenceforward will make no claim of
any kind to exercise any right whatever under the grant
herein made or under any charter or corporate right,
and any rights which might be claimed by said company,
party of the second part or its successors or assigns, to

hold beyond said period of time under the statute under which it was incorporated or any enactment prior to this date or which might have been derived from any other source, are herein and expressly waived."

The terms of the Chicago street-railway settlement of 1907 illustrate in an interesting fashion the more recent tendencies in franchise adjustments. They are in part as follows:

(a) The value of the tangible property and franchise rights was fixed at $50,000,000, and all additions and betterments must be made subject to the approval of a board of engineers composed of a representative of the city, a representative of the companies, and a third person agreed upon. Provision is made for publicity and scrutiny of new capital expenditures which may be added by the companies to the sum fixed above.

(b) The city may purchase on February 1 or August 1 of any year and operate the entire railway system on payment of the $50,000,000, plus the value of additions and betterments made under the scrutiny of the board of engineers as above described.

(c) In order to prevent the several companies from allowing their properties to deteriorate, after having the large capital value fixed, provisions were made requiring the concerns to set aside a certain portion of the gross earnings for depreciation and rehabilitation.

(d) Provisions were made for the maintenance of good and adequate services by the companies, and the fare was fixed at five cents for a continuous trip in one direction for persons over twelve, and three cents for those between seven and twelve years.

(e) Full publicity was to be secured by requiring the

companies " to file with the city comptroller annual reports according to forms prescribed by that official, showing the character and amount of their earnings and expenses."

While it can hardly be said that the Chicago settlement fully satisfied the demands of any of the contending parties, it certainly marks a distinct gain over the old situation in which everything was in a muddle. If the city decides upon public ownership in the future it will not have to take a leap in the dark, because it will have before it the terms of the franchise and full statistical details as to the operations of the concerns. Moreover, the companies are now under public supervision; and unlimited stock-watering and high finance are at an end.

Nevertheless this settlement is open to many serious objections, even from the advocates of private ownership. These have now become fully apparent and are pointed out in a recent speech by Dr. Wilcox. He criticizes the settlement particularly because the ordinances make no provision for a reduction of the capital account until the city is able to pay the full amount of the purchase price. He shows that, starting with a purchase price of $50,000,000 as of June 30, 1906, the street railways of Chicago stood on the books at more than $125,000,000 before the close of 1911, while the city's purchase fund with its meager accumulations would amount to only about $7,500,000 at the close of the fiscal year. In other words while the city was accumulating a purchase fund of $7,500,000 the purchase price increased $75,000,000. The worst of it, to Dr. Wilcox's mind, is that, of the present purchase price, a very large sum, estimated at about $35,000,000, represents old franchise and scrap values and property which has disappeared in the process of reconstruction. The Chicago ordinances should have provided a fund for writing off this dead capital before there were any surplus profits for anybody. Dr. Wilcox also criticizes the Chicago ordinances because they make no provision for the investment of the city's purchase fund, with the result that while the companies are all the time putting in new money and drawing five per cent. interest on it, the city has to content itself with letting its money lie in the banks at two and one-quarter per cent.

These facts are used by the advocate of municipal ownership to demonstrate the futility of attempting to safeguard public rights while leaving powerful corporations in possession of municipal utilities and in full sway in municipal politics.

By studying the varied experiences of our larger cities, experts on municipal franchises are coming to a certain consensus of opinion as to the principles which should lie at the basis of all grants of rights and privileges to public-service corporations. These principles have been brought together in admirable form by Dr. Wilcox under the title of " The Elements of a Model Franchise," [1] the main features of which may be stated as follows:

At the outset, it is necessary to decide definitely upon the term for which the franchise is to run. In this matter any one of three policies may be adopted.

The term may be expressly or impliedly perpetual; and unless the time limits are stipulated in the franchise or

[1] See below, Appendix I.

the reservation of the right to repeal or abolish is expressly made previous to or at the time of the grant it will be held to be perpetual. This type of franchise has recently fallen into disrepute, and is considered objectionable by everybody except the representatives of public-service corporations.

It is now the common practice to stipulate in the franchise a definite term; and the general rule is twenty-five years, to which exceptions are sometimes made in the case of grants for large and expensive undertakings. This form of short-term franchise is also open to one very grave objection. When the company approaches the end of its term and it is uncertain whether a renewal of the franchise can be secured, it naturally has no incentive to make large outlays for improvements or to keep its plant up to a high degree of efficiency. Depreciation is, therefore, almost certain to set in during the years immediately preceding the expiration of the franchise. The short-term franchise also tends to keep public-service corporations constantly in politics, in order to be in good favor with the franchise-granting authorities when the day of renewal approaches. Nevertheless, the short-term policy is a decided gain over the old method of granting perpetual and unlimited franchises.

The third policy with regard to the term, which now seems to be growing in favor with experts in franchises, is that which fixes no time limit at all, but leaves the matter indeterminate. The doctrine upon which it is based is thus concisely stated by Dr. Wilcox: "If we put together the principle that a public utility should be continuously and symmetrically developed to meet the needs of a growing community and the other principle that the street railway is a public business in which capital should be guaranteed a limited risk and should be satisfied with a limited profit, we may arrive at the right theory of franchises so far as the question of duration is concerned. The city cannot properly fulfil its function unless it maintains control over the several uses of the street.   It must have the power at any time to change or improve any public street, and to readjust the locations and the relations of the public-utility fixtures on, above, or below the surface of the street.   Moreover, inasmuch as the street-railway business is a public function, the city must remain in a position where, in the event that this function is not being adequately performed, it can either resume it or transfer it to another agent.'' When an indeterminate franchise is granted it is customary to make provisions safeguarding the rights of investors in the corporation, in case its franchise is terminated and the plant is taken over for public operation or transferred to some other corporation.

Whatever may be the term for which the franchise is granted, certain very definite stipulations should be made safeguarding the rights of the public. A clause should be included providing for purchase by the city at the expiration of the term or at any time during the life of the franchise, and this should be supplemented by careful arrangements for controlling the capital stock and all increases in the capital outlay of the company.   Otherwise the city may have to pay for a generous amount of water.

To meet the needs of a growing community, the conditions under which extensions of the company's plant shall be made ought to be carefully laid down, and some public authority empowered to order extensions under proper circumstances. Here the effect of the extension upon the net earning power of the whole corporation should be taken into consideration because it is easy for a company to demonstrate that any particular extension will in itself be a positive loss.

The capitalization of the public-service corporation is a matter which must be carefully and explicitly controlled. In case of a new company or a new plant this is a relatively easy matter, for it may be provided that the franchise itself shall be deemed to be without value, or the entire capital of the concern may be fixed at the total cost of organizing the corporation and constructing the plant. This should be closely supervised by the city, and under a system of publicity and expert accounting which will prevent the inclusion of fictitious values from the very outset.

After the original capital value is determined under public supervision, some method should be instituted for maintaining public control over all additional increments in the capital account. In the case of settlements with older companies holding under franchises granted years ago, the problem is more complicated. The chances are that the concern has already capitalized at its full value the franchise itself and sold its stock to innocent purchasers on that basis. The legal rights of the company have also increased in value with the growth of the community, and under these circumstances the mere physical cost of the plant is often only a fraction of the total capital charges outstanding against the company. The difficulties of the situation, however, should not prevent the city from obtaining a definite agreement as to the capitalization at the time of any resettlement with its corporations. Favorable arrangements may often be secured by granting further favors to the corporation in lieu of counting in as capital value the public follies of the past; and the taxing power may be employed to squeeze water out.

Adequate publicity and accounting for all the operations of the companies are now provided in advanced municipalities. Public-utility concerns should be required to make periodic returns to the city comptroller or some other designated officer, according to methods prescribed by public authority. These returns should include an analysis of all increments in capital values and operating expenses, so that the affairs of each concern may be absolutely transparent and all kinds of financial juggling in the dark effectually prevented.

Experience dictates that it is wise to require each public-service corporation to set aside a portion of its gross income for permanent improvements, in order to prevent the increase of the capital stock for the purpose of meeting depreciation. If this is not done, the company may allow its plant to sink in value and thus claim the right to issue a large amount of new capital stock to meet renewal charges.

A number of more recent franchises, which contain clauses authorizing public purchase, include a provision requiring the company to set aside each year a certain share of its gross earnings for amortization — that is for the discharge of the total capital indebtedness of the concern, so that, at the expiration of a fixed period, when the franchise reverts to the municipality, no payment need be made to the corporation.

The rights of labor may be stipulated in a franchise

if the public authority granting it is so disposed. The general laws covering Massachusetts street-railway companies limit to ten hours a day's work for conductors and motormen, and provide that this labor must be so arranged by the employer that it may be performed within twelve consecutive hours, except on legal holidays and other days when there is an extraordinarily large amount of traffic to handle. In the 1894 Detroit street-railway franchise it is agreed that conductors and motormen must be citizens of the United States and voters in the State of Michigan, and that ten hours, within twelve consecutive hours, shall constitute a day's work.

A recent Trenton franchise makes provision for the arbitration of labor disputes by stipulating that " whenever any controversy or disagreement arises between the company operating under this ordinance and its employees which interferes or threatens interference with the operation of the road, the question or disagreement shall be submitted to arbitrators — two to be selected by the company and two by the employees — and their decisions shall be final; if the said arbitrators shall fail to agree within three days, then a fifth arbitrator shall be selected by the mayor and the decision of the majority of said arbitrators shall be final and binding."

To meet the preposterous situation created by judicial decision in some of the States to the effect that rights fraudulently secured by a corporation survive the dissolution of the concern, some reformers now advocate including in the terms of franchises a provision that the company shall forfeit all of its privileges if it is convicted of bribery, jury feeing, corruption, and similar offenses. A committee appointed in San Francisco in

1908 to investigate the causes of municipal corruption recommended that " laws should be enacted for the cancellation of franchises procured by fraud or crime of the owners of the franchise or of their predecessors in interest." Such a provision, however, would doubtless prevent any company organized under it from selling its stocks and bonds.

Inasmuch as all public-service corporations use the streets more or less in laying mains and tracks and making repairs, it is most important that the right of strict supervision for such operations shall be reserved to some municipal authority.

During the past decade the principle of public regulation of rates, charges, and services of corporations has made rapid headway, and this involves many complicated questions which must be settled upon. Take, for example, the matter of street-railway rates. In some cities, like Cleveland and Detroit, political campaigns have been fought over " low fares," and it is often erroneously supposed that the passengers positively gain by the reduction of the rate from five to three cents, even when that rate is not applicable to all continuous rides in one direction. If they are home-owners this is true; but as we have seen in our larger cities the majority of passengers are not home-owners, and when the three-cent-fare zone has been established the almost immediate result is an increase in rents within it, which will offset any gain made by the reduction in rate. The establishment of rate zones also tends to increase congestion within the low-fare areas. Experience seems to show that the mere reduction of fares should not be the central point in the policy of regulation, but that long rides at one fare, adequate car service, and proper labor conditions should be the chief considerations.

In the regulation of the charges made by water companies several elements must be taken into account. For reasons of health, it is absolutely imperative that a copious supply should be furnished at a low rate, and while it is a growing practice now to fix the charges according to meter measurement, a great deal may be said for the older policy of making flat rates according to the number of sanitary conveniences rather than the exact amount of water consumed. The use of the meter, however, tends to check unnecessary waste; and, if a sufficiently low rate is fixed, the demand for economy is met and at the same time health and cleanliness need not be sacrificed.

In the charges of gas, electric, and water companies, one of the most perplexing problems is that of determining the relative rates to be charged to large and small consumers. On the one hand, it is contended that a uniform rate per unit should be charged to all alike, and on the other hand, it is claimed that this is a departure from sound business principles. A good case may be made on both sides of the question; but any conclusion will rest upon the attitude taken toward the public encouragement of small concerns and the maintenance of competition.

Finally, in regulating public-service corporations, the municipality must take into account the effect of such regulation upon the incentive of the company to improve its services. If the company understands that the improvement of its administration means only the lowering of rates and no positive gains in dividends — if it knows that its returns cannot be above a fixed amount no matter how great its economies — it has no incentive to introduce more progressive or more efficient methods. In order to meet this situation, there has recently been devised what is known as the " sliding scale," which allows a corporation to increase its dividends whenever it reduces its prices to the public. In Boston, for example, the price of gas was recently fixed by law at ninety cents per thousand cubic feet and the standard rate of dividends was placed at seven per cent. Whenever the company reduces the price of gas five cents per thousand cubic feet it may increase its rate of dividends one per cent. for the following year.

Among the other elements of the model franchise to be considered is the compensation which the city is to receive from its grant of privileges. It may sell the franchise outright to the highest bidder; or it may take a certain percentage of the gross or net earnings. It should be borne in mind, however, that whenever the municipality derives an income from the sale of franchises or from the revenues of franchise companies it is in effect taxing the consumer, not the corporation. The city must decide whether or not it intends to tax its citizens indirectly through public-service corporation franchises. Sound policy forbids this. The wisest city administration will not attempt to derive special revenues from its franchises, but will lay all its emphasis upon the excellence and cheapness of the service and the labor conditions in the operating concerns.

Although these elements of public control and supervision are being introduced into the newer franchises as fundamental safeguards for community rights, it must not be thought that municipal utilities resting on older and unlimited grants of privileges are wholly beyond the reach of legislative power. It is an ancient principle of the law that a business "affected with public interest" may be regulated in such a manner as to secure "reasonable" services and charges; and this principle is now being applied to municipal-utility concerns in two ways: the establishment of flat rates by legislative enactment and regulation through public-service commissions.

This exercise of regulating power is, however, always subject to judicial control under state and federal constitutions. That is, the courts, in final analysis, have the power of declaring any rate fixed by the legislature or by a commission void on the ground that it is unreasonable, and deprives the concern in question of its right to earn a reasonable interest on its capital. There is also a further limitation on the regulating power of the legislature. Where "in return for the franchise the company agrees to perform certain services or to make certain money payments and it is specifically stated that the right to charge a certain rate is granted in return for such services or money payment, a contractual relation between the public authority and the company arises which cannot be impaired by subsequent legislation."

Although the establishment of flat rates by legislative enactment is still quite common, the tendency is rather in the direction of vesting a regulatory power in the hands of state or local commissions, generally the former. Every advanced commonwealth in the Union now has its public-service commission with more or less control over the rates and services of the utility corporations, local and general, within its limits.

In some commonwealths the commission is merely an

investigating and reporting body with no authority to order things done; and in others it is invested with large and drastic powers, including the fixing of rates, the control of stock issues, the approval of franchises, the supervision of accounts, the prescription of definite services, and the ordering of extensions.

New York has two such commissions, one for Greater New York City and a second for the remainder of the State, each with wide powers over rates and services.

Wisconsin, by the public utilities law of 1907, places municipal concerns under the supervision of a state commission which is directed among other things to " value all of the property of every public utility actually used and useful for the convenience of the public." The Oregon and New Jersey laws of 1911 are based upon the Wisconsin statute in part and vest the control of municipal-franchise corporations in the hands of state boards. Section 24 of the New Jersey law runs:

No privilege or franchise hereafter granted to any public utility as herein defined, shall be valid until approved by said board [the board of public utility commissioners], such approval to be given when, after hearing, said board determines that such privilege or franchise is necessary and proper for the public convenience and properly conserves the public interests, and the board shall have power in so approving to impose such conditions as to construction, equipment, maintenance, service or operation as the public convenience and interests may reasonably require.

In connection with the regulation of utilities, as in other municipal affairs, the question of the limits of municipal home rule arises, and the line between state and local affairs is difficult to draw. Many municipal utilities, such as street railways, interurban lines, steam railways, telephone and telegraph systems, are merely parts of a far-reaching network. Consequently, there have been conflicts, in some States, between central and local authorities over the control of matters which might fairly be considered as within the jurisdiction of either.

The argument for a state board is undoubtedly weighty. It is likely to be composed of higher paid experts than any local commission; and through its experience with many cities it acquires a special skill and knowledge which no local body can acquire. It helps to remove the regulation of utilities from municipal politics and may thus minimize the influence of local corporations over other city affairs.

However, regulation by a state commission is, in many respects, a violation of sound principles of home rule; and a number of cities have local commissions of their own. Los Angeles, on a referendum vote in 1909, established a city utilities board with power to investigate the affairs and operations of local concerns, make physical valuations of property, recommend to the council schedules of charges, hear complaints against public-service corporations, and keep the records relative to such concerns. St. Louis, and Kansas City, Missouri, likewise have local commissions established under a general state law passed in 1907, authorizing cities and towns to create boards to investigate facts relative to rates and services and report findings to the city council.

The eminent authority on franchises, Dr. Wilcox, recommends that even where a state board is in existence, each city of more than 100,000 inhabitants should have its own commission or bureau invested with such powers as are in keeping with the supervision of state affairs by the central authority. This local body should have regulatory powers in case they are not vested in the state board, and should be authorized to make investigations, ascertain physical valuations, keep full records of past and present operations of companies, control stock and bond issues, supervise accounts, and in other ways secure the complete transparency of public utilities, so that there may be no hiding-places for high finance and political corruption.

CHAPTER VIII

MUNICIPAL OWNERSHIP

The theoretical arguments for the municipal ownership of all important public utilities are numerous and strong. A city, whose finances are in good condition, can borrow money at a lower rate than private companies. Thus, in the case of municipal plants, the annual interest charge, to be considered in fixing rates and improving services, is smaller; and the difference may be applied for public benefit in some form. This is no insignificant item in the case of utilities in populous cities where the capitalization mounts upwards into the millions.

There is, moreover, no incentive for "stock-watering" in municipal concerns, for the city can have no possible interest in overloading the capital of its plants. The art of inflation has been developed as a form of private enterprise. The temptation to take advantage of public indifference and capitalize monopoly profits has been so great as to overcome the scruples of most of our financiers. Indeed, the line between "legitimate" and "illegitimate" capitalization is difficult to draw, and experts in the legal profession can find ready justification for their clients who have laid hold of social values which have been neglected by the careless and ignorant public.

The tendency to overcapitalization in private companies as compared with municipal concerns is illustrated by a few figures collected by the National Civic Federation Commission on Public Ownership. In 1902, the outstanding stocks and bonds of private electric-light companies represented $271.51 capital per kilowatt-hour unit, while in the 815 municipal plants studied the capital was only $111.89 per kilowatt-hour unit. Of course a part of this discrepancy may be accounted for by diverse conditions of operation, but it is not wholly accidental.

Private companies everywhere strive with might and main to capitalize and earn interest upon every possible element of value in their plants and franchises. Generally speaking, the courts allow them to count as a part of their capital, whenever regulation on behalf of the public is proposed, the following elements: (*a*) any rise in value of the lands used for plants; that is, for example, if a company pays $10,000 for a lot on which to build a power plant and in time it grows in value to $50,000, the concern may claim the right to earn interest on the additional $40,000 before reductions may be made in charges; (*b*) the increase in the cost of duplicating the plant on account of higher charges for labor and materials; (*c*) established connections with customers, that is, in effect, good-will; and (d) franchise values, within limits. From six to ten per cent. interest upon their capital including the above elements, is claimed by operating companies, and frequently allowed by the courts, as the proper amount to be set aside before reductions in rates or expensive improvements in services can be required.

A third advantage, which may accrue from public ownership, is the retention of all monopoly values for the city. For example, a franchise is granted in a growing community to a street-railway company and within ten years the city has doubled in population; this means that the number of passengers carried by the company will increase out of all proportion to the additional capital required for the plant and rolling stock and that the earnings will be correspondingly larger. Under municipal ownership, this augmented income may be utilized to reduce fares or improve the service; but under private ownership it is a common practice for the concern to capitalize any new earning power and transfer the monopoly profits to private pockets. Of course, regulation and taxation may be employed to secure for the public a part of this gain; and the incentive to efficient service, which private ownership is supposed to confer, may be unimpaired. However, as everybody knows, the monopoly profits are the chief reasons for private ownership. If they are taken away, the opposition to public ownership will materially diminish.

Another noteworthy feature of municipalization is the ease with which regulations of service and rates may be secured and enforced. The accounts of the plants may be opened to all, and when the cost of any proposed improvement is estimated it is easy for the city to determine under what conditions rates and services may be changed. On the other hand, in supervising private corporations, public commissions are constantly confronted by recalcitrant officers who say that the orders are unfair, impossible of execution, and confiscatory. A regulation of any significance is certain to be fought in the courts at great public expense and with the usual delays which are incident to judicial processes in the United States. It is a poorly managed private corporation which cannot show by its accounts and the logic of its counsel the illegal character of an order issued by a commission. Even if the commission wins, it does so usually at a great expense of time, energy, and money. Under municipal ownership wars between commissions and companies may be avoided.

A negative argument in favor of municipal ownership is the extent to which city politics have been corrupted by private corporations seeking franchises or enlargement of their rights and privileges. It may be admitted for the sake of argument that utility concerns have been driven in most cases to employ bribery under the threats of blackmailers. This does not alter the fact that public-service corporations generally take advantage of every opportunity offered by the weakness of our city governments to increase their gains. They employ the shrewdest lawyers at handsome fees to draft their franchises and renewals and pit them against municipal legal officers — who are paid small salaries, hold their positions for short terms, and hope to find a lucrative corporate practice at the end of their official careers. Brains, legal skill, incentive to gain, and almost every conceivable advantage, are on the side of the private corporation. As Dr. Albert Shaw says, " The wear and tear upon the morals of a weak municipal government are greater by far when it comes to the task of granting franchises — that is to say, of making bargains with private corporations — than when it is attempted to carry out a business undertaking directly on the public account."

In addition to the bribery and corruption connected with securing franchises and dealing with public officers, there is also to be considered the direct influence of corporations in politics. The employees of public-utility concerns are often engaged at primaries and elections in support of claims advanced by the companies and also by other establishments in which they have an economic interest. Mr. John R. Commons, who investigated labor conditions in public utilities for the National Civic Federation, cites plenty of evidence to show that private ownership is as intimately involved in politics as is public ownership. Speaking on this point, he says: "Private companies are compelled to get their franchises and all privileges of doing business and all terms and conditions of service from the municipal authorities. And in carrying out their contract with the municipality they are dealing continually with municipal officials. Consequently it is absurd to assume that private ownership is non-political. It is just as much a political question to get and keep honest and business-like officials who will drive good bargains with private companies on behalf of the public and then see that the bargains are lived up to, as it is to get similar officials to operate a municipal plant. We do not escape politics by resorting to private ownership — we only get a different kind of practical politics."

Finally, it may be said in behalf of municipal ownership that there is no profit-making incentive to render poor service. Every improvement in the service of a private concern, beyond the minimum point comes out of profits. The commercial principle of a public-utility company is inevitably " Charge what the traffic will bear." While here and there a management will take pride in improvements and refinements beyond the exigencies of strict business, the incentive to make profits at public expense is usually too great for such philanthropic directors.

Over against these theoretical advantages of public ownership may be set the claim, made in behalf of private ownership, to the effect that our city governments are notoriously weak and inefficient and wholly incapable of assuming the responsibilities of large business enterprises. Plenty of evidence may be brought in support of this contention; but it is necessary to go behind the evidence; and when this is done it is found that the chief reason for the weakness and inefficiency of our cities is to be found in the assaults constantly made upon them by public-service corporations which thrive and wax fat by keeping incompetent and dishonest men in office.

However inefficient American city government may be and whatever may be the causes thereof, no municipality, as Mr. Walter Fisher says, " can escape from the necessity of controlling in some effective manner the management of its public utilities." Even the strongest opponents of public ownership are forced to admit the desirability and inevitability of public regulation of the charges and services of concerns which enjoy privileges in the streets of our cities.

When once regulation is accepted, its implications must be accepted also. Regulation of rates implies absolute publicity of accounts, the elimination of speculation, a knowledge of the physical operations of the concern, the value of its plant, its cost of operation, its profits, and all of its disbursements. This means that the city, if it is to regulate effectively, must have experts of as high a quality as those employed in private business. This means also that the relations of the city to the franchise corporations must be as constant, definite, and scrutinizing as its relations to its municipal plants. In order to do justice in requiring extensions, fixing fares, and prescribing improvements in service, the public officers must know exactly the nature and cost of each and every operation which the concern must perform. If stock issues are to be controlled, the regulating authorities must know precisely the cost of constructing new works and of repairing old works, in order to trace to their very ends all additions to the capital outlays.

Obviously, in the present stage of our municipal development, the incompetency of our city administrations is not a final and conclusive argument against public ownership. Efficiency is required to supervise, scrutinize, and direct the operations of private corporations whose interests all too commonly lie completely athwart the regulations prescribed in the name of public good. Our municipalities simply must become skilled in the arts of business management whether public or private operation be adopted.

Practical men, however, will waive aside theoretical arguments, no matter upon what real foundations they may rest, and demand to know the comparative merits of public and private ownership where they have been tried. This sounds plausible enough, but a little analysis will show that whoever waits to make up his mind until reasonably impartial men have settled this issue on a basis of fact and arrived at some common agreement, will reach no conclusion at all on the subject. The experts employed by the National Civic Federation's Commission on Public Ownership, in the investigation of 1907, differed profoundly in the interpretation of the identical facts, and, indeed, appear to have retained the same opinions which they held before making the inquiry.

Representatives of public-utility concerns, engaged by the Federation, were unwavering in their denunciation of municipal ownership. Mr. Edgar, of the Boston Edison Company and Mr. Clark, of the Philadelphia United Gas Improvement Company, announced at the conclusion of their survey of the facts: " We believe that no intelligent reader of the voluminous record of this commission's work will fail to see that it clearly proves municipal ownership to be productive of many and serious ills with little or no compensating good." Mr. Bemis, then superintendent of the Cleveland water-works, declared, on the other hand, on the basis of the same data, " It appears to the writer to be conclusively demonstrated from the above facts that in both water, gas, and electricity the municipal plants have done far better for the taxpayer and consumer than the private plants in anything like a similar situation. Prices have been lowered and the plants have been largely or wholly paid for out of earnings, where there were any, or may be considered to have been mostly or entirely paid for out of the difference between the prices charged by private companies in the neighborhood and the construction and operating costs of the municipal plants. . . . It is believed that the largest benefit of municipal management has come in the case of the majority of the municipal undertakings investigated through the freeing of the department from political evils and in freeing the city from the desire of investors in the plant to secure a weak or corrupt city government."

The conclusions of the Commission on Public Ownership were, on the whole, favorable to municipal ownership. It declared the principle that municipal utilities can be regulated by competition to be fallacious and held that public regulation or ownership was imperative — thus abandoning the cherished American doctrine that the public ought not to interfere in its own behalf with the rights of private corporations to conduct their own business in their own way. The Commission was of the opinion that where a public utility concerns the health of the citizens it should not be left to individuals; and that undertakings in which the sanitary motive enters largely should be operated by the public. On the general proposition of municipal ownership, the Commission concluded that it should not be extended to " revenue-producing industries which do not involve public health, public safety, public transportation, or the permanent occupation of public streets or grounds." It pronounced against perpetual franchises and in favor of conferring upon cities the " authority, upon popular vote, under reasonable regulations, to build and operate public utilities, or to build and lease the same, or to take over works already constructed." As to the merits of municipal ownership the Commission said: " There are no particular reasons why the financial results from private or public operation should be different if the conditions are the same. In each case it is a question of the proper man in charge of the business and of local conditions."

While this report appears moss-grown to the ardent advocate of municipal ownership, it really marks a radical advance in the position usually taken by bodies so conservative in character as the Commission selected by the Civic Federation. It refuses to condemn municipal ownership on the abstract grounds — the *laissez faire* principle — with which most opponents of public ownership are obsessed; it recognizes no inherent difficulties in the way of the successful public operation of utilities; and it would reverse the doctrine that the presumption should always be against the city in favor of private operation and would place the rights of the public first. Where this last step is taken and cities are empowered to own and operate, the movement for municipalization is strengthened by the knowledge that results may be obtained without long and tedious lobbying in legislatures or interminable litigation in the courts. Once give a city to understand that the presumption is in favor of its right to own and operate, and a most important step is taken toward municipal ownership.

As to American conditions, the Commission was unable to make a really scientific comparison of private and public plants similarly situated, because of the impossibility of securing data from the former and the confused system of accounting in the latter. Too much publicity as to capital, real and fictitious, condition of plants, cost of operation, depreciation, and profits, is not welcomed by private enterprises, and the Commission did not, in fact, secure the information upon which to pass an entirely satisfactory judgment. Perhaps after a few more years of regulation, such as exists under the public-service commission in New York City and under the

Chicago settlement, the data for studying private operation will be available. By that time also it is to be hoped that the accounting systems of cities will be immensely improved.

But when all the data are secured, the criteria for comparing public and private operation are bewildering in their complexity, and one can never be certain when he has included all of the significant elements. Take, for example, a study of public and private gas plants. It is not enough to compare cities of the same size. The area over which they spread must be taken into account. The nature of the soil in which the trenches are dug must be compared. Where gas users dwell in tenement houses the outlay for mains per thousand consumers is much smaller. Distance from the coal fields and sources of supply must be brought into the survey. Inquiry must be made into the sinking funds, franchise valuations, depreciation provisions. In the case of the public concern, it must be discovered whether the city took over a run-down plant of a private company or built a new plant on improved lines. The list of elements to be measured might be extended indefinitely.

It may be said positively that municipal ownership of itself does not guarantee any higher standards of service on the part of utilities nor improve the conditions of the employees. Neither is it to be held a gain for socialism in any sense, for it does not mean necessarily any increase in the power of the working class in government. On the contrary, corrupt rings, such as formed around the Philadelphia gas-works, may use the municipal employees to maintain a system of public exploitation from which all classes suffer alike. The excellence of municipal ownership depends upon the standards of the community in which it is tried and upon the character of the political organization which controls the city government.

Whoever wants a nicely balanced academic conclusion on municipal ownership, therefore, will find the facts of American city life disconcerting; but even in the absence of any such conclusion, the principle of public ownership seems to be slowly growing in favor. In 1905, the voters of Chicago elected Mayor Dunne on a program of immediate municipal ownership of the street railways; but there were financial and legal limitations which made impossible, at least in the minds of the political leaders, the fulfilment of the campaign promise. In the settlement which was shortly reached, however, provision was made for the acquisition of the property by the city under certain conditions; and Mr. Walter Fisher, the city's traction counsel, appealed to the advocates of municipalization to support the settlement " on the ground that under the proposed plan all of the difficulties in the way of the acquisition by the city would be removed and the price at which the city could purchase the street railways at any time would be definitely fixed."

In Des Moines, Iowa, the candidate for mayor in the campaign of 1910 stood for public ownership of the water-works and the ultimate acquisition of the street railways and was successful. In the election of 1911, in Los Angeles, the victorious Good Government party was pledged to practically all of the immediate demands of the Socialists, including municipal ownership. In the same year the city of Seattle voted bonds to the amount of $700,000 for the purchase, by condemnation proceedings, of a street railway concern which had been giving unsatisfactory service. The voters of Cleveland approved, on November 8, 1911, the issue of $2,000,000 worth of bonds to build a municipal electric-light plant to furnish current to private consumers as well as for the streets and public buildings.

The most striking thing about the recent developments in this field is the action of State after State in empowering its cities to assume proprietorship of their utilities. California, Michigan, New Jersey, and North Carolina are among the commonwealths which have conferred this authority upon their municipalities. Moreover, the debt limits imposed upon cities are being widened so as to permit the exclusion of the bonds of revenue-producing utilities from the regular debt limit, thus enabling them to incur the initial expenditures required for the construction or purchase of plants.

In studying the growth of the movement for municipal ownership one is impressed with the fact that neither logical arguments nor scientific determinations are the chief factors. In any particular city the movement is likely to start in this fashion. An electric-light company has an antiquated plant, its service is poor, its charges are high, its stocks are heavily watered, and it is suspected of " standing in " with the local political managers. Some enterprising newspaper or aspiring party-leader begins a war on the company, pointing out its defects and citing the supposedly favorable results of public ownership in some near-by or distant city. A few supporters of the abstract principle of municipalization make the issue a moral one, and the Socialists see a chance for some slight gain. Then the fight is on. The public, and generally not without reason, suspects the rectitude of the corporation's purposes, and votes for public ownership on the chance that things may be better and cannot possibly be much worse. The decisive element is popular sentiment, which is undoubtedly growing more and more collectivist in character.

At the present time, property owners are not all lined up against the advance of the collectivist idea. Business men are willing to oust an electric-lighting corporation if they can have better commercial and street lighting as a result. They are not generally prepared to sacrifice a practical convenience for a more or less remote abstract principle. Small property owners are not inclined to view with alarm the application of the doctrine of municipalization to a public utility. In other words, the property interests, not immediately concerned in a municipal campaign, are often willing to accept a socialistic proposal as an immediate gain and run the chance of taking care of themselves in the future when they are threatened by too great an extension of the principle.

The corporations affected in the struggle are not without weapons of warfare. There are now in existence organizations which undertake to wage campaigns against municipal ownership for companies in danger of being ousted. "The acceleration of public opinion" against new proposals has become a high art, and often it happens that men who are vehemently voicing their opinions one way or another in political meetings, saloons, and workshops are, all unawares, expounding "manufactured" or "canned" ideas. In a paper recently read before a meeting of some electrical operators, an expert who had specialized in the science of allaying the municipal-ownership fevers advised his hearers, as follows: "Listen to the song of the ad.-catcher. Buy some space in his paper and put something worth while in it. Don't think you have done your duty to the public when you say, 'Cook with gas,' and 'Electric irons cure Tuesday's ills.' The consumer's attitude is 'Electric irons make higher bills.' Put some life into your talks to the public. Show the editor you can say more about the progress of the city and your part in that progress than he can and see him get busy. Get the people with you once, and the biggest demagogue in the country can't win them away. You can't make hay when it rains — nor can you effectually mold public sentiment when you are under fire. The time to kill municipal ownership is before its starts — not a few weeks before election. A bit of news once a week about a failure; a few hundred sample copies of some magazine containing an article on municipal ownership — these are things that should mark the beginning of your campaign. When you are attacked, don't go to the council — go to the people and let them handle the council. It's the first blow that counts. If you want to dodge municipal ownership, hit first. I can name a dozen companies right now that have lost their fight because they were 'afraid to start an agitation.'"

It is in the field of water-works administration that the principle of public ownership has received the widest application in the United States. Of the sixteen plants in operation at the opening of the nineteenth century, fifteen have become public. Only eight cities out of the thirty-eight having a population of over 100,000 in 1900 left the ownership and operation of their water-works in

private hands. A government investigation in 1905
showed that of the 154 cities of over thirty thousand
113 or 73.4 per cent. owned or operated or owned and
operated their water system; and, furthermore, that of
the $831,368,707 invested in city industries, $535,957,-
239 represented investments in water-works. Within
recent years such large cities as Los Angeles, Kansas
City, Missouri, and Syracuse have changed from private
to public management, and a majority of the new plants
recently constructed have been public. The most interesting experiment of all is the 240-mile aqueduct built
by Los Angeles to bring Sierra floods down to supply
domestic water, furnish tremendous hydro-electric power
and irrigate 135,000 acres of dry land near the city.
The work was done by the city at a cost of over thirty
million dollars, and will bring in a net revenue of over
four millions a year.

On the general success of municipal ownership in this
field, Mr. Bemis, in the Civic Federation Report, says:
" In spite of the great reduction in rates in Syracuse on
going from private to municipal ownership, and the
phenomenally low charges for all residence consumers
under the present meter system in Cleveland, and the
moderate charges also in Chicago, the financial results
of municipal ownership, from the standpoint of the community and the taxpayer, are far better in the three cities
above named than in the case of the two private companies studied (Indianapolis and New Haven)." The
two cities with private plants also stood at the bottom of
the list on the score of health, as measured by the death
rate from typhoid fever. The private companies were
also found to have contributed largely to local campaign

funds when their interests were involved. As to the character of the mechanical equipment it is stated by the same authority that the plants of Chicago, Cleveland, and Boston will compare, in up-to-date and labor-saving machinery, with " the best that private water-works can show in any part of the world."

Notwithstanding the generally favorable opinion reached by the Commission of the Civic Federation, the special investigators of the Department of Commerce and Labor in their voluminous report on cities in 1905 complain that the accounting conditions in city water plants are wholly inadequate, and add that " one of the results of this condition of affairs is that it is possible for an advocate of any particular policy of furnishing public utilities, either by the cities or by private corporations, to make almost any statement concerning the comparative results of the operation of existing systems of public and of privately owned industries of the same class without any chance of verification by reference to actual statistics." The federal report urged the desirability of the city's adopting a definite policy with regard to the operation of water-works and the maintenance of a system of accounting. Of the various procedures, the following are suggested. Each has its special merits, but the particular point is that a city should know what policy it is pursuing and consistently follow it in all details.

(a) The city may conduct its plant on a purely business basis, paying its operating expenses, interest on the investment and sinking-fund and depreciation costs, taxes to the city, and charging the city (as well as private parties) for water used at regular rates.

(b) A policy of furnishing water to citizens " at cost "

may be adopted, and in case it is, there should be a full understanding of what elements are included in " cost."

(c) As a matter of public policy, a city may supply water to its citizens at less than cost, charging the balance up to taxes — a policy that has little to commend it.

In making charges to consumers, a municipality may employ a meter system, or rely upon more or less rough estimates based upon the size of the buildings, or upon the number of taps or conveniences used. On the whole, the meter system seems to be gaining in favor, although it is not without opposition on the ground that it discourages cleanliness, an argument that is without foundation where a minimum flat charge of $5 or $10 is made that will allow the customer all of the water he needs for reasonable use. It has been tried in Cleveland with satisfactory results. In New York it is employed, on the authority of the commissioner, on business and manufacturing premises.

The Water Commissioner of Kalamazoo recently put the following strong argument in favor of the meter system:

During the year ending March 31, 1911, with a population of upwards of 40,000, and with something over 5300 services and a revenue from water of over $38,000, we pumped a total of 710,474,683 gallons of water, as against 787,621,902 gallons pumped in 1893, with a population of about 18,000, and with only about 2500 services and a revenue of only $15,262.37, which permits the following deduction: With a population considerably more than double and with more than twice as many services, and with rates lowered more than 10 per cent., we increased our revenue over 150 per cent. and decreased the amount of water pumped 77,000,000 gallons. All this was accomplished by the enforced use of meters, and how any municipality that is struggling with the question of an inadequate supply of water will ignore the benefits they might derive from a complete metering of the plant and continue to pay out the citizens' hard-earned money, contributed yearly in the way of taxes, to get an increased supply of water in order that the wasteful may have more to waste, when all they have to do is to properly care for what they have, is too deep a mystery to be fathomed by the writer.

Where the people live largely in private houses and each family has its own meter, the actual measurement of the water used serves as an incentive to economy and the stoppage of waste but in cities where the population is grouped in large apartment houses and it is impracticable to have a meter for each family, actual measurement does not act as a check on waste, because the responsibility cannot be placed on any one. In general, the American policy has been to encourage a liberal use of water, and in 1900 the per capita consumption in New York City was more than twice the amount used in Paris.

In addition to encouraging the liberal use of water by private families, many cities have instituted public baths. In Europe, these baths are constructed in large numbers and on a generous scale, but the policy in the most enlightened cities of the United States has been rather to encourage the construction of bathing facilities in homes and apartments. In New York City, for example, the law requires the installation of water in each apartment in new tenement houses and this provision has led the majority of builders to include bathing facilities.

However, there is a place for public baths as well, and

New York has made the provision of bathing facilities obligatory upon the larger municipalities. As early as 1893, Milwaukee opened the first all-the-year-round bath-house, and this example was speedily followed by other leading cities — notably Buffalo, Boston, Baltimore, and Louisville.

In the field of electric lighting, the principle of municipal ownership has not been as extensively applied as in the supply of water, although it has been reasonably successful in some large cities, e.g., Chicago. Of the electric-light plants registered by the Census Bureau in 1900, only about 22 per cent. were municipally owned. In 1902 the federal investigation reported that only thirteen electric plants which had been started as public concerns had been transferred to private companies while about one-fifth of the public plants then in existence had originated as private enterprises. The percentage of the municipal plants increased from 9.5 per cent. in 1885 to 24.4 per cent. in 1906. The opponents of public ownership frequently publish lists of cities in which municipal plants have failed and been turned over to private concerns; but the Commission of the Civic Federation claimed, in 1907, that the allegations of failure in municipal plants were to a large extent based upon false statements or irrelevant facts.

Detroit, Michigan, has conducted an interesting experiment in municipal lighting, since the construction of the plant in 1893. Previous to that year a private concern had offered to light the streets at $102.20 per arc light for a ten-year contract. In its tenth annual report for June, 1905, the Detroit commission gave the cash cost of operation at $34.99 per arc light. Adding taxes,

interest, and depreciation charges brought the cost up to
$55.28 per lamp. Pasadena, California, in 1911, in-
stalled a large electric-light plant to sell current to private
parties as well as furnish it to the city. In the same
year Orange, New Jersey, established a municipal plant
and Binghamton, New York, voted in favor of public
ownership of this utility.

Memphis, Tennessee, took over the lighting of the
streets in 1902, and four years later the mayor reported
that whereas under private ownership the city had been
paying $49,270 for lighting its streets and public build-
ings, within a year after the installation of the public
plant it furnished to the city more than double the
amount of the light previously used and at the lower
cost of $33,500.

Some experts claim that the cost per lamp in Chicago,
where the plant is municipally owned, is about $10 per
year less than in New York City where the service is
purchased from a private company, but it is not apparent
that this claim rests upon accurate data. Municipal
ownership is applied in New York to the lighting of
some public buildings, and the Edison Electric Light
Company asserts that it will furnish the same service at
a lower rate.

About all that can be said with safety is that municipal lighting has been successfully maintained in many
American cities, in spite of the fact that they are often
forbidden to sell commercial light — which means a
larger capital outlay per unit of service. None of the
large cities has given up public ownership for private
enterprise, although in some of the smaller places this
transfer has been made. In a number of minor cities

threats of public ownership have been sufficient to scale
down to a surprisingly low figure the unreasonable
charges of private companies.   Indeed, it seems to be
quite an effective instrument in the hands of municipal
reformers in all parts of the country.

The comparative costs of important items in the operation of municipal and private plants, as given by the
federal census in 1902, are instructive.

Items	Total	Private stations	Municipal stations
Total	100.0	100.0	100.0
Salaries and wages.........	30.3	29.9	35.8
Supplies, materials, and fuel	33.7	32.6	46.2
Rents, insurance, taxes, etc...	17.5	18.2	8.4
Interest on bonds...........	18.5	19.3	9.6

In the public ownership and operation of gas-plants,
American experience has been extremely limited, and
by no means happy.   In 1900 there were only fifteen
municipal gas-plants in the United States, and six years
later the number had increased to twenty-five.   Two of
these plants, at Richmond, Virginia, and Wheeling,
West Virginia, were investigated by the Civic Federation
Commission, which reports concerning the former city
as follows: " Richmond has had municipal ownership
of its gas-works since 1852 and during that time has vied
with Atlanta, among all the cities of the South, in leadership in the reduction of price, while its expert accountants who have audited the books have reported that the
plant has not only been paid for out of earnings, but has

turned into the city treasury over $1,500,000 in addition." As to the Wheeling plant the Commission reported that it was honeycombed with bad politics but was a financial success in spite of this handicap. Professor Gray, of the Commission, found "the sentiment of the public and the press generally favorable to municipal ownership"; and he added, "The belief is universal that the works are running down. Nearly every one says that he prefers this condition to the dangers of monopoly with a private company."

The most commonly cited example of the failure of municipal ownership as applied to gas-works is that of Philadelphia where the plant was under public management from 1841 to 1897 and was systematically used by the spoilsmen in the maintenance of their political machine. Undoubtedly the "gas ring," so eloquently described by Mr. Bryce, was a standing menace to good government in the city, but those inclined to generalize hastily from this "horrible example" should remember that if disgraceful political conditions are an evidence of failure, private ownership and operation in many places must stand condemned as well. However this may be, Philadelphia decided in 1897 to give up the municipal experiment, and in that year leased the gas-plant to a private company subject to certain stipulations as to charges for gas and payments to the city. At the expiration of a long term the plant may revert to the city. In spite of some decided gains since the transfer, there are many experts ready to venture the opinion that had the city put the same effort into a rejuvenation of the old management that it has spent in its contest with the private corporation seeking the franchise, still greater gains would have accrued to the municipality. There appears to be, however, no decided municipal-ownership sentiment in Philadelphia, for when in 1907 an opportunity was presented to recover the plant by paying the cost of improvements to the company, advantage was not taken of it.

In the field of transportation, so extensively occupied by public enterprise in England and Germany, there have been no municipal experiments of any importance in the United States. In Seattle and San Francisco bonds have been voted for certain municipal railway lines, and in New York City municipal ferries are operated at a loss, for the advantage of the real-estate owners and residents of Staten Island. New York and Boston own their subways, but the operation of the concerns is in the hands of private companies. Generally speaking, therefore, we may say that this branch of municipal functions is monopolized by private corporations under more or less effective public regulation. With the growth of public-ownership sentiment, particularly on the Western coast,. it is probable that some significant ventures will be made soon in municipal-transportation systems. No doubt great economies might be effected by the consolidation of the power plants of electric-lighting and street-railway companies, but municipalization is not necessary to such a step.

CHAPTER IX

THE STREETS OF THE CITY

THE streets of a city have been likened to the skeleton of the human body which fixes and determines the general contour of the body. Once established, they are difficult and expensive to alter; Boston spent between 1829 and 1910 about $40,000,000 widening, straightening, and extending streets. They have been likened also to the arteries through which flows the life-blood of the city — trade and traffic.

But the streets are more than the skeleton and arteries of the city: they are the meeting-places of the people, the playgrounds for children, the highways of allurement to recreation and vice. "Here," says Dr. Soper, "persons of all ages and all tastes go to meet one another, to talk over the affairs of the day, to be entertained, to eat, to drink, to inspect shop windows, to do marketing, to buy and sell merchandise, and to perform a thousand offices which the exigencies of city life make profitable, healthful, or agreeable. . . . The city streets connect every household. The city man not only moves through the streets; he carries the dust of the streets into his home on his boots and clothing; he gets his food and air through the streets."

Indeed, the social significance of the streets can scarcely be overestimated. If they are wisely laid out,

smoothly paved, and well cleaned, great sums of money
can be saved in the speed and safety with which passengers and goods may be carried about the city, and
in the wear and tear on the vehicles of conveyance.
While the danger to health from mere dirt can easily
be overestimated, virulent tuberculosis germs and the
spores of lock-jaw are frequently found in street filth,
and the breathing of the gritty substances created by
traffic on the stone and asphalt surfaces is injurious to
the membranes of the throat and lungs. The dust of
the streets is harmful to fabrics and furnishings in
homes and in shops; its accumulation adds to the labors
of the housewife and storekeeper.

Then there is the esthetic aspect: the influence of the
streets on the habits of the people. In the congested
areas of the city, the people must spend a large portion
of their leisure time on the sidewalks, because their
homes are too small for comfort; and, if the city allows
its streets in these sections to remain unkempt and grimy,
a bad example is set for people who have to fight for
every bit of cleanliness they enjoy. The reflex influence on their homes is deteriorating. If a street is dirty
it invites the adjacent inhabitants to deposit rubbish
there; and thus filth becomes cumulative. If glaring
and hideous signs and advertisements are permitted indiscriminately, the people learn to think in head-lines
and look on the maiden of Old Dutch Cleanser as the
apotheosis of high art.

Apart from the proper laying out of highways, which
is considered below in the chapter on " City Planning,"
the first requisite of clean streets is proper paving. Here
several elements must be taken into consideration.

From the standpoint of cleanliness, asphalt pavement leads all the rest, because it admits of easy sweeping, flushing, and squeegeeing; but it has the disadvantage of not being able to bear the heaviest commercial traffic, particularly in warm weather.

On the score of durability, the smooth stone or granite block stands first; indeed, it is the only type of pavement that will survive the constant strain of loaded wagons. If the reduction of noise is the factor of prime importance, the wooden block is to be highly commended, but it speedily decays and requires constant repairs. Of the harder substances, brick is steadily winning favor, because it will stand up well under reasonably heavy traffic and is easily repaired. It has the disadvantage of asphalt, however, in that it is exceedingly slippery for horses in wet weather.

Cobblestone is to be utterly condemned, although millions of square yards are to be found in our cities. Macadam is likewise coming under the ban for streets which have to bear any considerable traffic, because it is hard to clean, produces a gritty dust of the most irritating kind, and requires almost constant repairing. Perhaps the only thing in its favor is the cheapness of construction and the ease with which it can be sprinkled; but when the cost and inconvenience of sprinkling year after year are taken into consideration the advantage of cheapness is easily offset.

Obviously it is unwise to attempt the introduction of a single type of pavement for all the streets of a great city. In the congested quarters, where the conditions under which the people are forced to live are such as to increase the amount of dirt that inevitably finds its way to the streets, asphalt should be used because it is easiest to clean. Indeed, in all residential districts, asphalt is the pavement which is steadily growing in favor, and promises to hold the future. Where the element of expense is too great for the wealth of the community, brick pavements or macadam treated with oil may be used with a reasonable degree of satisfaction. In the business streets where the traffic is heavy, stone and granite blocks are advised by the best authorities. Of course, in the determination of what streets are to be used for heavy hauling, a great deal may be done by carefully planned traffic regulations.

When the department which has charge of constructing and maintaining pavement has done its work, the immediate responsibilities of the citizen and the street-cleaning department begin. The citizen is mentioned first for the reason that his carelessness is the cause of a great deal of the unnecessary dirt in the streets. Here the old word about prevention is appropriate, and education is necessary.

In recognition of the part which the private citizen plays in littering up the streets, several of our cities have recently instituted " clean-up " days on which the citizens vie with one another in clearing up their yards, front and back; and the public is duly impressed with the importance of stopping street dirt at the source as far as possible.

Householders and janitors should be compelled to prepare the wastes for removal in such a way as to minimize the littering of the streets. Garbage should be placed in covered receptacles, and the too-common practice of allowing overflowing cans, waiting the garbage collector, to stand open, inviting flies, stray dogs, and cats, should be abolished; and the rule should be enforced.

Then, carters, peddlers, hackmen, and others who use the streets should not be permitted to scatter papers and other rubbish about indiscriminately. Being wanderers in the streets they feel no responsibility and it is incumbent upon the community to impress upon them the errors of their ways. Grocers and other shopkeepers are great offenders also, for they frequently permit their wastes to accumulate and blow about the streets. Contractors and builders often interpret their permits to include the right not only to encumber the streets but also to make them depositories for rubbish on a large scale. A part of this littering of the streets can be stopped by law, and education can help.

Drivers and private persons may be supplied with cards containing certain precise rules concerning the use of the streets, and in the schoolroom some simple ideas of conduct may be impressed upon the children. This was done with good effect a few years ago in Brookline, Massachusetts, where the children in a certain school were organized into brigades to watch the neighboring streets. "To each child was assigned a beat, and they at first found that they were picking up lunch papers, exercise papers, etc. The supply of these was quickly stopped. They then had to proceed with their educational campaign to their parents and older brothers and sisters, with the result that there was a substantial change in the appearance of the entire district."

The great burden of cleansing the streets, of course, falls on some branch of municipal administration.

Particularly is this true of the larger cities where the inhabitants are tenement or apartment dwellers and have no direct responsibilities for disposal of household wastes.

Two systems of collecting waste are now in vogue in the United States. About half of our towns rely upon private contractors who secure the work under some system of bidding. The second method is collection by a regularly organized staff of city employees under the supervision of an administrative head. The general tendency is toward the adoption of the latter method, because competitive bidding is frequently supplanted by collusion among contractors, and under direct municipal operation responsibility for unsatisfactory conditions is more easily fixed.

Under both systems it must be admitted that our present methods are far behind those of most European cities. As an expert sanitary engineer, Dr. Soper, remarks: " In spite of praiseworthy efforts here and there, the streets of but few cities are kept in a satisfactorily clean condition. . . . One of the reasons for the unsatisfactory condition of city streets lies in the fact that the business of keeping a city clean is rarely understood by the public or by the officials in charge of the streets. Street cleaning has not yet emerged from the state of a nondescript kind of emergency undertaking to the position of an effective art."

Even New York City, which is often cited as the municipality with the best street-cleaning department, has much to learn, for no radical advances have been made there since the revolutionary work of Colonel Waring who, during his administration of the department, beginning in 1895, put the service on a military basis, carried out by uniformed men organized into brigades. Colonel Waring also introduced the compulsory classification of wastes by requiring householders to separate ashes, garbage, and papers, cans, bottles, etc., for ready treatment by the collectors. He put the street-sweepers in white uniforms which won for them the name of " White Wings," and to the garbage collectors he assigned brown uniforms.

In many respects, the New York system which has been copied with variations by several other large cities, is crude beyond measure. The ashes are collected in open carts, and as they are dumped from the cans into the wagons they are blown about the streets into the eyes and nostrils of the dumpers and the pedestrians. Garbage is also collected in open carts which scatter filth in their trails as they jolt about the streets.

In enlightened European cities this intolerable state of affairs is avoided by simple methods. Paris, for example, employs large motor garbage wagons, provided with effective lids and built low in such a manner as to make the dumping of the heavy cans comparatively easy. Berlin, which lets the collection of wastes to a sanitary utilization company acting under strict city ordinances and the control of the police department, also requires the use of dustless, covered wagons. European cities also frequently require the mixture of garbage and ashes, which has several advantages. The lye and potash of the ashes help to disinfect the garbage while the juices of the latter make the ashes damp so that they do not blow about the streets. Moreover, garbage mixed with large quantities of ashes becomes nearly odorless and is less attractive to the disease-bearing fly.

The objection to this mixture of ashes and garbage is that it makes the latter useless for the disposal companies which buy it for commercial purposes. This objection is not altogether valid, however, because in Europe processes have been developed for making the mixture as profitable as the extraction of the fats.

Whether the garbage is separated from the ashes or not, the present antiquated methods of cartage commonly employed in the United States must be supplanted by the use of the newer type of covered, dustless, and odorless carts. The lifting of the heavy ash cans up to high wagons is a physical strain on the men which soon tells on them. The breathing of the dust which blows from the wastes seriously affects their lungs, as statistics of street-cleaners show. Moreover, the collection should be made with such precision that the cans need not be standing on the streets all hours of the day and night, and private citizens should be compelled to take in the emptied receptacles speedily on pain of fine for repeated offenses.

In addition to the removal of industrial and domestic wastes, the municipality is responsible for cleaning the streets. Here two methods may be used to remove the smaller deposits: sweeping into piles and cartage, or flushing into the sewers. A study of the most advanced methods in Europe shows that the latter method is gaining in favor. Occasional sprinkling to lay the dust and give the outward signs of cleanliness, and occasional oiling of the streets are becoming discredited as cleansing processes. The latter is particularly objectionable, although it furnishes some temporary relief, for it holds the dirt together and invites new accumulations by its sticky nature, thus creating a filthy layer which the pedestrian carries into the house on the soles of his shoes. Moreover, the theory that oil acts as a germ destroyer is sadly overworked.

Sweeping the streets with small hand brooms is likewise falling into discredit, although it is necessary for rough and broken pavements. It is expensive; it is offensive to the hand-worker and the pedestrians; and it can be defended only in cities too small and too poor to afford the initial outlay required for proper pavements and automatic sweeping and squeegee machines.

Our progressive cities are resorting more and more to flushing the asphalt, wood, and stone-block streets and our inventors are responding to the need by the production of remarkable motor machines for street washing and scrubbing. Attempts have been made to introduce vacuum cleaners, but in their present state of development they have not proved very practical or effective. Sprinkling to soften the dirt, followed by flushing to carry it away and squeegeeing to scrub, seems to be the method which promises the best results. The revolving street broom stirring up clouds of dust and the hand sweeper, with his sprinkling pot and broom and garbage can, have many days before them yet in the United States, but they are doomed in all foresighted communities.

After the streets are properly cleaned and the wastes of the city collected, there remains the problem of how best to dispose of the materials derived from the various

sources. Broadly speaking, there are three methods of
disposal: dumping at sea or on low-lying lands for the
purpose of filling in; destruction; and reduction.

The first of these methods, dumping, is the most common, and in spite of esthetic objections has much to be
said for it. Cities lying on the sea may easily dispose
of enormous quantities of wastes in a convenient manner
if the dumping is done far enough out to avoid con-
taminating the shores and if no nuisance is created by
the passage of the garbage barges in and out through
the traffic of the harbor. Dumping mixed wastes upon
low-lying land may be employed to reclaim large areas
which, if properly handled, may add to the collective
wealth of the city; ravines and marshes may be filled,
and building sites recovered from the surrounding
waters.

Where this method is followed, a careful survey should
be made of the country about the city so that the greatest
economic advantage may be derived from it. Above all,
the mistake should be avoided of paying contractors to
haul away wastes to fill private lands and reap enormous
profits through increased values. The wise application
of public ownership to waste dumping may make a nuisance a source of profit.

The objection that this method implies hauling unsightly and malodorous masses of materials through
the streets can be overcome by the use of low-hung,
covered wagons, constructed on proper principles, many
types of which may be now secured from a number of
enterprising manufacturers. The further objection that
the dumping-ground is an eyesore may be partially met
by selecting the spots least likely to prove noxious, by

a proper leveling of the materials and by following the dump-line closely with soil and grass seed.

A second method of waste disposal is the destructor system: the use of the mixed wastes either for fuel in a furnace, or their destruction in a furnace without any economic purpose. Applied science has been at work for a long time on the construction of a furnace which will permit the economical use of wastes as fuel, and some remarkable inventions have been perfected. For example, a system installed at Westmount, near Montreal, consumes mixed garbage, refuse, and ashes from a population of 15,000 at a low cost for labor, and from this waste develops two hundred horse-power for the municipal electric-light plant.

The destructor is a decided advance on the old crematory which merely consumes the waste without affording any economic return. It uses a high degree of temperature, consumes all kinds of wastes. is not odorous, and leaves nothing but ashes for final disposal. The crematory requires a large amount of additional fuel to evaporate the water in the garbage, cannot utilize all the wastes, and is generally a nuisance to the immediate neighborhood on account of the odors.

The third method is reduction, which can be employed for garbage only and consists in the extraction of the commercially valuable materials, particularly grease. The older method was the Merz process introduced at Buffalo more than a quarter of a century ago by which the garbage was reduced by cooking and the grease separated by the use of naphtha. A more modern process — the Arnold method — was established at Boston in 1895 and at New York in 1896. The plant at the latter

place is the largest in the world, having a capacity of
3000 tons a day, and is owned by a private company
which is paid by the city for its work. In 1905, Cleveland, Ohio, established a municipal reduction plant of
a type more advanced than the Arnold process, and by
successful operation has cut the cost of garbage disposal
to a very small sum on account of the revenue derived
from the sale of the products.

Columbus opened in 1910 a municipal garbage reduction plant, and the engineer reports for the first six
months of operation a net profit of $14,608.43 over all
costs of operation, from grease, tankage, and hides. The
cost of the collection equipment and reduction plant is
fixed at $295,530.82. The reduction plant alone cost
$189,542.23. At this rate, allowing 4 per cent. interest
on the capital and a reasonable amount for depreciation,
the city is a clear gainer by the system.

The recent Boston contract for the disposal of wastes
embraces the following terms: "The company proposes
to use the dry-heat system of garbage reduction, to be
carried on under vacuum throughout, which will eliminate disagreeable odors. If the city requires, the steam-
cooking process will be substituted. Incineration will
be carried on in Sterling refuse destructors of the English type, as furnished by the Hughes & Sterling Company, of London, through their American agents, the
Griscom Spencer Company. Paper and rubbish will be
incinerated after the valuable portions have been removed
by hand picking or mechanical separation. Each destructor unit will be competent to destroy a specified
mixture in the proportions of 40 per cent. garbage, 20
per cent. rubbish and 40 per cent. mixed household ashes,

but it is planned to use ashes and street sweepings for filling islands or swamp lands at the water-front."

New York City is now considering the wisdom of paying a private company a high rate for handling a commercially valuable product.

For the larger cities the following plan for the waste-disposal process seems to be recommended by experience:

Separate collection of rubbish and the extraction of valuable materials either by municipal employees or by a private contractor. New York City receives a large sum weekly from the contractor who sorts the rubbish and he makes a handsome profit out of the work.

Use of ashes to fill in low places and marsh lands, or, where a destructor system is employed, their utilization as fuel with the garbage. New York annually dumps about 300,000 tons of coal in the ashes off Riker's Island — an amount constituting nearly one-third of the total ashes collected.

Reduction of garbage by a municipal plant and the sale of the commercial products.

Variations will be made by combinations of these methods, but the alert city by giving proper attention to waste disposal and modern methods of street cleaning may keep its house in order without any serious burden on the taxpayers.

Generalizing from the statements of experts we may say that the following points should be observed by the city which would earn a reputation as a " spotless town."

Consider the element of cleaning when constructing streets and do not let low first costs obscure the later costs and the disadvantages inevitably associated with pavements that are dust producers or are hard to clean and maintain.

Water is the great cleanser, and when the streets are properly built, water and the sewers will do the work better and cheaper than the dust man.

Equipments may now be secured for street-cleaning and waste-disposal departments, which are not offensive to the eye or nose.

Those who use the streets may be compelled to minimize the litter they make there by ordinances properly enforced.

There should be a close connection between, if not a fusion of, the department which builds and repairs streets and that charged with keeping them clean.

The police should be brought into the work and required to report neglected streets and vile practices of private citizens.

The disposal of wastes should be considered as a whole and the possibilities of economic advantage for the city rigidly inspected.

The working classes in the congested quarters can have the back streets as well as the avenues kept clean — if they will.

The streets must not only be properly constructed and thoroughly cleaned, they must also be well lighted at night. The primitive element in street lighting was the provision of enough illumination to enable the pedestrian to pick his way from one place to another after night-fall. Some of our cities have scarcely got beyond this primitive stage, but new elements are winning recognition. Well-lighted streets and alleys tend to diminish crime and reduce the burden of police protection; they increase the value of the adjoining property; they prove profitable to business men by attracting trade; they are a general incentive to "civic pride"; and they are an encouragement to cleanliness. As a recent writer in *The American City* remarks: "Not only will well-lighted streets be kept cleaner as a matter of mere inclination, but they will be less littered and abused. There is extremely little wanton destruction or injury to property of any kind. Such cases arise mostly from thoughtlessness or association, and not only will good street lighting be an incentive to keeping the streets clean and sanitary, but it will further react upon the residents themselves with a wholesome influence to cleanliness."

As to the method employed in lighting streets, gas has steadily supplanted oil and other fluid lamps, and electricity is constantly gaining on gas. Indeed, gas is now seldom employed in the installation of new systems; it is rather being continued where already installed, on account of the contracts with private supply companies or the expense attached to the construction of new plants.

As early as 1899 there were three times as many electric plants as gas plants in use, and the proportion is now much greater. Moreover, as we have seen, the principle of municipal ownership is winning favor in this field, and demonstrating its practicability. Electricity has certainly distanced all competitors, and lighting interests are now devoted rather to experiments with more efficient and economical lamps and the substitution of ornamental fixtures for the old and unsightly wooden poles.

While the familiar arc lamp still holds the field, inroads upon it are threatened. The Tungsten lamp is attracting attention all over the country. For example, Warren, Ohio, a city of about 12,000 inhabitants, has installed a complete system of Mazda Tungsten lamps placed on ornamental standards, and fed (in the business portion of the town) through underground cables. The system was first tried out in certain residential streets and the success of the experiment led to the installation of a complete plant. A writer from that city says: " Our old lighting system consisted of 161 open arc Brush lamps of 9.6 amperes. The operation of this system up to midnight with a few all-night lamps cost the city $10,800 per annum, while the new lighting system, using the Mazda Tungsten lamps and giving all-night service all over the city costs $13,000 per annum; twenty per cent. more of our streets are lighted by this new system than were lighted before, while the streets formerly lighted are now illuminated 100 per cent. better than by the former method. The kilowatt consumption under the new method is thirty per cent. less than the old method." The ornamental Tungsten system has also been applied to certain streets in Dayton, Indianapolis, and other cities with apparent success.

Even where the arc lamp with its many improved forms is retained, more consideration than ever is given to methods of installation in the streets. Wires are being put underground, at least in the business districts, which are more encumbered with poles than the other sections; and the rough wooden poles are being supplanted by goose-necked and other ornamental iron standards.

The experience of Kansas City, Missouri, in the improvement of street lighting is interesting and indicates what may be done in any city. A group of enterprising merchants on a certain business street combined and installed a number of simple and plain standards at their own expense. The effect was immediate. About the same time a municipal art league took up the question of a uniform system of ornamental equipments, and as a result of a competition among artists secured a beautiful standard. Property owners and merchants then began to install this type of lamp at their own expense, and in due time the city will have a complete system of ornamental lamps which will afford better light and at the same time be pleasing to the eye.

The beauty of the street may be further enhanced by the planting and proper treatment of trees. The feverish commercialism that has built most of our newer cities has woefully neglected the tree. Although it is difficult to conceive of the imagination of a real-estate agent who can plan a vast new plot to a town without leaving any space for trees, it nevertheless remains a fact that huge areas are every day being added to our American cities without any provision for trees whatever. In these areas the summer sun beats down mercilessly on the playing children and the pedestrians, and the winter winds sweep through them, adding to their bleak and barren appearance. So great has been this neglect of trees in our cities that a tradition has grown up that they will not thrive in busy streets. Of course, this is not true, as many a fine shady street in the heart of some of our cities will show.

In this regard, as in many other matters of genuine public concern, our cities have relied principally upon private enterprise. Property owners have been permitted to plant trees in their yards or along their sidewalks at random, with more or less satisfactory results, and they have also been permitted to cut down trees along their property at will. Within recent years, however, the idea of public control has grown in favor, and a number of cities have created special departments to supervise the planting and care of trees. New Jersey led the way, in 1893, by passing a law dealing with shade trees in cities and authorizing municipalities to create commissions to take charge of the whole matter. In 1904 and 1908, Ohio and Pennsylvania respectively followed the example of New Jersey. Two years later Massachusetts extended an old tree warden act in such a manner as to provide a special tree authority for practically every city and town.

The Pennsylvania and New Jersey laws are optional and go into effect only when adopted by a city. Wilkesbarre placed the matter in the hands of the local park commission, giving it the power to supervise all shade trees except those in private grounds. Within less than two years nearly a thousand trees had been planted on seven barren streets and forty-five additional streets had been plotted for three thousand more trees. This was a practical demonstration of the fact that a city may be transformed in a short time by an enterprising tree commission.

The principles usually adopted on the creation of special tree authorities are as follows: The planting, trimming, and removal of trees can be done only with the consent of the commission, so that systematic plans may be carried out. By the employment of experts, the trees best adapted to the soil, the width of the streets, and the traffic, may be planted. The proper spaces may be secured between trees where uniform plans are drafted. The preservation of trees against the ravages of insects and time can best be done by a tree expert who gives his whole attention to the matter and keeps watch for pests and signs of decay. By having a public authority in charge of trees, plans for the whole city may be made and careful foresight may be exercised so as to prevent the newer parts, at least, from growing up as " wildernesses of brick and mortar."

Speaking on this point, the Newark tree commission, one of the most powerful and progressive in the country, says, in a recent report: " Adequate municipal control secures for the tree, expert planting, pruning, mulching, spraying, etc. Take the operations of pruning and spraying. When these have been left to private initiative, they have either been entirely neglected, or the operation so inexpertly performed (in many cases) as to result in the ruin of the tree. It is pitiful — the trees that have been done for forever by unskilled pruning and spraying. In a word, the treatment of trees is an expert profession; private initiative, as a rule, ignores that vital fact; intelligent municipal control accepts the fact and acts upon it."

CHAPTER X

GUARDING THE HEALTH OF THE PEOPLE

MUNICIPAL health administration is no longer concerned primarily with caring for the sick and dying — playing the part of an ambulance to a careless and uninformed public. Its chief business is not the abatement of intolerable nuisances or waging spectacular fights against periodical epidemics. Health departments properly equipped and based on correct principles — unfortunately too few in the United States — are veritable armies, waging war on the causes of disease, no matter how subtle or remote they may be, no matter whether lurking in the home, the school, or the workshop.

Nearly twenty years ago, we are informed by Dr. Lederle, health commissioner of New York, the board of health of that city began to announce its conviction that every undertaking that had to do with the *prevention* of disease was a proper function for health officers, and year after year that board has based its practical methods and its appeals for appropriations for new activities upon this principle. In other enlightened American communities this doctrine of prevention is winning acceptance; and under its influence the office of health commissioner is appealing to an ever higher type of expert — a veritable social engineer fully alive to the fact that "public health is purchasable, and within natural limitations a community can determine its death rate."

In other words, health and well-being are largely contingent upon modes of life and work, and therefore health administration, like every other branch of municipal government, becomes an aspect of a larger social and economic problem. And the health commissioner who recognizes this fact becomes a teacher of the community as well as its doctor. Pointing out how crowded tenements and badly built factories, malnutrition, and adulterated foods are daily recruiting the army of the stricken is more noble and more business-like than soothing the dying hours of civilization's victims and decently burying the dead. It is a cowardly health officer who shrinks from his higher duty and takes refuge in the narrow and unimaginative task of abating nuisances. "Every advance in sanitary science," says Dr. Lederle, "goes to strengthen the position that the problems of preventable disease and misery are largely social problems and must be met and solved by collective action on the part of the community."

Moreover, collective action is easier to obtain in the name of public health than in any other way. It is in this branch of the government that the American armor of self-righteousness and *laissez faire* is most vulnerable. No people responds more readily and more generously to a call for help in a war against contagion or in repairing the havoc of a disaster. Already our health departments are equipped with large and drastic powers over life and property; and when it can be shown that a law rests upon scientific notions of health, the courts, although always ready to resist legislative interference with private rights, will be inclined to uphold it and give its provisions generous interpretations. In fact, all things conspire to make public hygiene the gateway to revolutionary changes in the living and working conditions in the United States.

The Socialists by their appeal to the proletariate arouse the protests of those most directly affected by unhealthful environment. Employers of labor are beginning to see that improper living and working conditions — rather than original sin — are the chief factors making for inefficiency. Progressive hygienic science cannot rest content with attempting to cure when prevention is possible and is a more inspiring task. Educationalists are developing a sense of humor which will not allow them to devote time to Greek mythology when the subjects of their instruction have rotten teeth, defective visions, and adenoids. The top-lofty notion that anybody may do what he pleases so long as he does not gouge his neighbors' eyes out is no longer a defense against that "interference with the home" which prevents thousands of cases of blindness by forcing the observance of a few simple rules at child birth.

In fact, unless all signs fail, we are now on the verge of a wide expansion of public hygiene and health administration. But it is too soon to begin congratulations. New York City, which leads the country in the generosity of its expenditures and the scope of its health activities, devotes less than 2 per cent. of its annual outlay to health work as compared with approximately 5 per cent. for fire protection, 9 per cent. for police, and 17 per cent. for education. Public hygiene is shamefully neglected at our universities; and sanitary engineering is too largely a science of the disposal of wastes.

Turning now from generalities to particulars, we may

inquire into the principles followed in organizing health departments and fixing their powers and duties. In the matter of the form of the department, there arises the question whether a single-headed office or a board should be adopted. More may be said in behalf of a board for public-health administration than perhaps any other branch of municipal government. While the need for the concentration of responsibility is so great as to constitute a case for the single-headed office, public hygiene has so many interrelations with other departments that a strong argument may be advanced for a board composed of the health officer and heads of closely related branches. To speak concretely, it is impossible to draw the line between tenement-house work and health work. Hygiene is slowly penetrating the public schools; state factory legislation and inspection present aspects of health administration; and the police have their historic interest in the abatement of nuisances.

The desirability of some sort of coördination is so apparent that New York City attempts to solve the problem by creating a composite board, consisting of the commissioner of health, as head of the department, the police commissioner, and the health officer of the port — a state functionary. The commissioner of health is the responsible executive officer of the department, while the board is a legislative and consultative body with large powers, including the authority to amend or repeal any provisions of the city's sanitary code and enact ordinances " for the security of life and health in the city, not inconsistent with the constitution or laws of the State."

The powers of the ordinary health department start

with the legal notion of what is a nuisance, for the abatement of nuisances was the primitive health function out of which has grown the present wide-reaching concept of social hygiene. A nuisance is a matter for legislative and judicial determination, and health departments, while endowed with summary powers in the abatement of nuisances, must not collide with the restrictions inherent in the legal doctrines on the subject — doctrines which vary according to the degree of enlightenment of the courts. Moreover, legislatures and councils in enacting health laws must avoid coming into conflict with the Fourteenth Amendment to the Constitution of the United States which forbids any State to deprive any person of life, liberty, or property without due process of law. It is true, the Supreme Court has said that this provision does not abridge the police power of the State, that is, its power to enact laws for public health, morals, and welfare; but the Court decides when the limits of the police power have been transgressed by the law-making authority.

In addition to its general control over nuisances, the health department is invested with special authority for extraordinary occasions. It may destroy property, imprison persons, forbid traffic and intercourse; in short, do anything within human power to check the spread of contagious diseases. To meet such occasions the charter of New York confers upon the board of health special prerogatives in the following language: " In the presence of great and imminent peril to the public health by reason of impending pestilence, it shall be the duty of the board of health, having first taken and filed among its records what it shall regard as sufficient proof to authorize its declaration of such peril, and having duly entered the same in its records, to take such measures, to do and order and cause to be done, such acts and make such expenditures (beyond those duly estimated for or provided) for the preservation of the public health (though not herein elsewhere, or otherwise authorized) as it may in good faith declare the public safety and health to demand, and the mayor in writing shall approve."

These are the old and accepted functions of health departments everywhere, and it may be readily seen how innumerable special functions may be developed on the basis of these original principles. It would give an altogether mistaken notion of the recent advance and potentialities of public hygiene, to leave unmentioned the wider and more specific activities of health administration in our best cities. It is germane to our purpose, accordingly, to take note of some of the latter-day achievements in the field of sanitary science.

In the supply of city water, there are always lurking grave dangers to health which may be overcome by the combined vigilance of the water and health departments. Mr. Godfrey, in his interesting and informing book on city health, cites an instance which illustrates in a striking manner the way in which death may invade a community through the water mains: " In April, 1885, the town of Plymouth, Pennsylvania, contained eight thousand men, women and children. The general health was excellent, and the water supply from a clear mountain spring far above the town seemed unusually good. Like a whirlwind came the plague. Out of that eight thousand, eleven hundred and four contracted typhoid fever, and one hundred and fourteen died. Rich and poor alike were taken, and through every part of the town, highlands as well as lowlands, the fever raged. And this terror came from a single case of typhoid brought back from a great city whose polluted waters caused the fever. This case existed in one of the only two houses that could contaminate the water system. From this source came the decimation of the little town far below."

The constant danger of this peril at the water faucet lays a weighty burden on the two departments that guard the city's drinking water; and raises the location, treatment, and filtration of the supply to the first rank of applied sciences. Inasmuch as the amount of water secured from deep wells and thus filtered naturally is very limited, most large communities must rely on what is known as surface water, and it thus happens that the very first point of defense is the protection of the area from which the water is drawn. Every condition which may foul the supply must be swept away. Where there are neighboring communities whose wastes may pollute, the construction of sewage disposal plants must be made obligatory. Such plants are required for cities and towns whose sewage may in the slightest degree foul the waters of the metropolitan system of Boston.

When the sources of the supply have been scientifically controlled as far as possible, filtration for cleaning and removing bacterial life may be employed, at a cost of from 50 cents to $2.00 per person per annum, according to the estimates of experts. Generally speaking, two types of filtering plants are in use in the United States: "continuous" and "mechanical." The former usually consists of two large reservoirs through which the water is passed. In the first of these the water is allowed to settle so that the heavy sediment drops to the bottom and the purer water is drawn off into the second where it drains through strata of sand and crushed rock. " As the affluent passes through the upper layers," says Mr. Godfrey, " the sand stops the coarser materials left in the liquid and held in suspension there. Soon there forms above the original surface a filter composed of smaller sediments, a layer so fine that even infinitely small micro-organisms cannot pass. Many of them are probably held by the sheer adhesion of the sand. Add this adhesion to the filtering powers of the sediment layer and you have erected a strong barrier. Here is a fortress placed across the pathway of the invading germ, a barrier so effectual that water from sources polluted with disease germs has been safely furnished to thousands after such filtration."

The second type, the mechanical filter, which is gaining rapidly in favor, is built somewhat on the same principle but the passage of water is greatly facilitated by the use of harmless chemicals " whose action on meeting the water is such as to engulf all matters held in suspension, including bacteria, thus forming comparatively large masses which can be filtered without difficulty." The more rapid accumulation of sediment requires the use of several alternating beds which can be cleaned frequently. A good example of a mechanical filter is to be found in the new Grand Rapids plant constructed for purifying and softening the water of Grand River.

When one examines the careful processes used at a

scientific filtration plant, one sees the futility of the cheap household filter as a guard against disease. The former uses eighteen or more inches of sand in addition to the sediment, and the latter only a few inches of more or less effective materials. Nevertheless, when the city's water is muddy, thousands of people are inveigled into buying cheap filters under the delusion that they are guarding against disease, not knowing that muddy water may be safe to drink and clear water full of death-bearing germs.

The relation of water to public health, of course, makes the treatment and disposal of sewage a matter of first-rate importance. Where the city is, like Chicago or New York, on a great lake, or river, or the ocean, the process of disposal by discharge into public waters has been the accepted practice; but of recent years there has been no little uneasiness on account of the degree to which sewage saturation extends, and on account of the danger arising from the use of such waters for drinking and bathing and the possibilities of polluting oyster-beds. New York, for example, has recently expended a large sum of money for a thoroughgoing examination of the adjacent harbor with a view to ascertaining the amount of pollution from the sewage. The commission, undertaking this work, reported that the danger was not yet sufficient to warrant any radical change in the sewer system, basing its results on the most ingenious scientific tests. Chicago has constructed (1900) a great drainage canal to turn the sewage southward from Lake Michigan, and now the chief engineer of the sanitary district recommends the construction of immense purification plants.

A second method for disposing of sewage, which has enlisted the enthusiasm of many students of sanitary science and agriculture, is its utilization for fertilizing land. In England and on the Continent, and to some extent in the United States, this process has been employed for a long time, and with varying results. In Pasadena, California, for example, the sewage is used profitably to fertilize several farms. In other parts of the West where the irrigation and enrichment of the soil can be combined, sewage farms have yielded satisfactory results. Broadly speaking, however, it cannot be said that this method of disposal, in its present stage of development, yields large net returns over the costs of operation.

Other methods of waste disposal rest upon the principle that "purification is an oxidizing process carried out by bacteria living in the filter." The sprinkling or trickling filter is one application of this idea. It is a large bed of crushed stone upon which are thrown jets of sewage which carries with it enough air to oxidize the wastes. An accepted authority on this subject holds that the trickling bed "appears to be the ideal method of solving the essential problem of sewage disposal, the oxidation of organic matter. It exhibits the simplicity of all scientific applications which are merely intelligent intensifications of natural processes. A pile of stones on which the bacterial growth may gather, and a regulated supply of sewage are the only desiderata. We meet the conditions resulting from an abnormal aggregation of human life in the city by setting up a second city of microbes. The dangerous organic waste-material produced in the city of human habitations is carried out to the city of microbes on their hills of rock, and we

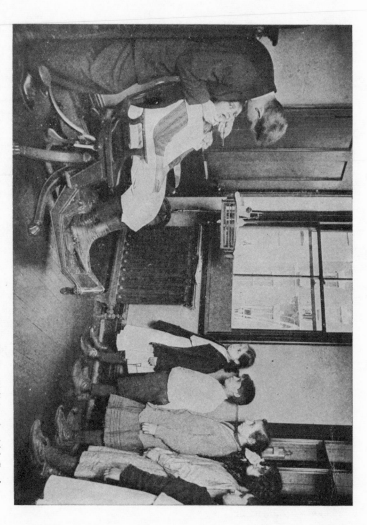

Dental Clinic in the Italian Industrial School of the New York Children's Aid Society.

rely on them to turn it over into a harmless mineral form."

This process of filtration is sometimes supplemented by drainage through sand beds or chemical treatment. Indeed, the purification of sewage by direct chemical treatment is proving highly successful and has a promising future. Jersey City has for some time purified its water supply by the application of a harmless bleaching powder which destroys the bacteria. While this is not the place for a technical treatment of a difficult branch of science, it may be said that in the present stage of public sanitation there is no reason why the water supply of a city should not be pure and the sewage wastes rendered absolutely harmless whenever they endanger life in any way. A vigilant health officer will see to it that the departments responsible for these public services have taken every precaution which sanitary science affords.

It has never been held by any school of political economy that the individual citizen was responsible for not exercising due care in case he contracted typhoid fever by drinking water from the municipal plant, but the doctrine of " let the purchaser beware " was for a long time applied in the case of foodstuffs and other commodities. According to this ancient and respectable notion, the purchaser was to blame if he bought glucose jams and jellies treated with coal-tar, and the surprising thing is that men, whose opinion on other matters is entitled to respect, still resist what they call paternal interference with municipal food supplies.

Nevertheless, our city health departments early came to recognize that they were bound to take notice of adul-

terations which were an actual menace to health; and
public sentiment is now so far advanced as to sanction,
by state, national, and city laws, public control of the
manufacture and sale of foodstuffs on broad social, commercial, and hygienic grounds. Standards for food supplies are being set up by law and the inspection of the
manufacture and sale of these supplies is committed to
the care of municipal health departments (supplemented
of course by state and federal assistance).

The department of New York City has under its jurisdiction more than twenty-five thousand retail and
wholesale establishments, including bakeries, butcher
shops, confectionery and grocery stores, and the concerns dealing in butter, eggs, chewing gum, cocoa, ice
cream, and all other important commodities, as well as
poultry slaughter-houses and cold-storage plants. All
that is necessary to secure adequate enforcement of the
statutes against impure and unwholesome foods is an
appropriation from the city large enough to provide the
requisite number of inspectors. Some of the " foods "
discovered by the inspectors on their occasional raids are
marvels of business ingenuity: brick-dust in cocoa,
molded bread crusts for coffee, and green plums for
olives.

The difficulties of properly inspecting perishable foods
and the recent increased cost of living have brought to
the front the proposition that municipal markets should
be established. Just as a great reservoir simplifies the
work of water inspection, so a centralization of food
supplies in a general and radial markets would render
public control easier.

It is the cost of food, however, that makes the matter

more serious, particularly for the poor, who must purchase in small quantities, usually from petty tradesmen,
three or four times removed from the producer. With
those living constantly on the margin, every penny
counts, and if the city can bring producer and consumer
face to face, thus eliminating to a considerable extent
the middlemen, it may materially help in the maintenance
of a proper supply of healthful foods at low prices.

Years ago many of our cities, especially in the South
and Southwest, had large markets, but their places have
been taken by private concerns, although a few cities,
like Boston, New Orleans, Baltimore, and Rochester,
still maintain some municipal trading centers. Nowhere
are the markets systematically organized, and no attempt
is made to cover the whole field adequately.

The subject is now receiving more attention, in answer
to the demand for some systematic organization of the
trade in food supplies, particularly meats and vegetables.
Dubuque, Iowa, maintains a market at which farmers
may sell without the interference of middlemen and the
result has been a decided reduction in the cost of staples.
" At the recently established market place in Des Moines,
between 100 and 200 farmers gather on the city hall
lawn and in the streets adjacent thereto between the
hours of 5 o'clock and 10 o'clock in the morning without paying any license or rent. They are permitted to
sell direct from their wagons to the city consumer.
The result has been that they receive approximately 50
per cent. more for their produce than the commission
men paid them before, while the city buyers get their
produce for approximately 50 per cent. less than was
paid formerly." In other cities, for example, Madison,

Wisconsin, recent experiments in marketing have not been so successful, and it is apparent that the problem cannot properly be met without a great deal of skilful management on the part of the municipal authorities.

No less important than safeguarding food supplies is the matter of securing cheap ice in summer-time. Some recent famines and monopoly prices in several large cities have raised the question of municipal control over the manufacture or storage of ice. The Socialist administration at Schenectady, New York, in the summer of 1912, attempted to supply ice cheaply, but was enjoined by the courts on the application of an interested party.

It is perhaps in guarding the milk supply that our city health departments have been the most active and successful, considering the gigantic task involved. New York City draws from over forty thousand farms scattered throughout seven States the enormous quantity of over 1,500,000 quarts daily, which is distributed by nearly six thousand wagons and over twelve thousand stores. The inspection of the dairies and the constant watching of the retailers is thrown principally upon the department of health; and the impossibility of discharging this duty efficiently without an army of officers has led the department to order the compulsory pasteurization of all except certain grades of milk.

The supply of milk for babies has received particular attention at the hands of private societies which have established stations where pure milk is sold and instruction given in the proper care and use of milk as an infant food. These philanthropic enterprises in New York have led the city to make considerable appropriations for the establishment of milk stations; and the maintenance of these stores for the sale of guaranteed milk is now a recognized municipal function.

Interesting efforts are also being made by private persons and health officers to educate the people in the care of children. In 1911, for instance, a splendid milk show, illustrating every aspect of the milk problem, was held in Philadelphia under the auspices of the department of public health with the coöperation of private associations. Most ingenious devices were employed to attract and fix the attention of the public on the significance of the exhibits.

The increasing interest in the milk question is only one indication of the growing determination to reduce infant mortality in our cities and to safeguard the health of future generations by giving proper attention to the young. Among other kindred measures the medical inspection of school children and provision for the correction of defects are now coming to be recognized functions of city government. "The eight years of school life offer the only opportunity to the community to examine all its members. Such inspection has a double interest, that of the physical health of the community and that of the intelligence of the community, since doctors have come to realize that physical health is a strong factor for or against mental development."

The timeliness of this new municipal function can hardly be questioned, for inspections in several of our large cities show that about 25 per cent. of the children have eye-strain; that more than two-thirds of them between the ages of seven and nine have defective teeth; that diseases of the nose and throat, particularly nasal obstructions, exist in from 6 to 25 per cent. of them according to age and social condition; and that malnutrition (running as high as 70 per cent. of the children in the schools in the working-class districts) is everywhere so common in our large cities as to be a menace to the physical welfare of the country.

During the years 1910–11, the Russell Sage Foundation of New York made an investigation into the progress of medical inspection in the 1285 cities, having organized systems of graded schools, and secured returns from 758 of them. Forty-five per cent. of these cities reported regularly organized systems of inspection in their schools, either under the board of health or the board of education itself. This medical inspection is, however, very superficial in many cases and is designed as a protection against contagious disease; for only half the cities reporting inspection (chiefly in the North Atlantic division) have any real physical examinations of the children. In a large number of schools the vision and hearing tests are conducted by the teachers, but more than one-half of the cities replying to the inquiry of the Foundation have school nurses. Only forty-eight cities employed regular school dentists. From this summary it is apparent that we are really only at the beginning of the protection of the health of the community at the proper point — the children.

New York City has in many respects led the country in this line of work, since the organization of the division of child hygiene in the department of health, in 1908. The functions of this new and important division include "the supervision of all midwives practising in the city, the prevention of infant mortality by the in-

Sewage Disposal Plant at Essen-North, Germany.

In operation since June, 1911. Eighteen Imhoff tanks, 30 feet in diameter, 33 feet deep; 180,000 inhabitants. Sewage flow, 17,000,000 U. S. gallons daily. Combined system. Flowing-through-time, 1 hour. Sludge-drying beds, 1.3 acres. Sludge-decomposition chamber, 230,000 cubic feet.

struction of mothers in the proper care of babies, the supervision of day nurseries, foundling asylums, and places where children are boarded out, the medical inspection and physical examination of children attending the public schools, and the enforcement of that part of the labor law which relates to the issuing of employment certificates to children between the ages of fourteen and sixteen." The commissioner of health of the city now recommends the extension of the inspection service to all free schools, the control of contagious diseases in the schools by nurses, the holding of school consultations with parents by medical inspectors to reduce the amount of home visiting by the nurses, and the establishment of school and dental clinics.

The need for dental clinics, particularly, is coming to be recognized, but in this matter we have scarcely made a start. Detroit has a free dental clinic for school children which was established by the health officer of the city with the coöperation of a number of dentists who volunteered to assist one hour a week each. Boston has a new magnificent clinic made possible by the Forsythe gift of $1,200,000. A clinic was recently organized in New York by private philanthropy in response to the discovery of the fact that over sixty per cent. of the children have defective teeth. In 1911, the New York health commissioner urged the foundation of six school clinics with three dentists at each clinic and three special dental clinics in addition.

These, however, are but meager responses to a great need. As Dr. W. H. Allen well puts the matter: " Many a city has had the experience of New York: (1) Physical examination of school children without proper examination of the teeth; (2) Piling up records of defective teeth with almost negligible facilities for securing treatment; (3) Permitting children's teeth to be extracted when they should be repaired and cleaned; (4) Heralding one or two dental clinics as evidence that dental needs have been recognized; (5) Promise of wholesale coöperation between dentists and public schools with practically no examinations or treatment of children." In other words we are far behind the leading European cities, which have founded adequate free dispensaries for the proper treatment of school children.

The danger is that when we begin our work seriously we will construct magnificent buildings and provide costly equipment for treating decayed teeth, instead of emphasizing, through effective instruction, the early care of the teeth and the habits which keep them sound. " One thing is certain," says Dr. A. H. Merritt. " If the teeth of the present generation are to be saved it must be during their school life. To defer it until they have taken upon themselves the responsibilities of adult life will be too late. Caries will have done its work. What per cent. of the parents of the children in our public schools are able to provide adequate dental treatment for their children when taught its value, no one can tell. But whatever it may be, there will inevitably remain a vast multitude of children who must depend upon the dispensary for all needed treatment."

The ideal system of medical treatment of school children will embrace careful and adequate physical and mental examination and the provision of proper facilities for remedying defects, so far as this is humanly possible. A system of records for each child throughout his school life should be provided and made accessible to the teacher and parents, so that all the elements bearing upon his physical, mental, and moral advancement may be understood.   The health or school authorities upon which this duty devolves should take immediate steps to have the defects remedied as speedily as possible, by the persuasion or coercion of parents and by the provision, through public and private institutions, of the necessary facilities.

These remedial facilities will include: free dental dispensaries; free or low-priced lunches in the schools of the poorer sections; the services of specialists in eye, skin, mental, and other diseases; the institution of specific corrective gymnastic exercises under experts for children found needing them; the classification of children on grounds of physical and mental differences and the establishment of special classes for the deficient; and the provision of open-air playgrounds and recreational centers in connection with the school buildings.   Under the ideal system, the scattered beginnings of which are to be found in various American cities, the old phrase " a sound mind in a sound body " will cease to be a bit of painful cant.

While this war of defense is being waged for the children, it would be well for every city to make sure that its school buildings and equipment, and the whole physical environment of the children in the schoolrooms, comply with high sanitary standards.   It is obvious folly for a city to battle with the results of slums and yet duplicate some of the evil features of congestion in its own buildings.   The investigation, mentioned above, conducted by the Russell Sage Foundation, showed that it was not uncommon to find cities in which schoolroom floors were not washed oftener than once in five months, and that one-fourth of the schools still have the common drinking cup. A surprisingly large number retain the old system of uniform desks for given grades so that the long and the short, the fat and the lean, are forced into one mold during the long hours of school. School hygiene is finding its place in the larger field of public hygiene.

The city can do even more than look after the welfare of the children immediately under its supervision; through the schools it can help educate the whole people in the modes of living which are conducive to physical well-being. Already nearly every State in the Union makes compulsory the teaching of hygiene with reference to alcohol and tobacco — this is obvious, and does not touch the pockets of slum landlords and the owners of unsanitary factories who, along with " demon rum," slay their millions. But the demand for full and scientific instruction in public and private hygiene is becoming imperative. As Dr. Allen remarks in his suggestive volume, " Civics and Health ": " Because the problems of health have to do principally with environment — home, street, school, business — it is worth while trying to relate hygiene instruction to industry and government, to preach health from the standpoint of industrial and national efficiency rather than individual well-being."

It is not only to the school children that instruction in public health should be given. Our health departments are already recognizing the place of sheer ignorance in creating unhealthy conditions, and are making special efforts through the newspapers, posters, leaflets, and visiting nurses to bring to the notice of the people the practices which are most conducive to well-being. The city of New York has, in its health department, a bureau of information which distributes reports and educational literature on health topics, acts as a center of inquiry for those who need the assistance of some of the preventative or curative agencies of the city, and generally assists the public in all matters coming under the jurisdiction of the department.

The Chicago health department maintains a permanent health exhibit, demonstrating by models the dangers to health in a great city. According to *The American City* —

One display which is found at all child-welfare and municipal shows, and various Chicago expositions, shows 3500 miniature dolls representing the unnecessary deaths among babies born in Chicago each year. In the center of this exhibit is an opening behind which a procession of the doll babies passes beneath the scythe held in the hands of the grim figure of Death. The scythe falls on every fourth doll, which immediately drops from view. It is operated by a person concealed in the box.

This startling demonstration of Death dealing with Chicago babies always makes a deep impression on exposition visitors, and causes them to realize as never before the great crime of the city in permitting every fourth baby born to drop into the grave before reaching the age of one year. One of the placards on this exhibit says that more than half the slaughter can be prevented if the public will only do its duty. Health officers from all parts of the country and others interested in matters of health find this exhibit, which is maintained permanently at the City Building, worthy of study.

Another instructive exhibit is the breathing dolls, a model operated to demonstrate the dangers of poorly ventilated sleeping chambers. In one of the small rooms a mother and baby are sleeping. They are shown to be breathing, and the air expelled from their lungs is carried out as smoke through the open door and windows.

Underneath this is a duplicate scene with breathing sleepers in a tightly closed room. Their breath, also represented by small puffs of smoke, completely clouds the room, clearly demonstrating the ill health resulting from pollution of a closed room.

New York, Boston, Cleveland, Rochester, Chicago, and other progressive cities have consulting clinics at the milk stations, schools, hospitals, and other convenient places for the special benefit of mothers seeking guidance in the care of infants.

Although we do not commonly associate fire fighting with the protection of public health, it should be remembered that the lives of millions of people — as well as property — are annually in peril from fires. This is especially true in the larger cities where the masses are congested in narrow spaces and particularly in factories and establishments located in high buildings. The appalling disaster, known as the Triangle Fire, which occurred in New York in 1911, resulting in the death of more than a hundred men and women, began high up in a huge manufacturing building. Similar horrors, on a smaller scale, are matters of almost daily occurrence in our industrial centers; and the annual death toll is on the average about 1500 a year, to say nothing of the five or six thousand injured.

A recent expert investigation shows that the actual fire loss, in one year, in the destruction of buildings and contents in the United States, was $215,000,000 or about eight times the per capita loss sustained by European countries from fire. It is estimated that in the period of thirty-six years, from 1875 to 1910, property to the amount of $5,120,000,000 was destroyed by fire in the United States.

This terrible annual loss in life and property is thus graphically portrayed by a fire-insurance expert: " If the buildings consumed were placed on lots with sixty-five feet frontage they would line both sides of a street extending from New York City to Chicago; and if we reckon the killed and injured by fire, a person in journeying along this street of desolation would pass in every thousand feet a ruin from which an injured person was taken, while at every three-quarters of a mile he would encounter the charred remains of a person who had been burned to death. Words are unequal to the task of depicting the awful sorrow which follows in the pathway of fire or of properly characterizing the act of those who are even innocently or ignorantly responsible for the waste of life and property so frequently chronicled in the fire record of the United States."

To combat this dreadful enemy, American cities have the most highly organized and the best-equipped fire-fighting systems to be found anywhere in the world. The administration of the fire department of a great city is usually entrusted to a layman appointed by the mayor, while the technical work of directing the fire-fighting battalions is committed to the care of an expert, known as the chief, who has seen long and honorable service. Under the chief are the several brigades and their officers stationed at the engine houses distributed at strategic places throughout the city. The men are organized somewhat on a military basis, and, as the soldier is often compelled in time of war to sleep on his arms, so the firemen are required to sleep at their quarters, and be ready for duty and even death at any hour.

The principle of selecting firemen by civil service, that is, on a merit basis, rather than political favoritism, has now found common acceptance in the larger American cities. And on account of the extraordinary hazards connected with fire fighting, cities quite commonly provide pensions for firemen who are injured or have grown old in the service.

In some of our cities, the excellence of the fire service is so high. that, in efficiency and *esprit de corps,* it outrivals all other branches of municipal administration and is the envy of the most successful private corporations.

As is in keeping with the advance of the country in mechanical inventions, the machines for fire fighting are being steadily improved. Collapsible ladders which can be raised to a great height are being introduced in cities having tall buildings. The motor fire engine is supplanting the fire horses; and on account of the terrific speed which can be developed by high-powered automobiles, the time consumed by a brigade in reaching a fire is incredibly shortened. New York City, for instance, is now revolutionizing the entire fire department by the introduction of motor engines. One of these machines, weighing nearly seven tons, was recently driven at a speed of thirty-five miles an hour and on reaching the place of trial threw an effective stream 462 feet into the air.

Among the newer developments is the introduction of

Giant Gasoline Pumping Engine.

what is known as " the high-pressure system " for business districts having high buildings. This consists of mains and pumping stations entirely separate from the ordinary water-plant, and is so constructed as to allow the development of a very high pressure. Separate hydrants are built at the street corners, and the chief, by communicating by telephone with the power house, may have the water pressure steadily increased to meet the needs of the particular fire. Cities on water fronts also commonly have fire boats equipped with powerful pumps and always under steam to assist at any fire within reach of the water's edge.

In order that as little time as possible may elapse between the discovery of the fire and the calling of the fire company, ingenious telephonic systems are devised. Arrangements are always made with telephone companies to transmit without a delay the news of a fire announced over their wires. Separate plants are, of course, installed for the fire department and New York is installing a special system, in the center of a park, that will maintain intact the telephonic communications of the department in the midst of a great conflagration that might cut off all ordinary systems and destroy the telephone exchanges.

As in most other fields of public activity in the United States, we have devoted more attention to the ingenuity of our instruments for fighting fires than to devices for preventing them. Happily, however, we are now beginning to think of fire prevention; and New York City has recently established a new " fire prevention bureau " which investigates the causes of fires, looks after the enforcement of the ordinances and laws against dangerous buildings and practices, issues instruction to private persons whose business or employment involves them in fire risks and in many other ways minimizes fire hazards.

Stricter building laws are being demanded, prescribing the kinds of materials to be used in various types of structures, regulating the installment of engines and machinery involving the use of combustibles, and controlling the internal arrangements and the construction of fire-escapes. Ordinances against smoking in forbidden places and in factories where inflammable materials are used are being enforced more strictly than ever, on account of the revelation of the number of fires due to careless smoking and the throwing away of lighted matches.

Finally, municipal authorities are demanding that insurance companies discontinue some practices which induce fires. A careful study recently made in New York showed that, in certain business districts, the number of fires varied with the prosperity of the concerns: in successful years the number was small, and in dull years the manufacturers got rid of their surplus stocks by insuring them heavily and then allowing fires to break out. The insurance companies, fully aware of these hazards, simply increased their rates in the unsafe districts, thus making the honest manufacturers pay the bills of the dishonest men and at the same time positively encouraging fires. Ordinarily, it is possible for a person to buy a few dollars worth of household goods, install them in a flat, and secure $1,000 worth of insurance from a reliable company over the telephone. If fire prevention is to succeed, insurance companies must change their methods.

CHAPTER XI

TENEMENT-HOUSE REFORM

As long as the people of the United States lived in the country or in small towns, the isolated house occupied by a single family was the unit in our living arrangements. And it was commonly assumed that any enterprising artisan could become a home owner by the practice of industry and economy. Accordingly, household sanitation was deemed to be a matter wholly within the management and direction of the family itself. Government interference was looked upon as an unwarranted invasion of the domestic " castle."

The attitude toward public control, which was natural enough under the conditions just described, has perdured, although the vast majority of the people in our large cities, as was pointed out in the first chapter, are not home owners, and millions are housed in multiple dwellings. Our typical proletarian does not possess a home; he does not determine the arrangements of his dwelling; and the only alternative presented to him, in case he does not like the treatment he receives from his landlord, is to move — an expensive and often inconvenient operation. Inasmuch as he has little or no control over the physical structure of his house and its management, he can find relief only through the development of public intervention. And the need for such intervention has been shown above in the chapter on "The People of the City."

Those who are opposed to drastic legislation dealing with tenement houses, or are indifferent to the imperative need for far-sighted improvements in the living conditions of the people of our great cities, often take refuge in the time-honored fallacy that the poor prefer to live in squalor and filth.   Every advocate of tenement-house reform has met more than once in the course of his labors the old argument that it is no use to provide well-appointed homes for the "lower classes," because they will right speedily reduce the better environment to their own level.   One of the favorite stories of the unthinking opponent of raising standards by legislation is that "the bathtubs are used by the poor to store coal or grow vegetables."

Over against this superficial criticism of the poor we may place the statements of a careful observer, who knows intimately the tenement district of New York, Mr. Lawrence Veiller.   Speaking on the general question of environment, he says: "The majority of the poor not only welcome improved housing conditions, but ardently desire them.   One of the most pathetic things in modern city life is the constant striving on the part of the poor to improve living surroundings. . . . It will generally be found that when the conditions surrounding the lives of the poor have been changed, the people have in a large measure changed with them."   Plenty of additional evidence has been brought forward by those who know their facts at first hand to show that, in spite of the doctrine of original sin, standards of life are being daily raised by legislation affecting environment.

Even the fiction about the use of bathtubs for coal storage seems not to have the slightest foundation, though one hears it confidently advanced by "nice people" who are supposed to know it as a result of personal experience. Writing on this tale of a tub, Mr. Veiller says:

No story, I imagine, has been repeated more often and none has less basis of fact — a hasty generalization from a single instance. Perhaps my failure during sixteen years' constant experience of tenement conditions in New York, throughout all parts of it, to observe instances of this nature has been due to the failure to find the bathtub, an institution that it has seldom been my good fortune to encounter in the ordinary tenement house. When one considers that few of the tenement population possess so great a luxury as a bathtub, and that it is their custom to buy coal by the pail because of their inability to pay for a larger quantity at one time, the story falls to the ground.

Over against this impressionistic picture one should, in all fairness, place those countless others, which stand out with photographic clearness, of the tenement-house mother laboriously carrying in pail after pail of water from the one faucet in the public hall, heating it in various receptacles on the kitchen stove and giving child after child its bath in an inconvenient wooden wash-tub.

In every attempt to improve housing conditions four factors must be taken into consideration.

In the first place, there is the tenant, who wishes to secure the most conveniences and comforts for the rent which his earnings will allow him to pay. Improvements are ill-advised, which overlook the fact that a material increase in rent means no gain to those for whom the benefits are designed. There are millions of poor now living near the margin of subsistence, and higher rent for the only quarters available to them is a benefit for which they cannot give thanks.   It must not be assumed, however, that the wages of the working class are in the long run a fixed sum, for they are in part determined by the cost of living and the efficiency of the workers.   Better tenements will raise the standard of living and tend to increase wages.   Better tenements will also increase the efficiency of the worker.

In the second place, there is the interest of the landlord, who naturally seeks to get as much rent as he can out of his properties.   Under a system of private ownership, regulations which are too strict and require too much capital outlay for the revenue to be derived will drive investors into other fields and thus the erection of new tenements will stop.   The effect of diminishing the number of new buildings will be to increase rents so that tenants will suffer.   From the standpoint of the landlord and investor, therefore, there are decided limits to the extent of regulation and charges, which the business of constructing and letting tenements can bear.

Again, there are the interests of the community at large, embracing those who are not immediately affected by tenement regulations.   In so far as vice, crime, disease, inefficiency, and death are due to bad housing conditions, the city and the nation suffer.   The diseases of the tenements are spread abroad through a thousand channels; vice and crime are heavy costs upon the purse and vitality of the people; inefficiency and a high death-rate are direct economic losses.   It is unquestionably true that some of the worst tenements in our great cities cost the municipality and the nation more indirectly than the landlords receive in rents. Because the problem is complicated we should not give it up; we should clarify our visions.

Finally, there are the interests of adjacent property owners. Unsanitary and disreputable tenements injure the values of adjoining property. This is responsible for a part of the demand for the regulation of height, adequate fire protection, and the limitation of area which can be covered by actual structures.

It is out of the play and interplay of these sometimes conflicting and sometimes converging forces that any policy of mere tenement regulation must come. American cities are not yet ready to follow the lead of European municipalities and lay out and construct municipally owned dwellings on a large scale. This is at present a part of the program of Socialism, although in Europe municipal housing is by no means confined to Socialist platforms and administrations. With the growth of Socialism in municipal politics and with the recognition of the limitations on mere regulation, some such experiments may be expected in the United States in the future. The Socialists in Milwaukee made extensive plans for municipal working-class dwellings, but their enterprises were cut short by their defeat at the polls in 1912.

The positive limits upon the regulation of tenements, by conditions which cannot be reached by tenement laws — that is, by wages, hours of work, and the unearned increment in ground values — are now being recognized by reformers, and housing programs for the future will embrace more drastic proposals than simple regulation and inspection. Indeed, there is no question that strict tenement laws, by increasing rents, actually tend to increase overcrowding rather than diminish it.

Leaving all of these larger proposals on one side for the moment, we may direct our attention to the present methods of dealing with unsanitary and congested areas of our great cities.

There are certain facts which any one, who wishes to engage in a campaign for better tenement regulations at the present time, should bear in mind. At the outset it must be remembered that vague impressions that conditions are bad will not suffice to stir the public and impress legislators who are always alive to the demands of the landlords. The actual facts about definite areas should be secured, the peculiar local conditions should be surveyed, and the precise evils to be remedied should be formulated in such a way as to indicate the kind of regulation best adapted to the purpose. " There can be no successful legislation based upon impressions," says Mr. Veiller. " Reforms not based upon carefully ascertained facts will be found to have no permanent value. You will but enact a law one year to have it repealed the next."

Laws affecting such powerful interests will be sure to be contested at every stage through the legislature, and their enforcement resisted at every point. An experienced worker in the field of tenement-house reform, Mr. Robert W. DeForest, former tenement-house commissioner of New York, thus sums up the situation: " Some enlightened landlords, with a sense of their obligations towards their tenants, are perfectly willing to suffer this small diminution of income. Others are not, and the others, who usually constitute the majority, in alliance with the builders and material men will always seek to prevent legislation which affects their pockets.

Tenement-house reform must always be militant, not only to gain ground, but to hold the ground that has once been gained."

In the fight for better tenement conditions, New York has had more varied and extensive experience than any other city in the United States, and has advanced further along the line of scientific control. The elements of a model tenement-house law may best be drawn, therefore, from the New York statutes which are the product of many years' work in formulating and administering housing laws. There are, of course, always local peculiarities to be considered, but it is difficult to imagine any new and serious problem in tenement regulation which has not come up in New York experience.

It is probable also that no other American city has ever had to cope with a worse state of affairs than that which confronted the New York tenement-house commissioner at the time of the establishment of his office in 1902. In his first annual report, July 1, 1903, Commissioner De-Forest said:

Tenement conditions in many instances have been found to be so bad as to be indescribable in print: vile privies and privy sinks; foul cellars full of rubbish, in many cases garbage and decomposing fecal matter; dilapidated and dangerous stairs; plumbing pipes containing large holes emitting sewer gas throughout the houses; rooms so dark that one cannot see the people in them; cellars occupied as sleeping places; dangerous bakeries without proper protection in case of fire; pigs, goats, horses, and other animals kept in cellars; dangerous old fire traps without fire escapes; disease-breeding rags and junk stored in tenement houses; halls kept dark at night, endangering the lives and safety of the occupants; buildings without adequate water supply — the list might be added to almost indefinitely. The cleansing of the Augean stables was a small task compared to the cleansing of New York's 82,000 tenement houses, occupied by nearly three millions of people, representing every nationality and every degree in the social scale.

In drafting a tenement-house law, it is necessary to define accurately, in the light of judicial decisions, the types of structures to which the regulations are to apply. The New York law as it stood in 1910 defined a tenement house to be any building or house or portion thereof, which is rented, leased, let, or hired out to be occupied or is occupied as the home or residence of three families or more living independently of each other and doing their cooking upon the premises, or by more than two families upon any floor, so living and cooking, but having a common right in the halls, stairways, yards, water-closets, or some of them. This apparently clear statement was later interpreted by a state court in such a manner as to narrow its application and exclude from the operation of the law thousands of tenements which the sponsors for the act intended to bring within its scope. Framers of laws must remember, therefore, that the general tendency of the courts in their anxiety to protect private property from governmental interference, is to limit, not to widen, the application of the principle of control.

Under the head of "Light and Ventilation," the New York law fixes the percentage of the lot which may be occupied by a tenement and the height of all new tenements. It contains detailed provisions relative to yards, inner and outer courts, and the lighting of public halls. It provides that in new houses the rooms shall be of a definite minimum size at least, and that in the living-rooms windows of a certain minimum area must be built. It also forbids what is known as the " dark room " in all tenements by declaring that no room may be occupied for living purposes which does not open upon a court, shaft, or the street, or into another room which is open to the outside air. This provision, which was bitterly fought, still allows an enormous number of inner rooms which have only an apology for light and air and are dangerous to the health of the occupants.

Under the general head of sanitary provisions, the law contains minute provisions as to plumbing, water supply, bathing and other conveniences, basements, jani-tor's quarters, water-closets, the cleanliness of buildings, stairways, basements, and courts. " In every tenement house hereafter erected," runs the law, " there shall be in each apartment a proper sink with running water. . . . There shall be a separate water-closet in a separate compartment within each apartment, providing that where there are apartments consisting of but one or two rooms, there shall be at least one water-closet for every three rooms."

It was urged before the Tenement-House Commission of 1900 that the installation of a bathtub in each apartment be required by law, but the Commission dismissed this suggestion and came to the conclusion that " to require a private bath for each family as a matter of law was not practicable, and might with difficulty be sustained if attacked in the courts." The requirement that running water should be placed in each apartment, however, makes possible the installation of bathing facilities at a slight additional expense to the landlord, and as a result between eighty and ninety per cent. of the new tenements contain private baths for each family.

Under these sanitary provisions great gains have been made for tenants. The common water tap for an entire building or for the whole floor has been abolished in the new buildings, and the construction of conveniences conducing to health and cleanliness has been required or encouraged. The filthy school-sink, dangerous to health and degrading to morals, has been forbidden. What New York has done in this regard is being followed by smaller cities, like Pittsburgh, for example, which now tolerate unsanitary conditions that are a disgrace to civilization.

Janitors of tenements, as might have been expected, have not gained in the same proportion as tenants, although the New York law does contain some scant provisions relative to their apartments. The housing of janitors is an outrage upon public decency, and would not be tolerated for a moment if they were not among the poorest and most defenseless elements of the community. Except in some of the best apartment houses in New York, they are housed in dark, damp, and dirty quarters substantially underground. The inadequate terms of the law as to light, air, and drainage are not even enforced and inspection is notoriously lax. The complacency with which tenants, even in apartments of the higher grade, look upon the wretched provisions made for janitors and their families is another illustration of the old adage that he who would be free must strike the first blow himself.

Under the head of " Protection from Fire " the New York law contains stipulations relative to the materials

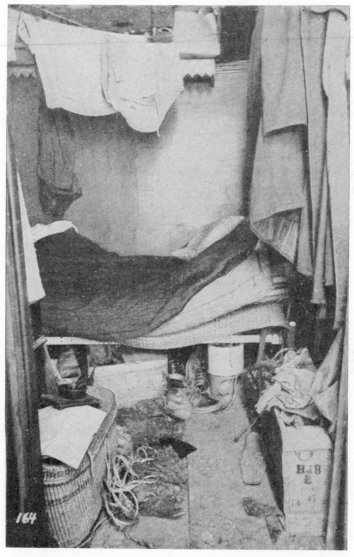

164

Courtesy of The Tenement House Commission

Inside Basement Room in a New York Tenement House.

used in the construction of tenements, the structure of halls and stairways, the erection of fire-escapes, and the storage of combustible materials. It is urged by some reformers that all future tenements should be fireproof, but the additional cost entailed by such a provision is so great as to check the building operations and force tenants to live in the older and less expensive houses.

It has been found by experience in New York City that the smaller tenements under six stories in height are reasonably safe if the stairways and halls are fireproof. The law requires, therefore, that only those new tenements exceeding six stories above the curb level must be fireproof, and that smaller tenements must have fireproof stairs and halls, enclosed in brick walls and constructed of iron, slate, marble, and other non-combustible materials. " This type of house," says Mr. Veiller, " has given eminent satisfaction in New York. It is practically the main type that has been built since the passage of the Tenement House Act in 1901. During the period of eight years, in the Borough of Manhattan alone 4506 new tenement houses have been built providing accommodations for 116,789 families, or approximately over a half a million people. There has not, however, in all this time been a single instance of a bad fire in one of these houses; nor has there been any loss of life from fire in one of these buildings nor any fire in which any considerable financial damage has resulted."

The cleanliness of the tenements depends in a large measure upon conditions which are not immediately under the control of the tenement-house department — such as the state of the streets and pavements, and the removal of garbage and other wastes. First, there are the physical aspects of the problem. Dirt from filthy streets is carried into the tenements on the boots of the tenants and is blown in through the open windows. Uncollected wastes stand about in open receptacles, filling the building with odors and drawing swarms of insects in the summer-time. Then, there are the psychological aspects. When the public places are dirty and untidy a bad example is set for the dwellers in the tenements. It is the easiest thing in the world to slide downward to the level of environment, and it is an energetic housewife, indeed, who is able to escape altogether the influences of filth outside her own door. Ruskin has suggested that we should sweep the back streets and leave the front ones to take care of themselves, but he overlooked the fact that influential citizens live on the front streets and the poor cursed by their poverty live on the back streets. By solidarity the latter may gain power also.

The law, however, may materially assist the tenement housewife by requiring that the halls, stairways, courts, and other public portions of the building shall be kept clean. On this point the New York law is full and specific. "Every tenement house," it runs, " and every part thereof shall be kept clean from any accumulation of dirt, filth, or garbage or other matter in or on the same, or in the yards, courts, passages, areas or alleys connected with or belonging to the same. The owner of every tenement house or part thereof shall thoroughly cleanse all the rooms, passages, stairs, floors, windows, doors, walls, ceilings, privies, water-closets, cesspools, drains, halls, cellars, roofs and all other parts of the said tenement house of which he is the owner to the satisfaction of the department of health and shall keep the said parts of the said tenement house in a cleanly condition at all times. . . . The walls of all court-yards, inner courts, and shafts, unless built of a light color brick or stone, shall be thoroughly whitewashed by the owner or shall be painted a light color by him and shall be so maintained. . . . The owner of every tenement house shall provide for said building proper and suitable conveniences or receptacles for ashes, rubbish, garbage, refuse, and other matter." How important the administration of the health department becomes under these general terms is apparent to all.

The provisions of the most elaborate law regulating tenements, do not, however, solve the problem of overcrowding; they merely make certain that the light, air, sanitary conveniences, and safety of the apartments comply with certain standards — that is, if adequately enforced. They do, in fact, tend to increase congestion by adding to the cost of construction and hence to rents. Families of eight or ten will continue to live in apartments designed for two or three, and the health safeguards, so far as light, air and ventilation are concerned, may be made nugatory in spite of laws requiring so much air space for each occupant. This is the point where wages and standards of life, which can be reached by no mere tenement-house regulations, enter into consideration.

Another evil of overcrowding which can be met by no legal requirements as to light, air, and sanitation arises from the practice of taking in boarders and lodgers for the purpose of supplementing the family budget. Curiously enough the poor who resort to this business are quite commonly penalized for their own thrift, because the landlords, finding their tenements more valuable on account of increased family revenues, raise the rents so as to skim off the profit from the supplementary income. Indeed, the lodger evil in the congested areas is in part responsible for high rents. Charging what the traffic will bear is one of the sound principles of business enterprise.

No satisfactory regulation for this serious evil has been yet devised. Indeed, it would be difficult to find one, for it involves interference with family affairs. Mr. Veiller suggests that, in tenements of a certain class, the taking in of lodgers and boarders without the consent of the landlord, should be forbidden, and the responsibility for this kind of overcrowding thrown upon the owner of the building. The difficulties of administering such a provision are obvious, and as it has not yet been tried out in any American city, its effectiveness is problematical.

A social aspect of congestion which cannot be reached by regulations regarding the structure of tenements is tenement manufacturing, or " home work," as it is commonly called. In every large city, there are hundreds of small masters who " farm out " work of every kind, to be done in the homes of the employees, usually by the piece. This kind of work includes knitting, sewing, shelling nuts, dipping chocolates, and other light employments which belong to the sweated trades. It is the poorest paid branch of modern industry, and a curse to the poor whose bitter want it relieves temporarily. It is difficult to control because the line between legitimate and illegitimate home industry is difficult to draw. The instant needs of the poor are always pressing, and adequate inspection is well-nigh impossible. This feature of housing reform, moreover, falls under the head of labor legislation more appropriately, thus illustrating once more the intimate connection between municipal government and larger economic questions.

Another aspect of housing reform is the prevention of prostitution in the tenement districts. As every one knows, prostitutes are recruited from the poor who through their necessity and ignorance are drawn into this "easiest way," as it is so erroneously called. If prostitution is allowed to flourish in the tenements the daughters of the poor are easily enticed by the flaunting finery of the women who have found a way to live in what appears to be luxury to the girl who toils long hours for low wages in the factory or store.

Largely on this ground, reformers have sought to drive prostitution from the tenements. Under the New York law it is forbidden in the tenements, heavy penalties are imposed upon the women who follow Mrs. Warren's profession there, and landlords are made responsible for the continuance of the business in their premises after due notice has been given them. " A tenement house shall be subject to a penalty of one thousand dollars," runs the law, " if it or any part of it shall be used for the purpose of prostitution or assignation of any description with the permission of the owner thereof or his agent." Detailed provisions are made for establishing the complicity of the owner or his agent, and the extent to which prostitution can flourish in tenement districts depends entirely upon the vigilance of the health department, the police, and the inspectors of the tenement-house department.

When a genuinely model tenement-house law has been secured, the battle is not half won, for enforcement is the rub. Particularly is this true when the terms of the law are too general and a large discretion is left to the officers charged with the execution of its provisions. It is imperative, therefore, that the requirements of the law should be exact and adapted with foreknowledge and care to the precise conditions to which they are designed to apply. The experience of more than one city has shown that where a tenement-house officer is allowed to fix, even within conservative limits, such matters as the height of buildings, the size of the rooms, or the window-area, he leans with unerring precision in favor of the interests of landlords and builders.

Take a single illustration. The New York law of 1895 provided that new tenement houses should not occupy more than sixty-five per cent. of the lot, except that under certain circumstances the superintendent of buildings might permit as high as seventy-five per cent. of the lot to be occupied. The effect of conferring this discretionary power is thus described by Mr. Veiller: " Now what actually happened? Within a year every tenement house that was erected occupied the full seventy-five per cent. of the lot. No one even thought of covering any less and from the very nature of things, nothing else could have been expected. If one architect presents a plan for a new building and the superintendent of buildings permits him to occupy seventy-five per cent. of the lot, a competing architect a few weeks later in submitting his plans will demand that he too be permitted to occupy as much. So gradually every architect insists upon his right to cover as much of the lot as his predecessors have done.

"There are, however, graver abuses connected with the grant and exercise of discretionary power. Nothing leads to municipal corruption so rapidly as leaving indefinitely to a single official the determination of what shall be done in individual cases without possibility of review. Favored architects in a short time, because of their friendship or political influence, or because of a corrupt understanding with the enforcing official, are gradually able to crowd out of business competitors without these advantages or who are unwilling to adopt the methods employed by their less scrupulous rivals. In a short time a situation develops by which a few firms of architects or builders control the entire business of a community."

Even if all the provisions of the law are as specific as possible and the discretionary authority of the executive officers as limited as circumstances will permit, it is extremely difficult to keep politics out of the department charged with inspection and law enforcement. Those who possess influence with the administration insist on having violations of the law overlooked, and it is easy for an inspector, if he is so inclined, to pass casually by dirty stairways and cellars, dark rooms, and filthy courts. So much depends also upon the standards of the department, for cleanliness, light, and safety are relative matters. The profits of the landlords will be pared down by a strict enforcement of the law, and landlords are voters, contributors to campaign funds, and party workers. Tenants are often too careless and too busily engaged in making a living to assume the responsibility of informing a health bureau about the unsanitary conditions of their tenements. Generally they do not know their rights. Men are largely indifferent; women are without substantial influence in the politics that counts. The well-to-do portion of the public having no direct contact with unsanitary conditions have no immediate motive for calling inspectors to book. The landlords and builders are always the positive element, and the pressure which they can bring against rigid inspection and law-enforcement easily overcomes the spasmodic efforts of tenants, reformers, and " the public at large."

These difficulties in the way of enforcing a tenement-house law must be taken into account by every person or organization laboring for improved living conditions. The tenement-house department charged with the enforcement of the law must be so organized as to cope with them as effectively as possible. Its corps of inspectors should be adequate; its records complete; its control over old and new tenements wisely safeguarded; and its powers for drastic action in cases of clear violations and unabated nuisances set forth in plain and unmistakable terms. In all these matters the New York tenement-house department may be taken as representing the most advanced type in the United States, for it is the oldest and has been built upon several years' practical experimentation.

The head of the New York department is the tenement-house commissioner appointed by the mayor and removable by him at will. Thus clear responsibility is secured. The commissioner appoints his immediate deputies.

The department is organized into bureaus. The first of these is the new-building bureau, charged with the duty of filing, recording, and examining the plans and specifications of buildings in course of construction and alterations in old tenements. No tenement house can be built in the city and no alterations can be made without the approval of the department. If the terms of the law are not met it is the fault of the administration.

The bureau of inspection through its large corps of inspectors examines all completed tenement houses and records violations of the laws and ordinances.

The bureau of records prepares and keeps on file the records and specifications of every tenement in the city. The records embrace the following items:

1. A diagram of each tenement house, showing the shape of the building, its width and depth, also the measurements of the unoccupied area, showing shafts, courts, yards, and other open spaces. Such diagram shall include a diagram of the second or typical floor of the building, showing the sizes and arrangements of the rooms, and all doors, stairs, windows, halls, and partitions.

2. A statement of the date or the approximate date when the building was erected.

3. The deaths occurring in the tenement house during each year and the annual death-rate therein. Such statement shall show whether such deaths were of adults or children, and, if occasioned by tuberculosis, typhoid fever, diphtheria, scarlet fever, smallpox, measles, or by any other contagious or infectious disease, it shall state the disease causing death.

4. The cases of sickness from contagious diseases occurring in the tenement house and the nature of the disease.

Such record shall also show whether such cases of sickness were of children or adults.

The powers of the New York department for drastic action are adequate. No new tenement or newly altered tenement can be occupied until the commissioner certifies that it conforms in all respects to the provisions of the law. Except in case of tenements where the average rental of the apartments is over $25 a month, the department must make a monthly inspection; the higher-grade houses are inspected at the discretion of the commissioner. The department may order any tenement house or part thereof " to be purified, cleansed, disinfected, removed or altered, repaired or improved." Whenever anything in or about a tenement house relative to plumbing, sewerage, drainage, light or ventilation is, in the opinion of the department, " in a condition or in effect detrimental to life or health, the department may declare that the same, to the extent it may specify, is a public nuisance," and may order it abated or altered to suit the demands of the law.

Notwithstanding the generous provisions of the New York law, the extensive organization of the tenement-house department, and the undoubted improvements which have been made during the last decade, it must be admitted that the living conditions in the tenement districts of the city are not only far from ideal, but positively incompatible with reasonable standards of health and efficiency. They are accurately characterized by Mr. Veiller in the passage quoted from his work in the first chapter. Indeed, leading tenement-house reformers, who heartily disapprove of anything savoring of the single tax or municipal ownership of tenements, now recognize the positive limitations of mere statutory regulations of privately owned houses.

In addition to the improvement of housing conditions by regulation, there are two other lines of action open: the construction of model tenements by private philanthropists and the provision of proper housing by municipal authorities directly. The efforts of philanthropists to relieve conditions by erecting model houses at a low rental, though imposing in themselves, are relatively unimportant and resemble the famous attempt to empty the ocean by a vigorous use of a pail. Writing in 1910, Mr. Veiller pointed out that during the past forty years philanthropists had constructed in New York " model " accommodations for about 18,000 persons while real-estate speculators had built tenement houses —" most of them of a very objectionable type "— for 1,267,550 persons. While Mr. Veiller's contention that the expenditure of the same philanthropic energy in the enactment and enforcement of proper housing laws would have prevented " most of the housing evils in New York City " will not meet with universal agreement, his conclusion as to the relative futility of private " model " tenements is evident.

In the field of public housing, there have been no experiments worthy of mention in the United States. Looking abroad we find two distinct lines of municipal action: the tearing down of slum areas and construction of municipal tenements, and the building of new dwellings in less congested areas or on the outskirts of cities, on approved sanitary and artistic plans.

The first of these has not been very successful, for the reason that land in the congested areas costs too much, the new buildings properly constructed cannot re-house all of those driven out, so that slum areas in other regions are increased and rents in the neighborhood of the municipal houses go up so materially after the public improvement as to add to the distress of the renters. The second plan — municipal houses constructed in less crowded and suburban areas — has proved more successful and is commending itself as the best method where municipal housing is undertaken. There the land can be bought at a lower price, no one is unhoused during construction, proper transportation facilities can be provided, and the city may take advantage of the increases in values, by purchasing largely in the neighborhood of the improvement.

Although the bourgeoisie in Europe supports these enterprises, American middle-class reformers are usually against any such experiments in the United States. They point with pride to the glaring administrative failures of our municipalities as compared with the brilliant successes of private enterprises — frequently overlooking, in this connection, the fact that private enterprise has failed as yet to house the population of a single great American city with anything like an approach to the decency which the mechanical achievements and wealth of our civilization ought to afford.

It is only in the brief Socialist administration of Milwaukee that any considerable attempt has been made in the United States to follow the example of English and German cities in dealing with the housing question. During that administration steps were taken to secure a large area of land on the outskirts of the city and lay it out for commercial and residential purposes. According to Mr. Thompson, city clerk under Mayor Seidel: "A form of lease will be offered to working people that will enable them by payment of a very small sum to secure possession of a little plot of ground and a dwelling. Further payments will be on easy terms and the arrangement will carry a surrender value, so that at any time any working man who takes advantage of the offer will be able to get back the money he has just paid in." The plan further involved new transportation schemes which would have provided quick and easy transit to and from the city. The defeat of the Socialists, however, in 1912 made it impossible for them to carry their plan into full execution, and it remains to be seen what will become of it.

Others besides Socialists, however, advocate some form of municipal housing. The eminent authority on municipal affairs, Mr. M. N. Baker, for example, favors municipal enterprise at least for the poorest tenants. He says: " While it has been proven that thoroughly comfortable and sanitary quarters can be provided at this price (seventy-five cents to one dollar per week per room) and realize five per cent. on the investment, still this good work does not meet the needs of that large class whose earnings are small, but who may be kept among the ranks of the self-supporting. We are, therefore, driven to the conclusion that, while it may be undesirable for the city to engage in the construction of buildings for a class of workmen who could get satisfactory accommodations elsewhere, yet it may be necessary for it to provide homes for the poorest classes, in case careful study should prove their proper construction to be unremunerative to private capital."

Judging from European experience, sporadic housing experiments by municipalities have not contributed largely to the mitigation of the serious evils of congestion. It is this fact that has driven England and Germany to undertake town-planning on a generous scale — that is, to grapple with the whole question of reconstructing and guiding the growth of cities in such a way as to make them comfortable to live in and pleasing to look upon. This newer theme is the subject of the last chapter.

CHAPTER XII

EDUCATION AND INDUSTRIAL TRAINING

THE American people have an almost pathetic confidence in education as a guarantee for the stability of republican institutions and a solution of all social problems. Our strong individualism has never allowed this faith in education to waver and apparently no voice is ever lifted against this species of large-scale collectivism. On the contrary, as time goes on, the increase in the common educational plant and its staff of teachers more than keeps pace with the growth of the country in wealth and population. The federal commissioner of education reports (1911) that " the expenses of public schools in the nation as a whole are three times as great as they were in 1890 and twice as great as in 1900." Taxpayers seldom, if ever, wage war against extravagance in education, and just as seldom, it seems, inquire whether the returns are comparable with the outlay.

In the more democratic communities, particularly of the Middle West, where the rather sharp segregation of the rich in private schools has not yet taken place, the direct taxpayers send their own children to the public schools and they are thus the beneficiaries of their own munificence. Everywhere the grants to the graded schools are generous, but they are not as generous as the appropriations to the high schools from which the taxpayers benefit particularly, because they are usually able to support their children through the longer course while the laboring classes are compelled by economic necessity to put their children out at work, at least on the completion of their elementary studies, if not before.

An examination of the tables printed in the report of the federal commissioner of education for the year ending June 30, 1911, shows a much larger per capita expenditure for children in high schools than in elementary schools. Of course, the expenses of higher education are naturally greater than for the more elementary work, but this alone will not account for the discrepancy. Louisville spent $24.75 per pupil in the elementary schools and $83.07 per pupil in the high schools; Seattle, $44.29 for the former and $102.03 for the latter. In other cities the difference is not so great. In Canton, Ohio, the figures are $25.90 and $41.92 respectively; and in Ithaca, New York, $30.45 and $40.43. Roughly speaking, however, twice as much per capita is spent on the pupils of the high schools as on those of the elementary schools.

The willingness of the taxpayers to pay for schools is complemented by the willingness of large numbers of the working class to make every sacrifice possible to enable their children to take advantage of the facilities offered; for education, they think, opens the way for an escape from the drudgery and anxieties which beset the life of the proletariate.

For these reasons, democratic and economic, the school systems of our cities present one of the most inspiring aspects of our municipal advance; and recent tendencies seem to show that we are on the eve of a new era, in

Hughes High School, Cincinnati.

which the social features of education will be emphasized, the practical needs of industrial democracy more carefully considered than ever before, and vital connections established between the curriculum and the world's work.

In 1909, the average daily attendance in our public schools was 12,684,837, a gain of more than two millions over the number in 1900. The number of high schools increased from 6005 in 1900 to 10,213 in 1910 and the number of pupils in them from 519,251 to 915,061. There are now over a half a million public-school teachers in the United States. The proportion of women teachers is steadily increasing — from seventy per cent. in 1900 to seventy-nine per cent. in 1909.

In that year, the total value of all public-school property was $967,775,587, an increase of over four hundred million dollars in nine years. Speaking on the items embraced in this increased expenditure, the commissioner of education says: " It seems safe to say that by far the most important one is that of better and larger school buildings. This has been preëminently a period of advance in the style and quality of our school architecture. Not only are larger buildings built, but many of them are constructed of permanent materials and are equipped with modern conveniences, better furniture, more extensive libraries, and various new departments for the teaching of the sciences and their applications in the daily affairs of life." The annual expense account of our public schools rose from $214,964,618 in 1900 to $401,397,747 in 1909.

The control of education in the American city is vested in a school board or committee. This body may be treated as a branch of city administration by vesting the appointment of its members in the mayor or council; or it may be constituted as a separate division of the city government by providing that its members shall be elected by popular vote. The former method is employed in Chicago and New York where the mayors appoint; and the latter method is in vogue in St. Louis and Boston where the school boards are elected at large.

It is difficult to say which is the better of the two procedures in actual practice. Cities change from one to the other in the hope — usually vain — of taking the school affairs out of the spoils system. No doubt politics in the gross sense is being steadily eliminated from our school systems, but it is in response to an enlightened public sentiment rather than to some method of selecting school boards.

In cities which have the appointive school committee there has recently been much discussion over the respective merits of the large board serving without salaries and the small board highly paid. Mayor Gaynor, of New York, recently proposed a change in that city to the latter type, on the ground that it was better to have a small board of well-paid members devoting all of their time to the work, but he encountered the objection of nearly every prominent educationalist of the country, including the presidents of Harvard and Columbia Universities.

The theory of the large unpaid board is that a number of public-spirited citizens are glad to give a portion of their time to the supervision of school administration and will constantly supply a " lay element " to counteract the professionalism of the schoolmen. Experts to do the actual work of teaching and administering and citizens to control matters of general policy — was the contention of Mayor Gaynor's opponents.

Over against this contention, the Mayor set the fact that it was difficult to secure public-spirited citizens who could give enough of their time to school affairs to gain that acquaintance with details which is necessary to any real control of general policy. To those who held that a small paid board would become a part of the spoils system in the city politics, he replied that it all depended upon the way in which a mayor exercised his appointing power, and furthermore that "machine" methods were not unknown in large boards where a few members almost inevitably dominate the majority by obtaining better mastery of the business minutiæ.

On the whole, there is a decided tendency toward a smaller school board. Boston reduced the number from twenty-four to five, in 1905. A general law of Pennsylvania passed in 1911 provided for a material reduction in the size of school boards throughout the State — in Philadelphia from twenty-one to fifteen and in Reading from sixty-four to nine. Kentucky, in 1910, fixed the number of the members of school boards in cities of the first class, that is Louisville, at five.

Along with the recent changes in the composition of school boards has arisen a demand on the part of teachers for some representation on the body that determines educational policies. The advocates of this proposition urge that, in order to make their wishes effective, teachers must now enter politics in some form and bring "indirect influence" to bear upon the board, whereas under a system of immediate representation they could make their wants and ideals known through spokesmen selected by themselves.

The functions of the school board are largely financial and administrative. It prepares the budget of expenditures for school purposes; and, in some cities, it makes appropriations without reference to the council for approval, being subject only to the limitation that the total shall not exceed a certain tax rate. In New York City, the board of education merely presents estimates which must be approved by the board of estimate and apportionment and the board of aldermen; in Chicago the school board certifies to the council the amount of money needed for the year, and the council must lay a tax that will cover the estimates. When it is remembered that New York spends about $30,000,000 a year, and Chicago about $20,000,000, the financial powers of the school boards may be appreciated. In addition to providing for current expenses and the management of the existing schools, the board of education must look to the future, secure new sites, erect new buildings, purchase supplies, and make provision for new activities in the schools.

It is in the construction and maintenance of buildings and the purchase of supplies that the spoils system has most frequently appeared in school affairs. Indeed, this opportunity for personal advantage has transformed many a local party leader into a " progressive educationalist "— approving every new scheme which carries with it expenditures for buildings and supplies. The politicians in the school board have their retinues of contractors, prospective and actual janitors and engineers, and ambitious teachers who would accept higher offices.

Many different devices are being constructed to thwart

the designs of the spoilsmen in education. The purchase
of supplies is being controlled by unifying the work under
the supervision of one responsible officer, such as the
supply commissioner in St. Louis, by standardizing the
supplies used, and by requiring competitive bidding after
public advertising. The construction of new buildings
is likewise being centralized and standard methods applied. And the merit system is being adopted in the
selection of teachers and other employees connected with
educational administration.

Turning from administration to the curriculum, we find
that the whole system of education in cities is in process
of reorganization and adaptation to more clearly defined
ends. When the furor for popular education began in
the United States, learning was as it always had been,
a class privilege; and democracy thirsting to share in
all high prerogatives, supposed that education was something definite and a good in itself rather than a wholly
relative matter. Consequently in expanding our crude
beginnings we took over bodily a curriculum that had
been useful and diverting to a leisure class — without
inquiring very closely what were the needs of a democracy or whether the " liberal arts " or parts thereof were
either liberal or arts. Then science fell upon us, and
botany and zoölogy were added to literature and " culture." Thus the high-school and graded-school program,
beginning as a historical accident, grew by accretion,
without anybody's taking any particular thought about
it as a whole or as an efficient instrument of democracy. But within recent years all has changed. Dog-
matism has given way to doubt and inquiry, and we are
now groping around in a search how best to relate edu-

cation to the needs of the people as citizens in a democracy and as breadwinners.

Inasmuch as about ninety per cent. of the pupils in the public schools go into some branches of industry and business, there has come a strong demand for the introduction of industrial and vocational training into the school system, and the elimination of what are regarded as the "ornamental" literary and theoretical courses.

This demand is supported widely for mixed motives. There are many teachers who are convinced of the utter folly of forcing upon the listless and uninterested pupil a lot of word-play courses which have no meaning for him and do not in any way prepare him for efficient action in that sphere of life to which by choice or by force of circumstances he will go. Enterprising manufacturers are anxious to take advantage of a shortened apprentice period which would furnish them trained workers who could be speeded up to a higher notch and thus add to their business profits. There are many "good" women who are distressed at the difficulties of getting efficient servants on account of the relative independence of the girls who enter industries, and they fain would prepare them for domesticity by proper vocational training. Then there are others who believe that the power to do, to create, is the basis of independence, and that it is the casual, unskilled, shiftless, unorganized and unorganizable workers who are the enemies of working-class standards of life, and that intelligence and skill are the very basis of social democracy.

Strong as are these arguments for industrial and vocational training, the new system has many opponents or at least, in its bald form, it meets with no little suspicion on the part of working men and Socialists. Seeing the sources from which its support comes, they suspect it to be another capitalist device for securing strike-breakers, speeding up workers, and winning larger profits. Nevertheless, the most discerning among these opponents are beginning to recognize the positive advantages that may accrue to the working class through the acquisition of technical and industrial skill, and are relaxing their opposition to industrial education and devoting their attention rather to the work of organizing the product. Indeed, there now seems to be little opposition to technical training as such, although there is a grave danger that teachers in the new system may come to look upon their pupils as mere producers of commodities.

The newer ideas of industrial and vocational training have not hardened into a dogmatic curriculum, and there is yet opportunity to see that " the humanities " are not all sent to the scrap heap. Certainly, there is a better chance that the skilled and highly paid workman will find the humanities than that the purposeless product of the schools, who knows a little Browning, will keep what he has. We cannot get art into life by a little word training in the public schools; it must penetrate our whole industrial and social structure; it must be visible in the streets, homes, and market-places. For this reason, there is not much danger that industrial education will increase the " materialism " of our civilization.

Industrial training, moreover, is susceptible of a wide interpretation and manifold application, and all the lessons of honesty, art, and skill may be taught through it as well as through " book-learning." It should be sharply differentiated from the old idea of manual train-

ing which was a sort of a plaything grafted on to the
regular curriculum in order that the pupils might learn
"to do things with their hands"— not a virtue in itself
any more than snuff-taking.   The newer industrial training includes three aspects: the laying of a broad and
practical foundation for industrial skill in the mastery of
principles, processes, and materials of manufacturing,
the study of the social and economic forces which condition the life and work of the people, and the addition
of some specific vocational training designed to fit the
pupils for certain trades, professions, or arts.

While the courses of study, the relation to the existing
public schools, the question of special trade institutions,
and similar matters are, and long will be, under discussion, the following statement made by Mr. B. W. Johnson, of the Seattle schools, may be taken to indicate a
general trend in current views: "My contention is,"
he says, "that children do differ in vocational aim and
that, therefore, industrial education must be a necessary
part of our elementary curriculum.   To realize this, the
present elementary period should be divided after the
sixth grade, and the seventh and eighth grades, together
with the first and possibly the second year of the high
school, become an intermediate school with elective
courses, one of which would be an industrial course leading to a trade or vocational school or back to the high
school or out to an apprenticeship and industry.   The
first six grades should be the elementary school proper
in which the course would be the same for all pupils and
based on child growth and the demands of society, and
should have as one of its elements industrial education,
manual training evolutionized, as a means of relating the

school to industry and of making the child more sympathetic and intelligent in regard to the work of the world."

The educational committee of the Chicago City Club in a report published in 1912 after a careful investigation of the whole field, recommends " the establishment of a two-year vocational school admitting boys and girls at thirteen years of age, who have completed six grades in ordinary schools; elementary industrial schools for over-age children below grade seven; optional and vocational courses in grades seven and eight; trade schools for boys and girls; day continuation schools; industrial, technical, and trade courses in the high schools; and the establishment of a central high school of commerce."

It looks as if this new system will develop in the following directions:

Training in the physics and chemistry of life: food, clothing, shelter, modes of living.

General industrial training, with emphasis on manufacturing for boys and domestic arts for girls.

Special trade and vocational schools for boys and girls.

Agricultural schools to meet rural conditions.

Higher technical and mechanical training as an integral part of the public-school system or linked with the private institutions, with public support.

With regard to special schools for girls, it is, of course, important that they should be taught the domestic arts, but it should be remembered that they have full civic rights in some States and are destined to have them in all, that they have a fair claim to an intellectual life of their own, and that millions of them must, as a matter of fact, enter the several branches of the world's work outside the home. Justice requires, therefore, the provision of equal facilities in a wide range of technical branches for both boys and girls. Nevertheless, the special position of women in modern economic life is woefully neglected by masculine school boards and the few "ladies of leisure" who occasionally serve on them. According to "The American Year-Book" for 1911: "Trade schools for girls are rare, and are almost exclusively located in the northeastern manufacturing States. Of eighteen schools of this class, recently reported, fourteen are in Pennsylvania, New York, and Massachusetts. Their courses of instruction are mainly limited to the various forms of dress-making, garment-making, and millinery."

To give point to industrial education, emphasis is now being laid on the vocational aspects of the problem, and a national conference on vocational guidance has already been held — Boston, November, 1910. The aim of vocational guidance is stated to be "not that of finding a place for a child but rather of leading both child and parents to a careful consideration of his industrial needs and aptitudes under intelligent guidance." Boston has organized a vocational bureau for the purpose of collecting and recording information as to the occupations of the community, educating parents and children in the advantage of special training for any occupation, counseling children and parents on their specific problems, and connecting the children with actual opportunities for employment.

Another advance in vocational training is in the establishment of relations between the schools and practical industries. According to Mr. W. R. Hood, of the National Bureau of Education: " Schools in which part of the time is spent at work under factory conditions constitute a new development in industrial training in this country. Fitchburg, Massachusetts, was the first city in the country to establish such a school as a part of the public-school system. In 1908, a modification of the ' coöperative plan,' introduced two years previously in the engineering department of the University of Cincinnati, was introduced into the Fitchburg High School. Boys were employed alternate weeks in the various industries of the city and were paid stipulated wages. The other half of the time was devoted to study in school. The school is now in the fourth year of its history and has been pronounced a success. Fitchburg's lead has been followed by several cities, though usually the term ' continuation school ' is applied. . . . Continuation schools are now conducted in Boston, New York, Providence, Chicago, and Cincinnati, and beginnings are made in some other cities."

There are undoubtedly hopeful signs in this whole movement for industrial training, but many of its optimistic devotees go so far as to expect a solution of the problem of poverty by the increased efficiency which it seems to guarantee. Professor Patten, for example, speaking of the evil of low wages and its effect on morality and culture, says: " There is but one remedy — an education that increases efficiency and thus augments income." Now as a matter of fact, increased efficiency does not necessarily mean an increase in income — piece-workers know this in the long run by bitter experience. It looks simple enough — the better man will get better wages; but suppose a relative increase in efficiency throughout the ranks of labor (which must be supposed or there would be no solution of the social problem under Patten's theory), competition among the workers would become keener and their wages might, unless other factors intervened, remain the same. There is absolutely no guarantee that increased efficiency on the part of the working class will in itself increase wages.

The efficiency theory of solving the social problem, that is, the problem of poverty, in fact, is hopelessly fallacious. It ignores the whole question of exploitation in every form; it ignores the forces which condition the distribution of income among classes; it ignores the absorption of wage increases by rent increases; it ignores the fundamental matters of seasonal and cyclical unemployment, crises, inflation and contraction in industries — in a word, the fundamentals of the modern system of production. Those who expect education in itself to solve any economic problems of moment are doomed to disillusionment. Those who hope to harden class lines by making the school a mere adjunct to the counting house and the factory have mistaken the temper of modern democracy. But this is no condemnation of industrial education.

The question as to whether the city should undertake the support of a special college of its own is now much discussed. The advocates of the idea are not agreed that the state and endowed universities meet the needs of the greater municipalities. The experiments of English cities, like Manchester, Leeds, Liverpool, and Birmingham, in municipal institutions of higher learning are attracting no little interest in American cities. New York City now maintains its City College for men and its Normal College for women, Cincinnati has its university, and some of the smaller cities of the Middle West are beginning to think of municipal colleges.

In an argument in favor of the city college, President Dabney of the University of Cincinnati recently said: "If equality of opportunity is the principle of our American institutions, as we assert, then opportunity must be provided for the poor as well as for the rich to get the higher as well as the lower education. . . . All our political principles and laws were made to fit pioneer or rural conditions. In the Middle or Western States the majority of our city voters are still country-bred people. We have very few experienced city residents and no trained leaders in municipal affairs. In fact, to a great extent our cities are, through the legislatures, directly governed to-day by the rural districts in accordance with the individualistic ideals and principles of country people. The people of the cities are only beginning to assert themselves and to contend for home government. The only way they will ever succeed in solving their own problems is through the education of their whole citizenship in accordance with the necessities of city, as opposed to country, life. To do this we must build city colleges to train men to study city problems and do the city's work."

Eloquent and incisive as is this argument, it is highly questionable whether municipal colleges, as now conceived, are helping any more in the solution of municipal problems than are the state universities or privately endowed institutions. In fact, if the ideal of the city college is merely to facilitate the manufacture of more lawyers, doctors, teachers, and other recruits to what Bismarck called the " black-coated proletariate," it has its place, but it does not thereby make any peculiar contributions to the advance of municipal science or practice.

In this respect, as in many others, we have much to learn from Germany where there are being now developed special municipal institutions dealing with the public rather than the private aspects of city life. For example, on October 30, 1911, Düsseldorf opened a college for municipal officers and those intending to enter municipal service. The courses of this new institution embrace every aspect of city life: the law of municipal government, labor and social questions in cities, sanitation, public works, city planning, and similar topics; and the teachers include not only professors, but judges, lawyers, and experts actually engaged in municipal administration. It would seem that the establishment of institutions for training and education in public service and the development of popular lecture and extension systems for general education would come more nearly meeting the needs of modern municipal life than the addition of more institutions modeled on the type of the traditional American college.

The old cant phrase about a sound mind in a sound body is now finding some practical application in our schools. Medical inspection and the close supervision of the physical condition of children are coming to be recognized as solemn public obligations and as we have noted above in the chapter on public health, the care of the school child's eyes, teeth, and body generally is being vested in public authorities, connected with either public health or school administration. Hospitals, dental clinics, and periodical physical examinations of school children are becoming elemental parts of our educational systems.

A plan of medical inspection in schools began in Boston as early as 1894 and spread rapidly to other Massachusetts cities. According to a report of the department of child hygiene of the Russell Sage Foundation, published in 1911, " in 552 cities vision and hearing tests are conducted by the teachers, and in 258 cities this is done under the direction of doctors. For the service of medical inspection in cities, 1415 doctors are employed, more than half the number being in cities of the North Atlantic States and more than one-fourth in the North Central States. School nurses supplement the work in 415 cities, ninety per cent. of the number being employed in the same two sections of the country. The services of doctors are donated in seventy-five cities and of nurses in twenty-one cities. In the remaining cities salaries to examining physicians range from fees according to services up to $4000 a year."

Generally speaking, much of this inspection is crude and too little effort is made to remedy the defects discovered. For example, it is estimated that in Cleveland, in 1907, only twenty-two per cent. of the children found to be defective secured attention and correction, in New York only twenty-five per cent., and in Somerville, Massachusetts, only fifteen per cent. There is plenty of room for improvement and it will come.

On the basis of medical inspection, it is estimated that about a quarter of a million school children in the United

States are predisposed to tuberculosis, and recognition of this fact has given a great impetus to the development of open-air schools. Providence, Rhode Island, claims to have been the pioneer in this new work. The windows of certain schoolrooms were opened there in 1907, much to the astonishment of the country. So novel was the experiment that newspapers gave columns to it and school committees came from far and wide to look at it. In 1908, three cities had outdoor schools; in 1909, five cities; and in 1910 twenty-seven schools and about fifteen cities had adopted this new feature.

Boston, New York, Chicago, Hartford, Rochester, Washington, D. C., Milwaukee, Buffalo, and Oakland are beginning experiments in this line. In 1910, the Women's Municipal League of Boston founded the Castle Island Open-Air School in which were placed 163 anemic children selected from among 5000 classified as debilitated by the medical inspectors. The average gain in the weight of the children in the open air was two pounds one and one-half ounces as against an average of one pound for the children of the same group who remained in the city. Many of the new open-air schools are conducted by private associations or at their expense, but the marked gain in the children attending them will inevitably lead to a wide extension of the idea to public schools. To take care of the children in actual need of such treatment, Chicago would require eighty-five such schools instead of the three or four now in existence there.

Children are not only debilitated on account of a lack of fresh air. Thousands of them in every great city are undernourished because their parents are too poor to buy proper food and are untrained in food values. This question confronts the school authorities: "Shall we try to teach these starving children, in the vain hope their parents will increase their earnings or their wisdom, or shall we feed them first and then teach them?" Slowly school boards are coming to the conclusion that some provision must be made for feeding undernourished children. Two high schools in Rochester have restaurants well equipped and serve hot lunches at cost. The Lincoln School at St. Paul, Minnesota, opened a penny lunch room on February 1, 1911, which proved to be almost self-supporting. Other cities furnish lunches to children at cost or free to those who cannot pay, giving out tickets of the same color to all so that no discrimination is shown.

In keeping with this general movement to provide the proper physical basis for education is the development of playgrounds and recreational centers, under trained physical directors, in connection with each public school. The peculiar social and economic conditions of the congested cities make it imperative that not only physical exercise but also the spirit of play should be regarded as a part of the training to be given to children. While the whole subject of recreation will be considered in the next chapter it is worth while mentioning here the peculiar function of the school as a part of the general system. The schools will always be important places for play, because the children are there during the formative years; they are more or less evenly distributed according to population; they have the buildings and equipment, and they are the natural centers of enlightened activities of every kind. Legislatures are now recognizing this, and several States require the construction of a playground with every new school building. Equipment for play and its proper direction have become an integral part of each well-constructed public-school plant.

Along with the emphasis on the physical basis of well-being, and the adaptation of the curriculum to the needs of an industrial democracy, there has gone a demand for the wider use of the school plant for social purposes: vacation schools, evening lectures and entertainments, and social centers.

Like many other educational activities, vacation schools began as private enterprises. Newark, New Jersey, took up the idea in connection with the regular school system as early as 1885, and during the last two decades school boards everywhere have been adopting the plan. Generally speaking, there are two types of vacation schools: "In the first type the aim is social, being merely to offer the children an opportunity to get out of the hot, crowded streets and into more wholesome surroundings in which they may play, sing, and do elementary hand-work and the like, under competent direction. Usually some instruction is offered in nature study, first aid to the injured, and similar subjects. Vacation schools of this sort are the more numerous and better known. The second type is academic in aim. In several cities, special classes are organized in vacation time for the purpose of enabling pupils failing in some of their studies of the previous year to make up work and thus escape repeating a whole year's work. In some cases, especially capable pupils are permitted to study in vacation time in order to advance a grade or save part of a year."

For the purpose of extending education far beyond the school years, and enriching the intellectual life of the community, several cities have established evening lectures at the public schools. New York began this work under a law passed in 1888, and it has now been undertaken in one form or another in Los Angeles, San Francisco, New Orleans, Worcester, St. Louis, Philadelphia, Columbus, Memphis, and other representative cities.

In New York City, the system is popularly known as "the People's University," and its curriculum embraces courses by specialists on literature, history, social problems, fine arts, science, economics, and travel, in addition to single lectures on topics of general interest. In 1910, more than one hundred courses were given and there was an aggregate attendance of nearly a million. The entertainment feature is emphasized in some cities, and effort is made to treat serious topics in popular form. In New York attempts have been made to reach a happy combination of systematic instruction and general entertainment. The introduction of moving pictures of an educational type has been begun with great success, and these afford some counter-attraction to the private shows of a questionable nature.

The wider use of the schools as social centers is such an important and promising feature and is so intimately connected with the recreational life of our municipalities that it will receive special treatment in the following chapter. Here it may be said that the public school promises to become the democratic center for the intellectual, artistic, and recreational life of the community; for more than forty cities have seriously taken up this aspect of school extension.

No description of our educational system would be complete which did not mention the public libraries. Every great city now has its central library for general reading and research, and hundreds of smaller cities, through private or public munificence, are emulating their larger rivals. In addition to central libraries, branches and extension departments are being created so as to bring the books within the easy reach of the people who cannot have access to the central storehouse.

A new type of librarian is being evolved who does not look upon readers as nuisances, but rather strives to keep his shelves full of the best literature and to circulate bibliographies which will invite readers' interest to current questions, as well as to fiction and lighter literature.

Libraries for children of all ages are being opened as departments of the larger systems. A few enterprising librarians have organized special civic and commercial divisions, devoted to works which interest students of public affairs and business men and manufacturers investigating technical matters. Furthermore, a number of cities have established municipal reference libraries stocked with official reports and special works dealing with the manifold problems which city councils and administrative officers have to face, thus making the experience of the world available for the public officer of the meanest city. It so happens that if the American people do not know about current history and literature and the best books on every phase of our social questions, it is their own fault.

Finally, it may be said that our municipalities are becoming more and more alert in everything that concerns public education. Private associations coöperate with the schools in their good works and suggest newer helpful activities. We have national associations on general and special branches of public education, child welfare, library administration, and the like. Recently there has come the new institution known as " the school inquiry " or investigation by experts, designed to ascertain just what we are getting in return for the enormous sums spent on education. To find out where we are is not a work of supererogation.

CHAPTER XIII

MUNICIPAL RECREATION

Two factors are responsible for the present insistent demand for the provision of municipal recreation: the concentration of our people in large industrial centers and the commercialization of amusements.

In the early days of our history the country was always at the back door even of townspeople, but the age of the " old swimmin' hole " and the vacant-lot ball field is over for vast numbers of our urban children. In the congested centers, there are few open spaces for playgrounds except those provided at public expense; and the young must play in the streets or in places which are furnished in connection with saloons or other commercial institutions where profit is the leading motive. Industrialism has no room for children, at least until they are old enough to go into the factory, and many a hard-hearted philanthropist has suggested that they should go early to the factory in order to escape the evils of the streets.

It is not only the children who suffer under the industrial revolution. The adults need recreation just as much, and commerce has seized upon this need in a thousand forms. Just consider for a moment the position of the typical family in the great city: those who are old enough to work, often including the mother, and children, are at the factory from eight to twelve hours a day, laboring at machines which require intense application, and continuous nervous tension. The home is a cramped tenement, or a small wooden house on a dull gray street and with a miserable apology for a back yard. These conditions produce a passion for relaxation — what John Collier calls "an emotional rebound which makes a desire for pleasure which is almost hysterical." The flashy "white city," the sensational moving-picture show, the "unlimited" dance hall, the saloon, the yellow press — these are the inevitable commercial responses to this desire for relief from the intense monotony of urban industry and life.

Where inadequate provision is made for wholesome recreation, petty acts of outlawry are committed which lead the way to juvenile delinquency and then to crime. It is the universal testimony of those connected with children's courts that the lack of wholesome play is the chief cause of early trivial offenses. In a report to the National Educational Association in 1910, Mr. Clark W. Hetherington said on this point, "after having studied for two years the careers of 480 inmates of a juvenile reformatory, personal data indicated that 75 per cent. to 80 per cent. might have been saved an institutional career had they had normal play experience. Social workers agree that the 'bad boy' is largely the product of restricted or misdirected play energies. Juvenile delinquency diminishes in districts where playgrounds are established."

This is also the testimony of that expert in urban affairs, Jacob A. Riis, who in an article in *Collier's Weekly* for February 11, 1911, on "Fighting the Gang with

Athletics," says: "In New York City the making of a people's park or playground has been invariably followed by a decrease in ruffianism and gang violence. The boy would rather be good than bad; he would rather play than fight the police. Chicago reports a definite decrease in juvenile crime of all kinds in the districts surrounding its play parks."

It is not only inadequate provisions for recreation that counts against the social welfare; the type of diversion created under the commercial motive is frequently pernicious in its influence. For countless thousands the saloon is the only oasis of good cheer in the dreary desert of hideous industrialism. The suggestive moving-picture show preys upon the craving for excitement. The recent Chicago Vice Commission found the steamboat " excursions," and gaiety parks to be two great sources for recruiting in the White Slave Traffic. Of the dance halls, the Commission reports: " There are approximately 275 public dance-halls in Chicago which are rented periodically to so-called pleasure clubs and societies or are conducted by individuals. . . . Many of these halls are frequented by minors, both boys and girls, and in some instances they are surrounded by great temptations and dangers. Practically no effort is made by the managers to observe the laws regarding the sale of liquor to these minors. Nor is the provision of the ordinance relating to disreputable persons observed. In nearly every hall visited, investigators have seen professional and semi-professional prostitutes. . . . In some instances they were accompanied by their cadets who were continually on the outlook for new victims." One of the main conclusions of the committee

Courtesy of The Playground and Recreation Association of America.

Lincoln Park Playground, Cleveland, Ohio.

that investigated the social evil in New York City a few years ago was also to the effect that it was necessary to furnish " by public provision or private munificence, purer and more elevating forms of amusement to supplant the attractions of the low dance-halls, theaters, and other similar places of entertainment that only serve to stimulate sensuality and to debase the taste."

The answer of the middle-class Puritan from his semidetached villa is, " Close these amusement places by the police force;" but fortunately those who are laboring to improve social conditions take another attitude. Indeed, there is nothing more remarkable in our municipal development than the recent response by public authorities and private associations to the call for sufficient and wholesome recreation in our cities. And it should be noted that the smaller towns of ten and twelve thousand inhabitants are likewise giving attention to the need for proper, supervised play.

There is now a large organization, the Playground Association of America, which holds annual conferences and devotes splendid energies to the study of recreational problems and the advocacy of increased facilities. It has committees of experts at work on every aspect of the amusement problem; it has published a volume " A Normal Course in Play " designed as a contribution to the education of trained leaders in recreation; and it has been instrumental in securing the introduction of courses in recreation in several of our larger universities.

The playground feature has naturally received first attention (although recreation for adults is just as imperative and as important), for the reason that even the hardest Philistine will admit the necessity of play for children. Boston claims to be the birthplace of the playground idea; and Massachusetts set an example to all the other commonwealths, in 1908, by passing a law to the effect that every city of over ten thousand accepting the provisions of the act must " provide and maintain at least one public playground conveniently located and of suitable size and equipment for the recreation and physical education of the minors of such city, and at least one other playground for every additional twenty thousand of its population." In December of that year forty out of forty-two cities voted under the law to provide playgrounds at public expense.

The Playground Association now reports several types of playground legislation. An Ohio law of 1908 authorizes the board of education in any city school district to " establish and maintain such summer or vacation schools, school gardening, and playgrounds as in its discretion seems desirable; " and the park law of the same State authorizes the park commissioners to construct and maintain children's playgrounds. A recent New Jersey law empowers the mayor of each city to appoint a special commission to organize and control the playground system of the municipality. A third and more advanced type of law is the Massachusetts act described above.

Under such laws and general acts, city after city has been establishing public playgrounds and these have been handsomely supplemented by private gifts. In 1907, there were ninety cities maintaining supervised play centers; in 1908, 177 cities, and in 1909, 336 cities. More than one-third of the cities over 10,000 now have such centers. In 1911, the Playground Association received reports from 257 cities which maintained 1543 playgrounds, employed 4132 employees exclusive of caretakers, and expended $2,736,506.16. In thirty-six of these cities nearly four hundred employees were engaged all the year round. In fifty-three cities over two hundred playgrounds were open all year, and in seventy-one cities nearly three hundred grounds were open for from five to ten months. Fifty-seven cities opened their grounds on Sunday and sixty-seven kept their grounds open in the evening. In nineteen cities bond issues in the aggregate amount of nearly four and one half million dollars were authorized for recreational purposes. City after city (for example, Philadelphia in 1910) is appointing its recreation commission to study the whole question, survey local conditions, and suggest the equipment necessary to meet the local requirements.

In this work Chicago has led all other cities. In 1903, the South Park Board of that city secured from the state legislature the power to create a number of new small parks, and thereupon made a careful investigation of the recreational needs of the congested area under its jurisdiction. Within three years the board had established fourteen parks, ranging in area from six to seventy acres, at an expense of over $6,000,000. By combining all of the recent devices of social settlements, kindergartens, and other recreational centers, the Board sought to make these new parks as attractive as possible to children and adults and at the same time to develop healthful recreation to the fullest extent. It accordingly provided ball fields, tennis courts, swimming pools, sand piles, swings, lagoons for rowing and skating, stands for band concerts, and outdoor gymnasiums for children and adults of both sexes. It furthermore established indoor recreation buildings equipped with bathrooms, lunch-, reading-, club-, and assembly-rooms. In the winter-time lectures, dances, and musical entertainments are given in the assembly halls. At present over ten million dollars have been spent by Chicago in this work.

In addition to the material equipment, the Chicago Board has given special attention to providing capable directors to supervise all of the various activities. To the athletic directors it has issued the following instructions which show the spirit of the new recreational ideal:

Whether we wish it or not, the gymnasium and the athletic field are schools of character, but the kind of character formed in these schools will depend in great measure upon the instructor in charge. On the athletic field, and in the practice of games in the gymnasium, the instructor should praise every tendency of a boy or girl to sacrifice himself or herself for the good of the team. Show them that this is the only way to succeed — by unity of action. If you can develop this spirit, you have laid the foundation of coöperation, politeness, and good morals. You have taught the fundamental lesson of thoughtfulness for others. Keep in mind that we are public servants, employed to serve the public as experts in all that our profession implies, and that we are engaged in a work which, if properly conducted, is perhaps better calculated to raise the standard of good citizenship than any other single agency in the hands of public servants.

It is of the greatest importance that all work be undertaken in the light of the objects sought, as follows:

First, to take children from the streets and alleys and give them a better environment and safer place in which to play. This will relieve the parents of care and anxiety — as well as truck drivers, street car men, policemen, and others who are involved in the care of children.

Second, to encourage working boys and girls and adults

to spend the idle hours in a wholesome environment and away from questionable amusements.

Third, to encourage both children and adults to give attention to personal hygiene — exercise and bathing chiefly.

Fourth, to furnish wholesome amusement for adults and others who do not participate in the activities of the gymnasium, athletic and play fields.

Plan your work, then, and carry it forward with the well-defined idea that you are striving, first, to attract both children and adults to your gymnasium, play and athletic fields; second, that after you get them there you must interest and hold them until the habit of frequenting your gymnasium is established; third, that you do all you can by means of your gymnasium program, athletics, plays, and games, to " set up " the frame, encourage bathing, teach skill, courage, and a wholesome respect for the rights of others.

While New York City has not undertaken anything like the extensive work of the Chicago Board and has woefully neglected the question of winter amusements, its public provisions for play and recreation are by no means negligible. It maintains a number of athletic fields under the direction of the park department; it supports indoor and floating baths; it provides for baseball at more than one hundred diamonds; it affords opportunities for boating in the parks through concessionaires; it has grounds for croquet, bowling, cricket, football, golf, tennis, lacrosse, polo and picnics; it permits skating upon a number of ponds in the parks; it gives band concerts in the summer in the parks and at the recreation piers which it maintains at several points along East River and the Hudson. Under the departments of parks and education it furnishes more than one hundred playgrounds, some with and others without, directors; it provides indoor gymnasiums in connection with the public schools, and is now making a beginning with independent public gymnasiums. The activities of the city are supplemented by those of private associations which open vacant-lot playgrounds and coöperate with the public authorities in developing " features " such as folk-dancing, directed excursions, woodcraft, and handicrafts.

A unique recreational center was recently established in Reading, Pennsylvania, in the construction of municipal open-air skating rinks which are used for roller-skating in the summer and ice-skating in the winter. The rinks are made of concrete slabs and a six-inch curb around each rink forms a dam for water so that it can be easily flooded for the winter season. Pavilions afford the skaters a shelter where they may rest, and at the same time provide dance-halls where free instruction in dancing is given. The pavilions and the rinks are well lighted by electric lamps so that skating and play may go on at night as well as by day. Sanitary drinking fountains are conveniently placed and in the summer the water is ice-cooled. " Roller skating is patronized almost exclusively by young folks, ranging in age from four to eighteen or twenty. Ice-skating is popular with both old and young and not infrequently a gray head can be seen cutting a figure eight to the delight of the youngsters. During the ice-skating season the ice is planed at intervals to remove the irregularities and ruts formed by excessive skating. . . . The rinks form a safe spot for sane and healthful recreation for hundreds."

A striking instance of the application of science in

planning recreation is offered by an "instantaneous census" taken of the playground regions in St. Louis. This census, according to the report of the park commissioner, "was made of the district within one-quarter of a mile of each playground in the city to ascertain how the number of children in the streets and alleys, at play or at work, compared with the number in the grounds at the same hour." In one of the regions it was found that there were four times as many absolutely idle children, neither at work nor play, as were in the playground.

The recognition of the need for room to play and equipment for gymnastic exercises has been followed by the discovery that the whole subject of recreation takes rank in importance with education and requires trained leaders for its proper development. A staff of expert physical directors and play leaders is now regarded as an essential element for a recreational center, and Chicago has devised special civil-service rules in order to apply the merit system to the selection of park employees. Educational institutions are responding to this call for experts by the establishment of special courses.

Another newer feature is the publication of guides to the recreational facilities of the city. Boston has recently issued a little manual on the parks and points of interest which might invite the citizens during their leisure hours. Seattle, which has spent nearly $5,000,-000 on parks, also distributes through the schools and hotels leaflets giving a full description of all the features. The Recreation Committee — a private association in New York City — issues a little pamphlet on the opportunities for recreation afforded by the municipality which describes the exact location of the several parks, playgrounds, athletic fields, and other facilities, explains how to reach them, and gives the amount of car fare required to go from the congested points to the several centers. This leaflet is supplemented by another giving the recreational features maintained by private philanthropy or for commercial purposes with a view to encouraging the patronage of the high-grade places. Such surveys have the double advantage of showing the features offered by the city and encouraging their use, and also of pointing out the weak spots in the system.

In the general trend toward public provision of recreation both as a positive good in itself and a counter force to commercialized amusements, attention has been drawn to the possibilities of using the public-school plant as a center for community activities of every kind. It is pointed out by Mr. W. R. Hood that "the average American school building is open not more than six hours a day for five days a week and thirty-six weeks in the year — about 1080 hours. If Sundays be excluded, there are in all approximately 3000 hours in a year during which the buildings might be used. This indicates a time waste of about 1920 hours, or 64 per cent. With the possible exception of the church, no American institution uses its plant so little." It is not surprising that advocates of recreational reforms have turned to the public-school buildings as the natural centers for developing those literary, artistic, civic, and athletic facilities which help to offset the dull monotony of modern industrialism, and create a spirit of democratic coöperation.

New York City began the use of the schools for lecture centers nearly a quarter of a century ago; and as early as 1899 that city opened a school building as a play center, particularly for athletic exercises. About the same time experiments were made, here and there over the country, in using the school buildings for general community purposes.

A definite movement to bring all features together under a large and generous purpose was begun in Rochester, New York, during the winter of 1906–07 by the formation of a school extension committee to secure the school buildings for social and civic clubs. On the petition of this committee the common council granted the funds and arranged for opening three centers. A director, Mr. Edward J. Ward, was selected to supervise the activities and develop them, so as to provide every kind of wholesome recreation. Soon there were organized " civic clubs for both men and women, debating societies, literary clubs, social organizations, musical entertainments, art clubs, athletic leagues, reading rooms, quiet game rooms and gymnasiums." The movement soon brought down the opposition of the politicians and others who were fearful of the results of a too-free discussion of social and economic questions in the schools. It is true that party politics as such was excluded, and care was taken not to offend religious susceptibilities, but, as was perfectly natural, these club-houses of the working classes became the centers for discussing labor and socialistic problems, much to the alarm of the good people. The result was the closure of the schools for a time, in spite of a great protest on the part of the working-class population which had hailed the provision of community centers outside of the saloons; but recently a tentative renewal of the experiment has been made, because the public demand could not be resisted.

Notwithstanding this discouragement, the movement has become nation-wide in its scope. Chicago, in 1910, appropriated $10,000 for the work, and in her annual report for the year Superintendent Ella Flagg Young says: "The distinctive gain was not so much in what was learned as in the social and moral conditions that were made attractive and that tended to draw the young people from the more dangerous class of amusements which they are likely to frequent." New York City has made some beginnings, and the superintendent reports for 1910 that "evening recreation centers were maintained from October to June in thirty-six school buildings. The aggregate attendance was 2,165,457, an increase of 18,196 over the preceding year. . . . The chief activities were quiet games, reading (books being furnished by the public libraries), gymnastics, athletic sports, folk dancing, literary and social clubs and study rooms for children who have no convenient place to study their lessons at home." Philadelphia, Milwaukee, and Cleveland also report some experiments, but in only a few places are real centers under competent recreational directors being developed.

A national conference on the subject was held at Madison, Wisconsin, in October, 1911, and as a result a national Social Center Association was launched, with Mr. Ward, who organized the Rochester system, as the secretary. The question of the danger of partizanship in the discussions at the civic centers was brought up, but the majority of the conference declared that, while partizanship ought to be excluded, every question of pub-

The great pool in the 60th Street Municipal Bath, New York City.

lic importance ought to be considered in the school. According to its constitution, the purpose of the association is " the promotion and development of an intelligent public spirit through community use of public school-houses and other public buildings for discussion of all public questions, and for wholesome recreational, educational, and civic activities." The ideal underlying the movement is set forth in the following words: " The social center represents all the people in all those interests which are common to all. It is the people's forum and permanent headquarters for citizenship and neighborly spirit. In it the people come to know one another and how to make their government work. The public-school plant now functions only in part. Its present service is parental. The social center makes it also function fraternally."

Generalizing from the programs of civic centers now available, one discovers the following features, which, though not common to them all, promise to be embodied in the ideal system as conceived by its originators.

An expert director organizing the programs and knowing the people of the community and their problems.

Athletic clubs.

Debating societies.

Reading rooms.

Lectures.

Moving-pictures and stereopticon shows.

Rooms for chess and quiet games.

Folk and other dancing classes.

Bureaus for information on every aspect of city government: health, paving, budget-making, etc.

Art exhibitions.

Election booths on election day (as in Los Angeles).

Budget exhibits showing the city's financial methods and problems.

Social rooms for neighborhood meeting-places, to take the place of the quiet corners in saloons.

Evening classes.

Social hours, with music.

As to the construction of the branch of municipal administration charged with opening and controlling recreational centers, the suggestions of the recent Philadelphia commission are valuable. It should include the officer in charge of the city property which is to be developed into playgrounds and also the chief health officer who, by his position and special training, can supervise the sanitary and hygienic aspects of recreation. It should have the power to plan the entire system and, with the approval of the financial authority of the city, open and operate all the centers. The principle of civil service should be applied to the appointment of recreational officers, as in Chicago; and the rule that employees should be residents of the city should not be enforced.

Notwithstanding the extensive development of recreational features, the commercial dance-hall continues to flourish and constitutes a regular menace to good morals, because it is intimately associated with illicit liquor selling and prostitution. It is estimated that 100,000 persons enter these halls in New York City every week, and it is a matter of common knowledge that few of the places are fit for decent boys and girls. An attempt has recently been made in New York to regulate these halls by statute; a local association operates several places which are properly safeguarded; and a recreation company has now been organized to conduct model dance-halls and motion-picture shows on a self-supporting basis. However, according to Mr. John Collier of the People's Institute, who has made a special study of the whole amusement question, " it seems to be generally recognized that, whereas the theater commercially viewed, has a legitimate future in America, the dance should be forthright provided through municipal initiative. Milwaukee under the Socialist régime has, during 1911, conducted frequent municipal dances which have been effective in diminishing the popularity of beer gardens throughout the city and have been incidentally self-supporting."

American cities have not followed the example of European municipalities in erecting numerous theaters and auditoriums. Denver is almost unique in possessing a large municipal hall in which public concerts are given. The attendance at these concerts is so great and the public interest in them so sustained that they have attracted an interest throughout the country. On witnessing an entertainment there in January, 1912, Madame Schumann-Heink was so impressed with this municipal enterprise that she voluntarily gave a free concert which was attended by about fifteen thousand people and from which about twenty-five thousand were turned away. Houston, Texas, gives summer and winter concerts, and uses an auditorium seating 8000 for lectures, entertainments, and moving-picture shows. Concordia, Kansas, has a municipal theater, a gift from a public-spirited citizen.

The idea of systematically reserving breathing spaces in our great cities where grass and trees may grow is really a recent development, although our forefathers did

occasionally lay out a beautiful green, such as the Boston
Common and some of the smaller parks in the older residential sections of New York.   It is true, the park idea
has been carried rapidly forward by nearly every city
of any consequence during the last few years, but, as
Mr. Charles Mulford Robinson points out, "when in
1853 the purchase was authorized of lands for Central
Park, New York, the acquisition and development were
most bitterly opposed; in 1869 there were but two well-
advanced rural parks in the whole United States; in 1886
there were only twenty.   In 1898 a student of park development who had been in communication with the
twenty-five principal American cities wrote to the author
that, except in the larger, the rise of ' general ' interest
in park development had manifested itself ' only within
a decade,' and that in ten years the park acreage in each
of these cities had been more than doubled."

Moreover, it is premature to congratulate ourselves on
the general adoption of an enlightened park-planning
policy.   With criminal negligence, New York City has
allowed vast areas of the upper East and West Sides to
be built up with crowded tenements and "apartments"
without those systematic reservations of open spaces
necessary to afford relief to the tenement dwellers.   The
State of Washington in 1909 sought to establish the principle by a general law that "no plot of an addition to a
city of the first or second class or other city having a
special charter . . . shall be filed, accepted, or approved
unless a plot or plots of ground not less than one-tenth
of the area of the blocks therein platted, exclusive of the
lands set apart for streets and alleys, be dedicated to the
public for use as a park or common or for parks or com-

mons and placed under the control of the city authorities for such use forever." But the governor of the State vetoed the bill.

This late development of the idea of reserving open spaces has made it extremely difficult to plan park systems now, on account of the high values of land in congested areas. Consequently, most of the large parks, recently acquired by cities, are out of the reach of the people — except on payment of a car fare, which is a serious item, often overlooked by comfortable persons. " In Boston for example, which now has the most complete system of any municipality," says Mr. Charles M. Robinson, " the reservations of Middlesex Fels, of the Blue Hills, and even of Franklin Park are quite out of town, and like the large park acreage lately reserved in the Bronx district of Greater New York, are plainly designed to add beauty to the present and future city rather than to benefit its poor." Recently Chicago had upwards of 700,000 people who lived more than a mile from any considerable park. The large acreage lately acquired by Indianapolis with much self-satisfaction is out of walking distance from the crowded areas of the city and designed as driving parks for gentlemen with automobiles rather than as recreational places for a tired industrial population. The greater parks of Los Angeles, St. Louis, and Kansas City are likewise out of reach.

There are some slight compensations for this evil. The necessity of locating new parks on the outskirts of the city has led to the construction of many beautiful drives and walks, as for example in Chicago and Boston. The various sections of the city, being jealous for their several park privileges, have required park commissions to distribute the new areas with more or less evenness in a chain about the city. This development is usually followed by the construction of drives from central points to the park areas, and of boulevards and walks connecting the several reservations.

It must not be thought, however, that our recent park advance has been entirely confined to suburban regions. New York City has preserved the small historic parks in the older sections of the city, and has recently spent millions in atoning for past neglect by destroying slum areas and laying out breathing spaces in the congested centers. Chicago is systematically developing small parks in the crowded sections, and Boston now has about one hundred small parks and playgrounds located conveniently for the people.

Another hopeful sign in our park development, is the attempt to introduce into the planning some system based on the needs of the city as a whole. It is more than timely, for according to Mr. Powers, Chief of the Department of Statistics for Cities in the Census Bureau at Washington, there is scarcely a city in the country that knows what property it owns, and is available for recreational purposes. It is to meet this situation and to adapt future plans to the ascertained needs of the city that many a municipality has created a special park commission for the express purpose of making a social survey as a basis for the distribution of centers.

How such a commission may work out its plans is well illustrated by the following extract from an article in *The American City,* for December, 1911, by Dr. H. S. Curtis: " About three years ago we determined to make a playground plan for Washington. In order that we

might secure such a plan, we went first to the District
Government and later to the United States, trying to discover what land was owned by each of these public bodies
within the District. But we found immediately that
there was no complete list. . . . The one complete list
was the list of property exempt from taxation. . . . We
next made a study of the cemeteries. We found that
thirteen of these had been abandoned in the District in
the last thirty years, and we secured one of them. We
then took the hydrographic survey map and studied all
the depressions and shallow water about the city. We
found that there was a certain place about forty feet below grade which the ashes collector offered to fill in,
cover with a foot of soil, and put a fence around, if we
would allow him to put his ashes there. . . . We then
took Baist's Plat Books and located every vacant area of
one-half acre or more within the city. We put these
areas in on an outline map of the city in different colors,
and entered the public schools on the same map, the white
schools in red and the colored schools in blue. When we
had put down the enrolment for each of these schools
we had a good practical estimate of the child population
of each section. We then studied all of these sites with
a view of securing a system covering the city, so that
there might be a play place within half a mile of each
child." Obviously this plan, which might be improved
upon according to local circumstances, would furnish an
excellent rough guide in the location of small parks as
well as playgrounds, and, indeed, it has been used by
some recent park commissions in studying city park-
planning as a whole.

The proper use of parks constitutes one of the trying

problems for a park commissioner. On the one hand, he is besieged by those who would reserve the parks as quiet places for shady drives and cool walks, properly beautified and diversified in landscape and water arrangements. On the other hand, he is beset by the imperative demand from the congested centers for recreational centers for young and old. The advocates of recreational features urge that the parks are for the people and that whereas a few hundred enjoy the drives, thousands use the playgrounds and fields. Dr. H. S. Curtis is the authority for the statement that an acre and a half playground in Washington has a larger attendance than Rock Creek Park with its 1600 acres, and that Tompkins Square on the East Side of New York, is perhaps daily used by more people than Central Park.

Here, as elsewhere, there must be compromise. There should always be places for drives and walks, benches for tired pedestrians, smooth lawns, and shady nooks for mothers and children — they are good for the nerves and acquaintance with them should be cultivated. Therefore, the cry that every open spot should be skinned for teeter boards and sandpiles must be resisted by the park commissioner. The fight should be for more separate recreational centers, not for the destruction of the parks as places of rest and beauty.

In fact, lawn and woodland may be conserved and some recreational features developed in the parks, under restrictions. The rules of many parks permit parties and picnics on certain days to use the lawns, and some portions are set aside to be used with more freedom than others where the " Keep off the Grass " sign confronts the visitor at every turn. In Cleveland the park authorities recently developed special days — a "Romping day" for children, a "Turners' day" for the German societies, a "Cleveland day," in memory of the founding of the city, and an "Orphans' day" when the children of the institutions were given a ride through the parks and treated to a picnic lunch at Gordon Park. A judicious use of the parks under restrictions may at once preserve their natural beauty and make them serve recreational purposes. Nevertheless recreation ought to be considered as a special function — not a subsidiary work of the park superintendent.

CHAPTER XIV

CITY PLANNING

CITY planning is a new municipal interest in the United States. On the call of the New York City committee on congestion, the first National Conference on City Planning and the Problems of Congestion was held at Washington, D. C., in May, 1909. The attendance at the sessions and the consideration given to the subject by the public generally were such as to warrant the repetition of the experiment. A second conference was held at Rochester, in 1910, a third at Philadelphia, in 1911, and a fourth at Boston, in 1912. Thus every year students, experts in city planning, and officials of cities are brought together to compare ideas and take stock of the latest developments in the improvement of cities.

The third conference at Philadelphia through the influence of Mayor Reyburn was made the occasion of a city-planning exhibit —" the first of its kind to be held under municipal patronage in America." Models showing the most recent achievements in Europe were constructed, and photographs, maps, and plans were prepared to illustrate the treatment of transportation and other problems by the progressive cities of the old world. The boulevards of Paris, English garden cities, Ulm municipal houses, and Liverpool docks were shown by ingenious contrivances which enabled those who attended the exhibition to visualize the good works of other lands.

In addition to the National Conference on City Planning, we have several allied organizations which deal with one or more related phases of the general subject. The National Housing Association, the American Institute of Architects, and the American Society of Landscape Architects give more or less attention to the subject, while the American Civic Association is organized largely for the purpose of collecting and disseminating information in respect to the improvement of the physical conditions of urban life.

In our leading cities local associations are vying with each other in securing experts to prepare handsome and impressive volumes showing imposing buildings, grand avenues, and splendid plazas — volumes which are often followed by no practical results and which, after a little furor, are allowed to repose peacefully among the municipal archives. For example, New York City, a few years ago appointed a city improvement commission to make a study of the plan of the city and suggest improvements. "The result of their labors was published in a handsome volume which failed to provoke any popular interest, and there is little reason to suppose that their recommendations will carry any authority in whatever schemes for improvement the city of New York may have to deal with," says Triggs in his work on town planning. Several years before the disastrous fire of 1906, San Francisco had an expensive commission which elaborated large plans, but when the cataclysm leveled buildings all over the city and offered an opportunity for correcting the mistakes of the past along the lines suggested by the commission, nothing worthy of mention was done.

Indeed the careless and superficial way in which the phrase " city planning " has been bandied about, and the evident futility of many expensive surveys, have led serious workers in the field of municipal improvement to sneer at the idea and treat it as outside the range of practical affairs. At first glance, it looks as if it were the old story over again of " much cry and little wool."

This attitude of opposition to city planning has some further justification on account of the fact that city planners, with some notable exceptions, have very largely confined their efforts to creating civic centers — beautiful show places — that is, to putting diamond crowns on leprous brows, as Ruskin would phrase it. Take, for example, Mr. Charles M. Robinson's valuable volume on " The Improvement of Towns and Cities," published about a decade ago. In it are to be found suggestive chapters on sites, streets, advertisements, trees, parks, architectural development, civic esthetics, and popular education in art, but the word housing does not occur in the index and the subject receives no treatment in the text. In other words, a serious work on municipal improvements ignores the most fundamental of all great urban problems — the housing of the people and the treatment of vast slum areas.

The attacks upon city planning have been useful, however, for recently experts in the subject have begun to see the incongruity and immorality of calling a city of festering slums and fire-trap factories " beautiful " simply because the places which " respectable people " see — the parks and public buildings — are ornamental. It is fair

Courtesy of The Commissioner of Accounts, New York City.

Plaza at Entrance to Williamsburg Bridge, Brooklyn. Note prominence of bill-boards.

to say that Mr. Robinson entertains a noble conception of a city beautiful, although his early work on the subject treats of only the superficial aspects. Mr. Frederick Law Olmstead, one of the most distinguished experts on municipal planning, also takes a most comprehensive view of the subject, for in his speech at the Philadelphia conference in 1911, he said: "The fact is we are concerned with a single complex subject, namely, the intelligent control and guidance of the entire physical growth and alteration of cities, embracing all the problems of *relieving* and *avoiding congestion* — congestion of people in buildings and of buildings upon land, congestion of transportation facilities or of recreation facilities, congestion in respect to the means of supplying light, air, water, or anything else essential to the health and happiness of the people — but also embracing in addition to the problems of congestion, each one of the myriad problems involved in making our cities year by year, in their physical arrangement and equipment, healthier, pleasanter and more economical instruments for the use of the people who dwell within them in carrying on that part of the work and life of the world which is not to be done in the open country."

A still more positive note of dissatisfaction with superficialities is to be found in an address by another expert in city planning, Mr. George B. Ford, delivered before the seventh annual convention of the American Civic Association, printed in *The American City,* for March, 1912. Mr. Ford, after emphasizing the significance of properly treating problems of transportation and business, adds: "Although this work is of immense importance in itself, it does not so seriously affect the life of the city dweller, and in particular his wife and children, as does the question of habitation. A city is worthy just in proportion as its habitation is good. No city begins to be well planned until it has solved its housing problems." Mr. Ford then turns to the question of the proper location of public buildings in which he would see majesty and dignity combined; but here again he cautions us against overemphasizing these features of city planning, saying:

Locating these public buildings or grouping certain of them in civic centers before the problems of living, work, and play have been effectively solved is one of the strangest anomalies that America has ever witnessed.

Yet, strange as it may seem, this is just what has been done in many American communities. As we look through the American city-planning reports, splendid and inspiring as they are, we find that many of them have given their first consideration to showy superficialities — things worthy in themselves, but terrifying when we wake to a sense of responsibility to our fellow man and realize the rottenness of the foundation on which we build.

What has been the keynote of most of these city-planning reports? Beauty. Beautiful public buildings, beautiful squares and streets, beautiful lamp-posts, beautiful parks. The City Beautiful is a most desirable object, for we do crave beauty; but can we with equanimity stand by and help the city spend its money on these frills and furbelows when only a step away the hideous slum, reeking with filth and disease, rotten with crime, is sapping the very life-blood of the city? Can we calmly help the city spend on extravagant public monuments that money which has come from the taxes on the poor man's hovel while the worker in the factory is rushing to an early grave because the city has failed to see its duty in providing him with those working conditions which are his absolute right? Yet such are the questions we have to confront.

Fortunately, recent city-planning reports are showing more appreciation of this responsibility. The Boston Metropolitan Commission report of 1909, the recent Pittsburgh reports, the Philadelphia Exhibition, and, to a certain extent, the Chicago, the Rochester, and New Haven reports and others, have begun to show an understanding of what city planning really means. A number of these reports have developed parks and park systems, chiefly, however, from the standpoint of beauty. A lesser number of the more recent reports have taken up the question of playgrounds; only five or six have gone into the matter of transportation and transit; and only two or three of these have gone at it in anything like a big way. And when it comes to housing — that most vital subject of all — practically not one has even begun to deal with the problem. Yet we say that city planning is well launched in America, and we are apt to think that we are leading the world, little realizing that the inexorableness of justice will demand that we start all over again and begin next time with the fundamentals.

When we think of the amount of money and the amount of energy which has already been spent in America in the last ten years in working out these most attractive city plans and we realize how far it has come from really solving the problem of the development of these cities, it must make all the more apparent our duty in the future to try to make amends to our fellow citizens for our perverted use of their money in the past.

Leaving these generalities and turning to specific matters, we find that all of our representative cities are busy with city plans in some form. For many years Boston has been working toward a unification of the various authorities concerned in controlling the physical structure of the city. In 1893, a park commission was created which spent, within a few years, more than ten million dollars for reservations and connecting boulevards. Later three other commissions were formed to deal with railroads, transit, and highways; and these were afterward supplemented by a board of survey for Boston. In 1911, under an act of the state legislature a metropolitan plan commission was appointed to report on the necessity of a plan for the entire metropolitan district and devise ways and means for carrying the designs into execution. In its investigations, the commission considered the great waste due to the division of the metropolitan area into thirty-eight towns and cities, the loss accruing from the narrow streets and the disjointed system of transportation, the unsatisfactory housing conditions of Boston, and the problem of relating the several improvements now projected under different authorities. The commission recommended the creation of a permanent metropolitan planning board with power "to consider the relation of traffic highways and traffic open-spaces to transportation, of transportation to parks and playgrounds, of parks and playgrounds to the homes of the people, of the homes of the people to manufacturing districts, of manufacturing districts to transportation, and on and on through that unending relationship and interrelationship which stamps the character of modern life, and upon the profitable and skilful provision for which depends in many instances the success or failure of a public improvement and the return or dividend on a public investment."

Meanwhile, there was introduced in the Boston city council an ordinance creating a commission on city plan-

ning with large powers. "It shall be the duty," runs
the ordinance, "of the said commission to plan such
developments and improvements in the city of Boston as
have to do with the structural and sanitary safety of
buildings and all kindred matters usually included under
the head of building laws; the prevention and relief of
congestion of population and traffic; the control of fire
hazard; the proper distribution of buildings for the purposes of residence, manufacturing, trade, and transportation; the beautification of the city; the preservation of
its natural and historical features; the extension of water
supply and sewage disposal; the preservation, development, and management of lands and buildings for public
uses; the coördination of transportation whether of
passengers or freight and whether by railroads, railways,
highways, or water; the development of the water front;
and the distribution of telephone, gas, electric light, and
other public utilities, and such other matters as may
properly be understood to come within the scope of city
planning."

A movement for a city plan was instituted in Chicago
recently by the Commercial Club which prepared through
a committee, coöperating with several leading experts, an
elaborate set of designs for a civic center, new avenues
and boulevards, the treatment of the lake and water
front, and the coördination of transportation facilities.
In 1909, the mayor of the city appointed a large commission " to study and devise an official plan for Chicago,
using the Chicago plan originated by the Commercial
Club as a basis, and to provide for the needs of the present and direct the development of the city toward an end
both practical and ideal." Through the press and pub-

lic discussions, the idea of controlling and reconstructing the city under intelligent direction is being spread among all sections of the population. Mr. W. D. Moody, managing director under the mayor's commission, has prepared a manual of the plan of Chicago which has been adopted by the board of education as a regular textbook in the eighth grade. This manual emphasizes the place of conscious planning in modern city life, outlines what may be done in Chicago, and stimulates the imagination by showing what art and planning have done to make beautiful places in Europe. This is attacking the planning idea at the proper point, for one of the chief reasons for the failure of many excellent ideas is the indifference and ignorance of the public. When the people want a beautiful city, they may have it, holds the author of this unique school text-book.

The first practical application of the Chicago plan is along the lake front which, the commission urges, should be owned absolutely by the city. Parks and public bathing beaches are being planned along it, and the question of terminal facilities is being considered as a whole. The city council has taken the legal steps necessary to provide for filling in and reclaiming the lands along the shore, and, unless something unforeseen intervenes, Chicago will have within the next few years a completely reconstructed water front which will afford excellent recreational centers and at the same time give business and transportation more coördinated and more economical facilities than ever before.

St. Louis has a city-plan commission whose program embraces the following elements: " (a) Improvement of the river front; (b) extension of streets and the supervision of the opening of subdivisions; (c) improvement of surroundings of Union Station; (d) a system of widening and opening various through streets so as to make the city more cohesive and less disjointed; (e) control of nuisances; (f) a playground, park and boulevard system; (g) location of public buildings; (h) encouraging the location of manufacturing establishments in designated districts; (i) extension of conduit districts for wires; (j) extension of granitoid sidewalk districts, and for the regulation of same in the residence districts so as to provide for the planting of trees and for sufficient soil space to assure their growth; (k) such other improvements as will tend to make St. Louis a better city."

The New York congestion committee, appointed by the mayor in 1910, while not bearing the name, was in reality, more nearly a city-planning commission than many which have pretentiously borne the title, for, although it published no hand-tooled volumes on civic centers, it seriously considered the vital questions of city planning — housing, taxation of land, and distribution of factories. Moreover, its remedial measures went more nearly to the root of the matter than " suggestions for a permanent planning commission," or " proposed appropriations for beautification of city approaches." One of its bills, presented at the legislature, embodied the idea of reducing the tax on buildings and increasing that on land in such a way as not to penalize, but to encourage, improvements. Another measure proposed conferring upon the city authorities the right to create zones and impose restrictions as to the height and structure of buildings within each area. Although neither of these bills passed the legislature, their introduction and public discussion mark a decided advance. Moreover, the keen suggestions of the New York committee as to the causes of congestion and maladjustment in our great cities are more enlightening than pictures of " vistas " and " mall terminal fountains."

Philadelphia, as noted above, held a city-planning exhibition in connection with the national conference in 1911, and it has a comprehensive report on playgrounds for the whole city, prepared by the mayor's commission in 1910. In July, 1911, the city council passed an ordinance imposing upon the mayor the duty of supervising the plans for the future development of the city and authorizing the appointment of a permanent commission to coöperate with him. The matters to be considered by the commission are railroad and transportation facilities, river and harbor improvements, municipal auditoriums and assembly centers, parks, boulevards, and avenues, and the promotion of trade. This commission has been appointed and is at work.

Some of our smaller cities are becoming interested in planning, if for no other reason than the " boosting " of the town. A few years ago, the Grand Rapids board of trade appointed a committee which attacked some of the obvious evils : smoke nuisance, filthy vacant lots, hideous bill-boards. It arranged a series of public meetings and induced the city council to appropriate $8000 for a comprehensive plan for the urban center as a whole. The city-plan commission, which was thus created, called in experts and made a survey of Grand Rapids problems, including traffic, the river front, housing, park systems, and streets.

The Rochester chamber of commerce has likewise

taken up the question of city planning and in 1911 published "A City Plan for Rochester," prepared by Mr. Arnold W. Brunner, architect, Mr. Frederick Law Olmstead, landscape architect, and Bion J. Arnold, traction expert. Albany, through the joint action of its civic bodies and city authorities, has begun a city survey and has already published a report on the water-front problem. In October, 1911, the Kansas City City Club, in coöperation with other local associations including the municipal art league, started an energetic campaign for "a civic center, better public buildings, better streets, more playgrounds, better transportation facilities, and a more attractive city."

Hartford, Connecticut, was among the first cities taking up the idea of a permanent planning commission. By an act of the legislature in 1907 a commission was constituted composed of the mayor, the president of the board of street commissioners, the president of the park board, the city engineer, one alderman, one member of the common council, and two private citizens. The law provided that all questions relative to the location of public buildings, streets, squares, and parks, should be referred to this committee for investigation and report before final action. The city, through the commission, may condemn land for public purposes and resell, with or without reservations as to future use, any lands not needed for the projected improvements.

Washington, D. C., is, of course, unique among American cities, for it was originally founded upon a generous and artistic plan drafted by L'Enfant, and now has a comprehensive scheme for future development prepared a few years ago by a committee of experts. This com-

mittee, after studying European capitals and surveying
the plat and environs of the city, presented to Congress
a magnificent set of plans and drawings, illustrations and
models for the rectification of many maladjustments, the
plotting of new areas, and the location of new public
buildings.   Owing to the coöperation of congressional
committees and the public, it seems that their general
ideal for the growth of the city will be realized.

In order to encourage cities to take up more systematic planning, a few States have expressly authorized
the creation of planning commissions.   A New Jersey
statute of 1911 empowers the mayor of every city of the
first class to appoint a commission for the purpose of
preparing plans for the future development of the city,
and permits the expenditure of at least $10,000 a year
in the employment of experts and the making of surveys.
The. Wisconsin legislature, in 1909, passed an act authorizing cities of the first, second, and third classes to create
planning commissions composed of four city officials
and three citizens.   When such a commission is organized the council of the city must refer to it any question concerning " the location and architectural design of
any public building, the location, extension, widening,
enlargement, ornamentation, and parking of any street,
parkway, boulevard, park, playground, or other memorial
or public grounds," and receive its report before final
action.   Plats and replats of land within the city or
within one and one-half miles must also be submitted to
the commission.   The actual execution of public improvements not within the jurisdiction of some department of the city may be entrusted to the commission at

the discretion of the council. On its own motion the commission may make a map of the city.

By an act passed on June 10, 1911, supplementing the law of March, 1909, the legislature of Pennsylvania created in each city of the second class a department of city planning to be in charge of a commission of nine persons, appointed by the mayor, and serving without pay, but authorized to employ engineers and other assistants. The act requires the clerk of the council to furnish to the city-planning commission, upon its introduction, every ordinance or bill relating to the location of public buildings, or the extension, widening, ornamentation or parking of any street, parkway, park, playground, or other public ground. The commission, however, merely has an advisory power in such matters. It is instructed to make and lay before the council a map or maps of the city or any portion thereof, including territory extending three miles beyond the city limits, showing the streets and highways and other natural or artificial features, and also locations proposed by it for new public-buildings, civic centers, streets, parks, playgrounds and other improvements. The commission is authorized to make recommendations to the city council with regard to the conditions and future needs and growth of the city, transportation, the distribution of public buildings, and the planning and laying out for urban uses of private grounds brought into the market from time to time. All plans and plots of lands laid out for public use or for sale within the city limits must be submitted to the commission and receive its approval before being carried into execution.

It is difficult to make many observations on the general subject of city planning which are helpful in concrete cases, but it is interesting to note, from a study of the recent works and plans prepared by experts in the United States and Europe, the main lines of attack which are being proposed. New York City, the heart of whose population is congested on a long narrow island, presents one set of circumstances in the matter of housing and transportation, Pittsburgh scattered along river banks and up and down high hills another, and Indianapolis spread out over a wide plain another, and so on throughout all the cities of the country. Nevertheless, certain problems must be treated in each case: transportation, the location of public buildings and factories, and housing.

Naturally, all the recent plans deal extensively with streets, water fronts, terminals, and other means of traffic and intercourse. The business reasons for this are obvious, for as the Pittsburgh civic commission points out in its report on the main thoroughfares of that city prepared by Mr. Olmstead: "All delays and congestion of traffic . . . add to the expense of manufacturers, the costs borne by wholesale dealers; in short, inadequate traffic facilities in Pittsburgh as in other cities, add to the cost of doing business and of living." Then there is another element — congested traffic and difficulties in transit make for congestion of population near the factory districts.

Broadly speaking, three general methods of laying out streets are suggested. There is in the first place the "gridiron" "checker-board" plan which is so common in the United States and has little to recommend it. It is true that it affords a maximum area for building, but, except in a few rare instances, lack of room for growth is not a characteristic of American urban sites. Another quality, which has done so much to commend it to the American imagination in esthetic matters, is that it is so simple that any childish engineer can follow it.

In the second place, there is the diagonal avenue scheme which is the basis of L'Enfant's Washington plan, and is followed in a more or less thoroughgoing fashion by some other cities, as in the case of Indianapolis. This scheme has many features to recommend it. As Mr. Charles M. Robinson points out, it offers " economy of communication, vistas of much possible beauty, open squares and spaces that are grateful to the eye and of no little sanitary value." One has only to compare the difficulty of crossing Philadelphia and Washington diagonally, for instance, in order to grasp in an instant the immense convenience to the traveler which is afforded by the converging avenues. The checker-board scheme is discouraging to the landscape architect on account of its wearisome monotony, while the long sweep of the diagonal avenue invites artistic treatment.

The third type of street plan is known as the " ring or concentric plan." The best example of this type must be sought in Europe where it is made famous by the Vienna circle street within and girdle street without. " The former contains not only the public buildings, which in the aggregate give to it an air of splendor, but it contains the leading houses of business and amusement. Enclosed by it, is the small area of the old town, the network of highways and byways striking the Ringstrasse at forty points; without, extend fifteen main radials. The street railways coming in by these center their operations on the Ring, circling along its length until each passenger has been left at the point nearest his destination. Thus the Ringstrasse has been likened to a great receiving and distributing reservoir; but it has also a majesty that has lately rendered Vienna famous. It resembles an enormous circular stage devised for the spectacularly scenic entrance and exit of the Viennese throng."

Of course, local circumstances make impossible the exact copying of either of these plans. Diagonal Broadway in New York cuts across the gridiron with excellent effect; and narrow checker-board streets are nearly always found within the areas enclosed by the grand avenues. The ideal system is probably a combination of the three schemes: one or more great civic centers with imposing public buildings to which radial avenues run, encircling boulevards connecting parks and residential environs, and gridiron sections diversified by diagonal streets.

However, it is well-nigh impossible to reconstruct an old city already based upon the gridiron plan, at least not without enormous cost, and this method of solving the traffic problem is not favorably received by American city planners. They are now making actual analyses of the traffic currents, ascertaining the number of streets too narrow for street cars and wagons to pass conveniently, the amount of traffic blockading at given points, the number of vehicles and pedestrians daily using the main streets, and the daily loss at congested points. On

Proposed Civic Center for Cleveland, Ohio. Two of the buildings are already erected. From the plan by Daniel H. Burnham, John M. Carrère and Arnold W. Brunner.

the basis of ascertained facts they suggest a differentiation of streets; the use of some for traffic in one direction and others for traffic in the opposite direction. They advise changes in terminals when they discover the long hauls and congestion caused by inconvenient locations. They propose widening certain streets by shearing off the buildings or cutting down the sidewalks. The difference which a little widening of a street makes in the convenience to vehicles and pedestrians is often astounding.

Approaches to cities are also receiving special attention. In this matter business and esthetic considerations must be taken into account. One thing which the investigations of experts have shown is that enlightened self-interest does not often know its own business, and that coöperation is necessary for selfishness to reap its full measure. Only a complete survey of the distribution of the freight of a given railway in a city can determine the proper location of terminals. A central location physically may not be the proper center for freight distribution. The amount of loss due to cross hauling cannot be ascertained by imagination — but only by actual measurement. The same is true of passenger traffic. But undoubtedly there are grave difficulties here on account of the shifting character of business.

Then there is the esthetic consideration. A certain English city about to be honored by a visit from Queen Victoria found that there was not a single street leading from the railway station to the city hall which was decent enough for Her Majesty to traverse. One might venture to say that there are very few railway or water approaches to a great city in the United States which are fit for the common citizen to see, without offense to the eye.

City planners are attacking this problem. Along water fronts they advise the recovery of land by filling in, the double banking of the front so as to afford a traffic level and a park level, and the diversification of the lay-out by park areas. Railway approaches are much more difficult to treat on account of the fact that the public has no rights there akin to the reserved rights in water fronts. Nevertheless, city planners are also at work on the problem. They advise the abolition of the dangerous grade crossing, and frequently the elevation of tracks; and in the laying out of parks and centers they try to have one or two oases of beauty along the ways of the steam roads. The electrification of railways is facilitating the improvement of approaches and when the blight of the coal-burning engine is taken off the land, a marked encouragement is given to the owners of property along the lines to improve their belongings.

The treatment of parks, playgrounds, and spaces for public buildings is likewise a special care of the experts. Indeed, the construction of new public buildings, city, state, and federal, is, in some fortunate cities, the opportunity for creating an imposing center which often leads to the building of worthy approaching avenues.

It is, however, in seeing to the reservation of proper breathing spaces in new plots of ground added to the city, that the plan commission may do better work. Some far-sighted German cities have laid out sites for public-school buildings, art galleries, museums, baths, and other communal buildings and centers fifty years ahead, and control development with a view to beauty and service for the coming generations. America is disgracefully backward in long-sighted works, but city planning promises to come to our aid.

But the most fundamental of all the problems confronting the city planning experts, is that of relieving congestion, and the conditions which produce this state of affairs must first be understood. Many superficial causes have been assigned for overcrowding in modern cities. It is sometimes remarked that congestion is due to the fact that people prefer to live huddled up in tenement quarters, where the amusements and diversions of life are more abundant, than to endure the humdrum existence of the small towns or country. Of course, it is true that there would be no problem of congestion if people did not come to the cities; but this view overlooks two important facts. In the first place, it ignores the economic forces at work divorcing the people from the soil and carrying them into the cities. And in the second place, it offers no hint as to the problem of congestion; for whatever may be the forces bringing the people to the cities, it is a condition, not a theory, with which we have to deal. The city cannot refuse to attack the problem simply because it does not approve the motives which have led people to come within its borders.

A large and active school of reformers contend that the problem of congestion may be solved by proper systems of transportation and low fares for long rides, supplemented, perhaps, by workmen's trains early in the morning and late at night. That facilities for rapid transit admit of the wider distribution of population cannot be doubted, and often noteworthy improvements in congested centers are observable after the establishment of a new suburb connected with the factory districts by rapid transit lines. Nevertheless, modern students of the municipal transportation problem are coming to the opinion that even a perfect system of transportation will not solve the problem of overcrowding, unless it is accompanied by other measures.

Two of the most recent scientific investigations of the subject, the report of the New York committee on congestion and Dr. Pratt's study of the industrial causes of congestion, give three fundamental causes for overcrowding: congestion of factories, low wages and long hours, and land speculation. The tendency of working people to live within walking distance of their employment is natural and inevitable. Their long hours make them averse to spending any considerable time in crowded trains or street cars going to and from their work — and large numbers of them cannot afford to spend ten, or even six, cents a day in car fare.

Dr. Pratt shows that the great volume of manufacturing in New York City is carried on in Manhattan below Fourteenth Street within a space which constitutes about one one-hundredth of the city's total area. The forces making for congestion within this area are cumulative. Working people, who are constantly haunted by the specter of unemployment, must live within an area that offers the most chances for jobs. The factory at hand closes down for a week, or indefinitely, and the employee feels more secure in having other opportunities open near by. This same advantage also invites manufacturers to come into the already overcrowded area, because they want to take advantage of the fluid labor market, from which they may draw their labor supplies freely, and into which they may pour their discharged laborers with little or no compunctions of conscience. It is perfectly clear that as long as manufacturers are permitted to establish their plants wherever they please within the city's area, they will gravitate towards the congested centers, terminal transportation facilities and other similar advantages being equal.

The fact that low wages and long hours contribute heavily to congestion hardly needs any statistical demonstration. No person who works eight or ten hours a day wants to spend another hour or two going to and from his work. The longer the hours the less time the workman is physically able to spend in reaching his work — to say nothing of the wear and tear upon his nerves and efficiency. Then, too, the lower the wages, the smaller will be the amount which can be spared for transportation. The truth of these statements is supported by the results of Dr. Pratt's survey. On the basis of statistical study, he concludes that there is " an intimate and seemingly causal connection between increasing wages and constantly widening distribution." Generalizing from his statistical tables, he adds:

These tendencies, which need not be dignified by the name of laws, may be formulated as follows:

A working population tends to live in the immediate vicinity of its place of employment, although extreme congestion of population forces workers to seek homes at greater distance from their work places.

The distribution of a working population is greatly influenced by such industrial factors as hours of work and wages. The degree of distribution may be termed residence-mobility.

The residence-mobility of a working population varies inversely with the length of the working day or week. The longer the working day the intenser the congestion.

The residence-mobility of a working population varies directly with the wages of labor. The workers earning the lowest wages are the most congested.

The nationality or race of the workers has no appreciable effect upon the residence-mobility of a working population.

Female workers tend to live nearer their places of employment than male workers. Female workers, therefore, exhibit a less degree of residence-mobility than male workers.

The factors influencing residence-mobility seem to operate with less vigor in the case of female workers than in that of the male workers.

The third cause of congestion is land speculation. The private acquisition of unearned increment in land values is of course strongly emphasized by the advocates of the single tax. Leaving aside the question of the justice of private ownership of land in great cities, there is no doubt that the holding of land for purely speculative purposes, particularly on the outskirts of cities, tends to check the flow of the population from the overcrowded high-rent areas. By the shifting of a large portion of the burden of taxation from improvements to land, the holding of vacant lots would be discouraged and a decided stimulus would be given to the building of tenements and residences. Nevertheless, it is difficult to see how the taxation of increasing land values unaccompanied by control over the location of factories and a general improvement in the condition of the working class so far as the hours and wages of labor are concerned, would of itself approach the solution of the problem of congestion.

Indeed, this is recognized by recent students of the question of congestion. The report of the New York City committee on congestion, published in 1911, marks a distinct advance over the views entertained a decade ago by reformers who looked to tenement-house legislation and the improvement of transit facilities as the really important methods of relieving congestion. This report recognizes the complexity of the situation and comes to the conclusion that any real solution of the problem of relieving and preventing congestion must embrace a long program of measures. Among the projects cited in it are restriction of the height and volume of buildings, including the area of the lot that may be occupied; the forcible distribution of factories; the taxation of land at a higher rate than buildings; stringent legislation against overcrowding and unsanitary conditions; the education of citizens in such a manner as to interest them in removing from congested centers wherever possible; municipal housing and the active coöperation of the city in housing enterprises; the construction of garden cities and garden suburbs; the encouragement of labor unions in maintaining the standard of wages and hours; and national assistance in the distribution of immigrants.[1]

In approaching those graver questions of city planning which involve a more or less drastic interference with private rights in land, city planners grow cautious, although they admit that the land question is, in fact,

[1] For the recommendations in full, see below, Appendix II.

one of the basic elements in city development. Nevertheless, we are beginning to see in the United States, some assertions of the rights of the community as against the unlimited exploitation of land-values by private persons who insist in building when and how they please in order to reap the largest returns, present and prospective.

Of course, the restriction of the height of buildings in accordance with the width of streets is a principle that has already been adopted; but recently the idea of a positive public control over the use of urban land is finding acceptance. A conservative housing reformer, Mr. Veiller, who strongly opposes municipal ownership, now urges that " there must be the definitely conscious purpose of bringing about a system of classification of buildings within the city, and the laying out of the city and its buildings with regard to the uses to which different parts of the town are to be put. Unless this is done, city planning as we understand it in America, will have little effect on the housing problem." Remedying our worst conditions, he adds, requires " the determination of the rational depth of the lot and the adaptation of street widths to height of buildings, the establishment of a practical and rational zone system and the division of the town into quarters for various definite uses."

The districting of the city into zones is an idea which has been extensively applied in Germany with great success. Take Cologne for example. There, according to Triggs, " the whole city area is mapped out into zones, for each of which special building regulations are made. In the center and business part of the city twenty-five per cent. of all building land must be left free; in the second zone, immediately surrounding the central one, thirty-five per cent. must be left free, but buildings may have four stories; in the third zone, if the building is not more than thirty feet high, thirty-five per cent. only need be free, if higher, fifty per cent.; in the fourth zone, which is the zone of villa residences, the buildings may be detached, with about thirty-three feet between each, with gardens in the front, and fifty per cent. of the site must be left free. But this zone is not separate and apart, like the wealthier villa suburbs of an English city; it is cut up into sections and so intersperses between the second and third zones that the dwellers in the poorer districts are always within reach of beautiful surroundings, and in touch with their richer neighbors."

Although this zone principle has met with no general acceptance in American cities, housing reformers are beginning to approve it, and the New York committee on congestion definitely advocated its adoption. In a measure which it supported in the state legislature, the city was to be authorized to divide its areas into districts and make appropriate restrictions for each.

Realizing that the land problem lies at the base of the significant changes which they would make in parks, public spaces, streets, and playgrounds, city planners are now advocating the principle of " excess condemnation," which allows the municipality to acquire land surrounding any proposed public improvement and resell it after completing the work, thus reaping the increased value due to public enterprise. This principle is commonly applied in England, and the following example is given of its workings by the eminent New York architect, Mr. Arnold Brunner: " It was found that communication between Holborn and the Strand was difficult. These two thoroughfares were separated by a tangle of streets and by most undesirable property. Accordingly, a new avenue was planned and it was found that cutting through this network of streets left little irregular-shaped pieces of property. Some were little triangles, others long slices, many of them unfitted for building purposes. Accordingly, the city of London not only acquired the property necessary for the new street but also bought a strip 100 feet wide on each side of it. These bordering strips were then cut into pieces of property suitable for building. The value of this property when it was bought was low; the neighborhood was undesirable. The new avenue which the city created entirely changed the character of the neighborhood and these building lots, bordering the King's Way, as the new street is called, became very valuable indeed. The city then sold these building lots at the market price with the result that this great improvement is paying for itself, the city as a city making the legitimate profit which resulted from the new values that it, itself, had created."

A constitutional amendment based on this principle was submitted to the voters of New York in 1912 and defeated largely by the up-state rural vote; but it has been reënacted by the legislature and will be submitted again. Several States, however, have adopted the principle of excess condemnation and applied it with success. It is embodied in the Hartford city-planning law mentioned above. The Wisconsin act also confers upon the cities of the three classes indicated the power to acquire by gift or purchase lands within their corporate limits for establishing, laying out, and extending memorial grounds, streets, parks, squares, playgrounds, and similar purposes, and provides that "after the establishment, lay-out, and completion of such improvements, [the city] may convey any such real estate thus acquired and not necessary for such improvements, with reservations concerning future use and occupation of such real estate, so as to protect such public works and improvements and their environs, and to preserve the view, appearance, light, air, and usefulness of such public works and to promote the public health and welfare." Under a law of 1907, Pennsylvania cities may acquire land within two hundred feet of property taken for public purposes and may resell under restrictions similar to those laid down in the Wisconsin act. Massachusetts, in 1911, adopted a constitutional clause arranging for cities to exercise the power of excess condemnation in connection with public improvements and acquire land in the neighborhood "sufficient for building lots which can then be leased or sold." Under such laws cities may retain some of the value created by their improvements and protect them against vandals.

Another treatment of the land question in city planning is that proposed by the single-taxers, many of whom believe that the taxation of land values to the limit will of itself produce "naturally" that improvement in structures, distribution of population, and location of factories and public buildings which are commonly included in a city plan. The theory of the single tax has been considered above in the chapter on taxation and municipal finance, but in this connection it should be noted that it is often suggested as a method for inducing the development of cities on correct lines. For example, Mr.

Frederic C. Howe, one of the most eminent exponents of the single tax and the author of several works on municipal government, recently declared: "Without any reservation, I have come to the conclusion that the orderly and symmetrical building of cities and the housing of urban population can be corrected through taxation of land values more easily and more fundamentally than in any other way. By the taxation of land values I mean the abandonment of all taxes now levied against houses, buildings, improvements of all kinds, machinery, goods, stock in trade, and personal property of every kind and description and the placing of all local taxes on the value of land."

Finally, there is the proposition that the municipality should own outright all or a part of the land within its borders and be empowered to purchase adjacent areas and reap all the values which accrue from its growth generally. It is the enormous cost of land which prevents the execution of the most important projects of the city planners, and outside of the Socialist ranks there are now several prominent experts in municipal affairs who favor public ownership of land on a large scale. Speaking on this subject, Professor H. R. Seager says, "There is reason to think that especially in large cities absentee landlordism is becoming more and more the rule for the simple reason that more and more people are coming to live in tenements and apartment houses. If this is the case, there may be good ground for the contention that the system of private property in land is ceasing to serve any useful purpose in cities which the system of public ownership would not serve as well and that the time is ripe for a gradual transition to the latter."

The best example of municipal ownership of land on a large scale is afforded by Germany, where the leading cities, like Berlin, Munich, Leipzig, Strassburg and Hanover, own large areas within and without their limits. Berlin, for instance, which has an area of nearly sixteen thousand acres within its boundaries, owns in all about forty thousand acres, including almost ten per cent. of the land within its gates. Munich owns twenty-three per cent., Leipzig, thirty-two per cent. and Hanover, thirty-seven per cent. of the land within their borders and large areas without. Ulm "considers the land policy to be at the root of the housing question. In 1904 it owned about sixty per cent. of its area, while in 1906 it owned about eighty per cent. It is thus in a position rigidly to control its movements. The city is continually buying land, and recently bought the old fortification, thus bringing into use a large amount of private land that was not before available. In order that it might share the increased valuation it secured a law giving to it a part of the increased value. The city controls land speculation by reserving the right to buy back all land within a hundred years at the price at which it was sold. The scheme generally followed to prevent overcrowding is to allow twenty per cent. only of a site in outlying districts to be covered by buildings, seventeen per cent. by the street, thirteen per cent. by the back gardens and fifty per cent. by the front gardens."

City planning, like every other municipal undertaking which vitally affects the life and labor of the people, has all of the limitations inherent in the dependence of the city upon the larger social and economic tissue of which it is a part. If the prime cause of congestion, as defined above, is low wages, and the best authorities agree that this is true, how can the city expect to do more than touch the fringe of the question? If long hours, low wages, and extensive periods of unemployment are responsible for a large part of the crime and misery of the city, how can a municipal government hope to make any radical changes when the underlying economic forces are beyond its reach.

All this is not said in disparagement of city planning or any of the newer enlightened activities of American municipalities. A great deal can be done by the city to make the living and working conditions within its borders better, but when the city has done its utmost, many fundamental evils will remain untouched at the real source. That is why non-partizanship, aiming at mere business efficiency in administration, and good city government movements are to be considered as temporary, not permanent, advances in American politics. The social policy of the city cannot be forcibly torn from the larger social policy of the nation which conditions the very problems with which the municipality must deal.

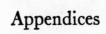

Appendices

APPENDIX I

Outline of Sections for a Model Street Railway Franchise, by J. W. S. Peters and D. F. Wilcox, of the National Municipal League Committee on Franchises.

1. The grant — Renewal of existing franchise — For specific routes — General nature of construction — Obligation to begin and complete work.

2. Publication of franchise — Referendum required — Other consents required and time allowed for securing them — Property owners — The courts — Approval of state commission — Permits from city departments.

3. Future extensions — When permitted — When required — Subject to conditions of original grant — Subject to amortization plan from date of construction — Built by city or special assessments.

4. Gage of tracks — Joint use of tracks by interurban roads — Free territory in business district — Joint use of poles and other fixtures — Switch connections with other railroads.

5. Terms of purchase clause — Price fixed in contract — Appraisal of physical property — Cost of reproduction — Unexpired franchise values — Paving — Depreciation — Appreciation in value of land and cost of labor, materials and street work — Displaced investments — Development charges — Investments from surplus earnings — Going value — Cost of future extensions — Cost of future additions and betterments — Cost of relocations — Supervisory control of new expenditures on capital account — Bonus for early termination of grant — Bonus for turning property

over to new company — Method of payment — In cash —
In general city bonds — In street railway certificates with
security franchise — Purchase subject to outstanding mortgages — Accumulation of purchase fund out of compensation for franchise — Purchase of company's bonds for extensions and betterments — Purchase of company's bonds
called at request of city or at market price — Amortization
out of earnings to retire capital and reduce price — Disposition of property when purchased — Transferred to new
grantee — Owned by city and leased for operation — Operated by city.

6. Duration of grant — Terminable at any time, after
minimum period, or at fixed intervals, upon purchase of
plant by city or city's licensee.

7. Service requirements — Standard of regularity —
Standard of frequency, minimum schedule, varied schedule,
" Owl " service — Transfer accommodations — Through
routing — Maximum and minimum speed — Carrying capacity required — Subject to future ordinances — Subject
to regulation by public service commission — Character of
cars — Passenger houses — Lost articles — Right to use
cars assured.

8. Health and convenience — Standards of cleanliness
and ventilation, heating, and lighting — Subject to future
ordinances, orders of public service commission, and police
regulations.

9. Safety requirements — Standard set for brakes, fend-
ers, and wheelguards — Location of tracks in street — Distance between tracks — Care of poles and wires — Subject
to future ordinances, orders of public service commission,
and street permits.

10. Public control of the streets — Plans to be filed —
Tracks and fixtures to be adjusted to public improvements
and other utilities — Tracks and fixtures to be removed and
routes changed to meet new traffic conditions — Municipal
ownership of tracks — Viaducts and bridges — Reconstruction requirements — Terminals — Subways.

11. Motive power — Provision for present or future changes.

12. Paving and paving obligations — City's right to do the work itself — Track foundations — Width of street occupied by tracks — Overhead trolleys — Underground trolleys.

13. Maintenance of street surface — Cleaning the streets — Sprinkling — Removal of snow and ice — Repair of paving — Repair of rails and conduits — Cleaning and sprinkling as city's agent.

14. Prevention of noise and jar.

15. Protection of city from damage claims.

16. Penalty fund to enforce company's obligations.

17. Rates of fare — Lower fares — Higher fares — Five-cent fares — Uniform rate — Differentiated rate — Free service — Higher rate for night service — Special rate for rush hours — Transfers — Tickets — Through service — Regulation of rates — Automatic readjustment of rates according to franchise schedules.

18. Advertising — To be artistic — Free for public proclamations — Not to be used for propaganda by company.

19. Carrying mail, express, and freight — Loading of cars — Operation of cars — Hand baggage — Hauling materials for street work — Special city service.

20. Special and chartered cars — Observation cars — Funeral cars.

21. Forms of accounts — Investigations — Reports — Publicity.

22. Filing of corporate documents and reports.

23. Limitation of bonds — Sale in open market — Discounts — Brokerage — Relation to purchase price or capital value.

24. Construction account — Approval of construction contracts — Certification of cost.

25. Valuation for rate regulation and return on capital to be same as purchase price fixed in contract.

26. Disposition of earnings — Operating expenses —

Maintenance and depreciation — Taxes — Interest on Investment — Reserve — Profits.

27. Limitation of cost of power and supplies — Limitation of salaries paid to officers.

28. Reserve for accidents — Mode of disposing of accident claims.

29. Insurance.

30. Maintenance and depreciation — Rehabilitation of old lines — Renewals — Normal wear — Obsolescence.

31. General taxes — Franchise taxes — Car license fees — Special assessments — Compensation to city.

32. Minimum allowance on capital — Amount of investments — Rate of interest — Distinction between stocks and bonds.

33. Amortization of capital.

34. Temporary use of special funds for additions, betterments, and extensions.

35. Contingent reserve.

36. Division of surplus profits — Sliding scale.

37. Employees' benefit fund.

38. Sale of property no longer needed.

39. Supervising authority to approve plans, hear complaints, audit accounts, pass on company's contracts, certify expenditures, inspect equipment, see that franchise obligations are complied with — Public utility commission — Supervising engineers — Local transportation bureau — Arbitration — Trustees for funds — Trustees to control stock of holding company — Commission for laying out and constructing rapid transit lines.

40. Obligations to employees — Hours of work — Conditions of work — Wages — Arbitration of labor disputes.

41. Protection of company against interference with its property — Cars to have right of way in streets — Right of company to sell power as a by-product.

42. Forfeiture clause.

43. Acceptance of grant.

44. Rights of city in case of receivership.

Exhibit A. Specifications for the railway and its equipment — Character and weight of rails — Gage of tracks — Strengthening of bridges where necessary, etc., etc.

APPENDIX II

RECOMMENDATIONS OF THE NEW YORK CITY COMMISSION ON CONGESTION OF POPULATION FOR RELIEVING THE PRESENT AND PREVENTING FUTURE CONGESTION OF POPULATION AND ROOM OVERCROWDING.

1. *Restriction of the Height or Volume of Buildings Other Than Tenements.*

(a) That no building hereafter to be erected in Manhattan, south of the south side of 181st st., shall exceed a cubage or volume of 174 times the area of the lot, and that no building be altered to exceed this cubage. This means that no building shall exceed a height of 174 feet covering the entire area of the lot. If each story were 12 feet in height this would permit of a height of 14 stories with a basement, which would not in any way seriously affect existing land values since a large part of the value of the site is due to accessibility to the multitudes on thoroughfares for stores and commercial purposes, on the first floor.

(b) That no building hereafter to be erected in any part of New York City, except in Manhattan, south of the south side of 181st st., shall exceed a cubage or volume of 120 times the area of the lot, and that no building in this district shall be altered to exceed this cubage. This means a restriction to about ten stories covering the entire area of the lot.

(c) That every building over four stories or 50 feet in height to be occupied as a factory, loft, warehouse or other miscellaneous buildings be of fireproof construction.

(d) That when the height of any building except one to be used as a factory, loft, warehouse or other miscellaneous buildings does not exceed one hundred feet (instead of twelve stories, or more than one hundred and fifty feet, as provided in the present building code), the doors and windows and their frames, the trims, the casings, the interior finish when filled solid at the back with fireproof material, and the floor boards and sleepers directly underneath may be of wood.

(e) That when the height of any fireproof building except one to be used as a factory, loft, warehouse or other miscellaneous building exceeds one hundred and fifty feet, no wood may be used in the floors or as sleepers even if treated by some process now approved by the Board of Buildings to render them fireproof, nor for the inside window frames and sash, doors, trim and other interior finish as permitted by the present building code.

(f) That no factory or loft building hereafter to be erected shall exceed a cubage or volume of one hundred and thirty-two times the area of the lot, and that no building hereafter altered to exceed this cubage or volume shall be used for factory or loft purposes.

2. *Restriction Upon the Lot Occupancy of Buildings Other Than Tenements.*

(a) That at the rear of every factory and loft building hereafter erected, there shall be provided a yard open and unobstructed from the street level to the sky across the entire width of the lot and of a depth equal to one-tenth of the height of the building, but in no case less than one-tenth of the depth of the lot, or if the lot be under one hundred feet in depth, of a depth of less than ten feet, and that no premises or building hereafter erected shall be converted to or occupied as a factory or loft that does not conform to this requirement.

(b) That there shall be a yard extending across the rear of lot of every dwelling hereafter erected to be occupied by more than one family equal to 10 per cent. of the depth of the lot, unobstructed from the ground level to the sky, and all rooms of such dwellings shall open and ventilate upon a street, yard, or court, not less than 4 feet wide or upon an offset to such court the depth of which does not exceed the width of same.

3. *Restriction Upon the Height of Tenements.*

(a) That no tenement house hereafter erected shall exceed in height the width of the widest street upon which it stands and that no tenement shall be increased in height, so that it shall exceed in height the width of the widest street upon which it stands.

(b) That no tenement house hereafter erected in The City of New York, except in the Borough of Manhattan, south of the south side of 181st st., shall exceed four stories in height, except that for every fifteen percentum of the lot area left unoccupied less than the maximum occupancy that is now legally permissible an additional story shall be permitted and a tenement house may be five stories high without being of fireproof construction if it occupy fifteen percentum less of the lot area than is now legally permissible.

(c) That every tenement house hereafter erected exceeding four stories or parts of stories or fifty feet in height above the curb level shall be a fireproof tenement house, and that no tenement house be altered so as to exceed such height without being made a fireproof tenement house.

(d) That tenements in outlying districts of the City be restricted to three stories in height and an equivalent restriction be put upon the volume or cubage of all buildings other than tenements, and that the Board of Aldermen and Board of Estimate and Apportionment should determine these districts or zones for a period of twenty years.

4. *Modifications of the Tenement House Law Respecting Three-Family Tenements to Encourage the Construction of These Small Tenements with Few Families, as Follows:*

(a) That buildings not exceeding 30 feet in height, need not have fire-escapes or stairs extending to the roof.

(b) That in tenement houses hereafter erected, not exceeding three stories and cellar in height, and arranged to be occupied by not more than one family on a floor and three families in all, in lieu of stairs there shall be an iron ladder to the roof placed at an angle of 60 degrees, and constructed as required by the Tenement House Law, and that the width of stairs in such a three-story tenement be two feet and nine inches.

(c) That a scuttle shall be provided for a three-family tenement, twenty-four by thirty-six inches, with a scuttle cover provided with a counter balance weight.

(d) That in tenements not exceeding three stories in height, the stair-wells may be reduced to a width of ten inches to extend from entrance floor to the roof.

(e) That windows in three-family tenements may be placed in vent shafts in existing buildings when windows are used to afford additional light in halls, provided that such windows are stationary and frames are fireproof and glazed with wire glass.

(f) That in three-story buildings where the bulkhead to the roof is omitted, fire-escapes and balconies with connecting ladders be placed on the rear of the building in accordance with such regulations as may be adopted by the Tenement House Department.

5. *Measures to Prevent Room and Apartment Overcrowding.*

(a) That no room in any tenement house hereafter to be constructed shall have a superficial area of less than 90 square feet, and that in every apartment there must be at least one room whose superficial area is at least 150 square feet.

(b) That no apartment in a tenement house or two-family house shall be so overcrowded that there shall be afforded less than 400 cubic feet of air space for every adult, and 300 cubic feet of air space for every child under 12 years of age occupying such apartment, and that a penalty of a fine not to exceed $25 shall attach for each violation of this provision. The provision of the present Tenement House Law regarding room overcrowding applies to rooms, but it is not feasible in the judgment of the Commission to enforce this in rooms, since they vary so in dimensions and cubical contents, and the Commission therefore recommends that apartment instead of rooms be made the measure of occupancy.

(c) That a placard should be posted by the Tenement House and Health Departments in a conspicuous place in every apartment of tenement houses, and in two-family houses respectively, calling attention to the fact that the law forbids more than the stated number of adults and children to occupy the apartment, and to the penalty attaching to a violation of this law.

(d) That no lessee of any apartment in any tenement house shall be permitted to take lodgers without notifying in writing the owner or responsible agent of the tenement or dwelling, who shall immediately report to the Tenement House Department, and that a penalty not to exceed $25 shall attach for each violation of this provision.

(e) That the owner or responsible agent of every tenement and two-family dwelling be required to report to the Tenement House Department and the Department of Health respectively any violation of the law against overcrowding on the part of his tenants, where he is unable personally to prevent such overcrowding by serving the tenant with a written statement (of which the owner is to keep a copy), that he is violating the law, and that the lessee of an apartment in a tenement house secure a license from the Tenement House Department and the lessee of an apartment in a two-family house secure a license from the Department of Health before taking lodgers.

(f) That a Bureau of Occupancy be created in the Department of Health charged with the enforcement of the law against overcrowding in apartments of two-family houses.

6. *Measures to Secure Better Conditions of Labor.*

First — The enlargement of the State Department of Labor in New York City by providing:

(a) A Deputy Commissioner of Labor for New York City.

(b) More Factory Inspectors.

(c) Appropriate legislation to enable the State Department of Labor to enforce its regulations.

Second — The creation of an Industrial Commission for New York City composed of three persons, one to be nominated by the Employers' Associations of the City, one by the Labor Unions of the City and one to be selected by the Mayor and all to be appointed by him. The duties of this Industrial Commission to be:

To investigate labor conditions and wages paid both skilled and unskilled workers of every class in the City, whether organized or not, and to investigate disputes when strikes or lockouts are threatened and after they occur.

Third — The creation by legislation of a series of employment offices in the larger cities of the State with special provisions for well equipped offices of this nature in New York City, or the creation of a Municipal Employment Bureau with several branches in New York City, including at least one in each Borough, which should keep a record of the opportunities for employment in New York City and outside, and furnish this information free or at a minimum charge to all looking for employment.

Fourth — The creation of a National Department of Labor, which should be coördinate with the Department of Commerce, the duties of this Department to be two-fold:

> (a) To give the widest publicity throughout the State and country to the opportunities for work by a system of Labor Bureaus or Exchanges in different sections of the country.
> (b) To give the widest publicity throughout the country to the conditions of labor, and wages paid, permanency of employment and local conditions.

7. Measures to Secure a Better Distribution of Factories.

(a) That 500 cubic feet of air space be provided for every employee of any factory instead of 250 cubic feet of air space, as at present, and not less than 600 cubic feet of air space for every employee when employed between the hours of 6 in the evening and 6 in the morning, under the provisions of the present Labor Law.

(b) By adequate improvement of the waterfronts in all Boroughs with piers and docks for factory purposes and with warehouses.

(c) That freight lines be built connecting all the Boroughs as soon as possible.

(d) That the ferriage charges for trucks on Municipal Ferries be equalized to the present minimum.

(e) Further provisions for carrying trucks on Municipal Ferries by altering the existing boats so that they can carry four lines or rows of trucks, and by requiring that boats to be constructed in the future have the same capacity for trucks.

8. Recommendations Regarding Parks, Playgrounds, Schools and Recreation Centres.

(a) That the City acquire land early in advance of future public needs.

(b) That land for parks in the outlying Boroughs should

be paid for partly by the property benefited, partly by the Borough in which located, and partly by the City at large.

(c) That adequate appropriations be made for the maintenance of parks and playgrounds and for their supervision.

(d) That adequate appropriation be made to the Department of Education to provide a teacher for every 40 pupils in the elementary schools on the basis of the registration, and within one-third of a mile of the homes of pupils ten years of age and under, and three-quarters of a mile of the homes of pupils over ten years of age, and further that a suitable schoolroom be provided on the same basis for every 40 pupils registered.

(e) That no school building outside of Manhattan should be over three stories in height nor have accommodations for more than 1,500 pupils, and that not more than 40 seats should be provided in ordinary classrooms in any elementary school.

(f) That adequate yard area should be purchased with every school site, so as to accommodate the children of the neighborhood.

(g) That the Department of Education be requested to give more instruction in physiology and hygiene, and impress upon the children the evils of room overcrowding and its physical effects.

(h) That greater provision be made for school farms and training in gardening.

(i) That the City provide more parks and playgrounds and recreation centres in the outlying districts.

9. *Measures to Keep Land Cheap and Promote the Provision of Good and Cheap Housing.*

(a) That the rate of taxation upon all buildings be half the rate of taxation upon all land, and that this reduction be secured by an equal change in each of five consecutive years.

(b) The question of recommending an unearned increment tax has been strongly advocated before the Commission. The principal argument advanced in support of the imposition of such a tax is that in nearly every instance where real estate values have increased such increases have been due wholly to public improvements and to the general development of the City, and in no way to action on the part of the property owner.

Some members of the Commission have strongly urged that this Commission should advocate such a tax to be levied annually on the increase in the assessed valuations of land — the proceeds of the tax to constitute a fund to be used exclusively for the construction of rapid transit undertakings.

The Commission have refrained from making such a recommendation because they believe that the subject requires greater study and investigation than they have been able to give it, and because there is a division of opinion among the members as to the expediency of such a tax at present. The Commission, however, refer this question to the officers of the City Government, with the request that it be examined and considered by them, and that public hearings be had in order to determine what action, if any, should be taken by the City with respect to this tax.

(c) That as a means of ascertaining the true price of land and of taxing it justly, the true price be required to be registered when the property is sold, so that the taxing officials may have definite information upon which to base their assessment.

Since a comprehensive system of transit is preferable for uniform and universal transfers and unified operation, and since subways and elevated lines furnish the key to urban transit systems and the control of these expensive links will, sooner or later, bring complete control of all street railway transit facilities, the following measures are advocated for the adequate development of the City's transit system:

(d) That the existing perpetual franchises should be terminated as opportunity offers by forfeiture, where, through neglect or non-compliance with the law, they should be forfeited, or through condemnation or through purchase or through negotiation, substituting modern short or indeterminate franchises for them.

(e) That the transit system of the city should be extended so as to utilize to their full capacity the subways, bridges and elevated lines, and so as to bring people from the outlying Boroughs directly into the principal business districts with quick service and for a single fare.

(f) That lines should be run into all sections of the City, although some such lines may not pay money profits at first, because they will be extremely profitable from the point of view of conserving the general welfare and prosperity of the citizens, and in developing the City.

(g) That the City extend its lines to the Queens side of the Queensborough Bridge and through the Steinway Tunnel into several portions of the Borough of Queens, and if this fails that the franchise for the use of the bridge and tunnel should provide for the operation for one fare, of extensions, into Queens.

(h) That all franchises for the operation of surface, elevated or subway lines shall contain a provision for transfers to and from all such lines which they own, operate or control.

(i) That a subway should be constructed as early as possible into the Borough of Richmond, to provide equal transit for its extensive area, and that pending the completion of such a route forty tickets should be sold for $1.00 on the Municipal Ferry to Richmond for the relief of people of small or moderate means who live there. This is advocated because the City has constructed at enormous expense bridges connecting all other boroughs with Manhattan, and the use of these bridges is free, while there is no free connection with Richmond.

(j) That the Rapid Transit Law be so amended as to confer upon the Public Service Commission and the City authorities the same powers with respect to surface lines as they now have with respect to rapid transit lines.

(k) The preparation by the City through the Board of Estimate and Apportionment of a plan for the entire City which shall include the following items:

(1) The restriction of factories to certain districts.

(2) The provision of transit lines and means of carrying freight upon the basis of such a districting of the City.

(3) The determination of the main lines of streets and secondary streets as suggested by Mr. Nelson P. Lewis, Chief Engineer of the Board of Estimate and Apportionment.

(4) Provision of sewers and methods of sewage disposal and substructures for pipes.

(5) Provision of adequate sites for parks and playgrounds and recreation centres and Municipal buildings in various parts.

(6) Acquisition of adequate land by the City for all public purposes.

(l) That as a means of reducing rents, and with the sanction of the Board of Estimate and Apportionment in each case, streets in outlying districts may be 30 feet wide, and houses be set back from 15 to 20 feet from the curb line so as to permit the widening of streets subsequently at a small expense.

(m) That subways for passengers be provided at crowded street crossings.

(n) Excess condemnation of land, through which the city may acquire more land than is required for a specific improvement, and resell or rent the surplus.

10. Measures to Promote Health and Safety.

(a) That when in the judgment of the Tenement House Department the minimum requirement of window space and other means of ventilation and lighting required by the law are not sufficient in any tenement house apartment to make rooms sanitary and habitable, said Department shall be empowered upon a certificate being signed by two medical inspectors as to the above facts to cause the vacating of said apartment or part thereof in the manner prescribed by law.

(b) That a staff of medical inspectors who are qualified physicians shall be assigned by the Department of Health to the Tenement House Department, who shall pass upon all cases of vacating of an unsanitary tenement house or part thereof in which there may be any contagious disease or which is unfit for human habitation, except in the case of new tenements awaiting a certificate of compliance.

(c) That the Tenement House Department of The City of New York shall at such times and in such manner as may to it seem best cause an inspection and examination to be made of all tenement houses, and wherever it shall be found that any such tenement house or part thereof is infected with contagious disease or that it is unfit for human habitation or occupancy, or dangerous to life or health by reason of want of repair or defects in the drainage, plumbing, lighting, ventilation, or the construction of the same, or by reason of the existence on the premises of a nuisance likely to cause sickness among the occupants of said house, the Department shall issue an order requiring all persons therein to vacate such house or part thereof within not less than twenty-four hours nor more than ten days, for the reasons to be mentioned in said order, and that the Board of Health should cause a similar inspection and examination to be made of all buildings other than tenements.

(d) That whitewashing of tenement house walls every year be required by law.

(e) That in tenement houses not exceeding four stories in height and not having more than two families on each floor, with courts of the width now required, a family be permitted to occupy the basement.

(f) That the Commissioner of the Tenement House Department be made a member of the Board of Health, with a vote on all matters pertaining to his Department.

(g) That manufacturing in tenement houses be adequately regulated and if possible prohibited by law.

11. *Measures to Promote the Distribution of Population Through Municipal Control Over Charities and by Public Outdoor Relief.*

(a) The creation of a Board of Trustees of Public Outdoor Relief to be provided with an office, administrator and investigators, who shall supervise the dispensing of outdoor relief to the dependent members of families of consumptives when after investigation into the circumstances of all such persons, it is established that the dependent members of the family of such consumptive or consumptives are not able to maintain themselves, provided however, that the dependent members of the family of such consumptive or consumptives move into a section of the City where the population is not greater than three hundred to the acre in the ward, and provided, also, that the dependent members of the family of such consumptive or consumptives are living under such surroundings as are approved by this Board or their representatives.

(b) That this Board of Trustees of Public Outdoor Relief shall have power to dispense outdoor relief to indigent widows with children, if such widows are competent to care for their children, provided, however, that they care for their children themselves and that they live in a ward having a density of less than three hundred to the acre and under such surroundings as are approved by this Board of Trustees of Public Outdoor Relief, or their representatives.

(c) The creation in the Comptroller's Office of a bureau for the supervision of all charitable institutions in The City of New York whose property is exempt from taxation under paragraph 7, of section 4 of the Tax Law.

The Chief Officer of this Bureau should be called the examiner of institutions and be appointed by the Comptroller to investigate the work done by these institutions and methods of accounting and report to the Comptroller from time to time as to whether these institutions are doing work which entitles them to exemption from taxation and should make recommendations to the institutions regarding the conduct of their work. The Comptroller should be authorized to appoint for the work of this Department as many expert accountants, examiners of accounts and other employees as he deems necessary.

(d) That the City encourage the removal of charitable institutions, except emergency hospitals and similar institutions, from the congested districts.

(e) The extension of the principle of the City Farm Colony and the acquisition of tracts of land by the City in the outlying boroughs for the extending of the work of the City Farm Colony and for teaching adults methods of earning a living such as agriculture and gardening.

(f) That the private charities of the City be urged to dispense their relief so as to encourage the distribution of population from congested districts and to encourage the recipients of their relief to learn other trades than those of congested city life.

12. *Recommendation Regarding Immigration.*

(a) Abolition of the time limit on the Government's right to deport aliens for cause.

(b) Progressive legislation looking toward the effective control over aliens by the Federal Government.

(c) That the Bureau of Industries and Immigration of the State Department of Labor be urged to encourage the immigrants to become farm laborers and to discourage the segregating of immigrants in congested sections of this City.

(d) Measures to prevent artificial stimulation of immigration.

(e) The establishment of City and State farms on the principles of those State institutions which have proved successful.

(f) Publication of information as to the opportunities

in high schools and elsewhere to learn the English language.

(g) Change of Federal and State laws to provide for the immediate deportation of convicted aliens to relieve the overcrowding conditions of our State Penal Institutions, in which there is a large proportion of alien convicts.

13. *Recommendations Regarding Delinquency in Congested Districts.*

(a) The closing of streets in the congested districts during certain hours of the day so that the children of those districts may use them for playgrounds.

(b) That the Department of Education be urged to arrange talks for mothers on the danger to children of occupying rooms with lodgers.

(c) That more physical exercise be provided for children in the Public Schools.

14. *Recommendations Regarding Public Squares and Buildings.*

(a) That there should be in every borough at least one large area for the public administration buildings in the Borough and a series of sub-civic centers with groupings of administration buildings.

(b) That there should be in each borough a grouping of public buildings such as schoolhouses, libraries, etc., except fire stations, in a park with open grounds around them.

(c) That the City provide recreational playhouses or at least sites for these in the civic centers.

APPENDIX III

BIBLIOGRAPHY

GENERAL. There is no exhaustive bibliography of American city government. Professor R. C. Brooks' admirable " Bibliography of Municipal Problems and City Conditions " (1901) is now sadly out of date.

H. E. Deming, " The Government of American Cities," lays particular stress upon home rule and the relation of the city to the State generally.

J. A. Fairlie, " Municipal Administration," a technical work covering all important branches of the subject. " Essays on Municipal Administration," by the same author, contains studies on the city council, municipal ownership, and kindred topics.

F. J. Goodnow, " City Government in the United States," is a brief treatment with an emphasis on political and administrative matters; " Municipal Government," by the same author, is a larger work in which a comparison of American and European methods and problems is instituted.

F. C. Howe, " The City the Hope of Democracy."

W. B. Munro, " City Government in the United States."

L. S. Rowe, " Problems of City Government," gives special attention to the newer social questions raised by the growth of cities.

D. F. Wilcox, " Great Cities in America ": a review of the governments and special features of Washington, New York, Chicago, Philadelphia, St. Louis, and Boston. " The American City," an earlier work by the same author, is a study of special topics such as public utilities, recreation, finances, home rule.

As guides to current municipal developments, the student will find the following magazines useful: *The American City* (a monthly publication, New York) and the *National Municipal Review* (the quarterly journal of the National Municipal League). A concise survey of current municipal events is printed in each issue of *The American Year-Book*. For social matters *The Survey* (New York) is invaluable.

THE PEOPLE OF THE CITY. For statistics on population and labor conditions consult the Census Bulletins, and the reports issued from time to time by the Department of Commerce and Labor at Washington, D. C. The best brief survey of urban industrial life in America is R. Hunter, " Poverty." For the condition of the children see J. Spargo, " The Bitter Cry of the Children." The publications of the Russell Sage Foundation of New York City, particularly " The Pittsburgh Survey," in several volumes, are indispensable. For women and children see the " Report on Condition of Woman and Child Wage Earners in the United States," 19 volumes (Washington, Government Printing Office, 1910). J. A. Fitch, " The Steel Workers." E. Pratt, " Industrial Causes of Congestion."

MUNICIPAL DEMOCRACY. E. Merriam, " Primary Elections," a study of the direct primary. W. B. Munro, editor, " The Initiative, Referendum, and Recall " (National Municipal League Series). W. H. Allen, " Woman's Part in Government Whether She Votes or Not."

COMMISSION GOVERNMENT. C. R. Woodruff, " City Government by Commission " (National Municipal League Series), includes several chapters by Mr. Woodruff and a collection of papers by specialists. E. S. Bradford, " Commission Government in American Cities," is a survey of the facts and an analysis of their significance. *The Annals of the American Academy of Political and Social Science* for November, 1911, contains a large number of papers by persons having a first-hand knowledge of the subject. R. S. Childs, " Short Ballot Principles," a study of the theory underlying the short ballot, and commission government incidentally. C. A. Beard, editor, "Digest of Short Ballot Charters," a collection of typical commission-government charters and digests of the leading documents. F. H. Mc-Gregor, "City Government by Commission," a study of the system and a statement of its merits and demerits.

POLICE ADMINISTRATION. L. F. Fuld, "Police Administration," a scholarly and technical study. W. McAdoo, "Guarding a Great City," a popular presentation of all the problems of police administration by a former police commissioner of New York City. On the social evil there are three reports of high value: "The Social Evil in Chicago" (1911), by the Vice-Commission of that city; "The Social Evil: With Special Reference to the City of New York," a report by the Committee of Fifteen (1902, new edition, 1912), edited by E. R. A. Seligman; "The Report of the Vice-Commission of Minneapolis" (1911).

MUNICIPAL FINANCES. F. A. Cleveland, "Chapters on Municipal Administration and Accounting," is a discussion of the management of municipalities, including budget-making, accounting, and municipal ownership, with special reference to New York and Chicago. *The Annals of the American Academy of Political and Social Science* for May, 1912, is a collection of expert studies by eminent specialists in efficiency and accounting. "State and Local Taxation," the annual report of the conference of the National Tax Association, is a current review of the whole subject. The Bureau of Municipal Research of 261 Broadway, New York City, has published a number of suggestive and practical pamphlets on all aspects of finance, budget-making, and accounting.

PUBLIC UTILITIES AND MUNICIPAL OWNERSHIP. D. F. Wilcox, "Municipal Franchises," 2 vols., is the most extensive treatment of the subject and should be in the possession of every student of municipal government. C. L. King, "The Regulation of Municipal Utilities" (National Municipal League Series), is a valuable collection of papers by specialists. R. H. Whitten, "The Valuation of Public

Service Corporations," is a technical study of this important topic. F. Parsons, "The City for the People," an older work devoted to showing the advantages of municipal ownership. "Municipal and Private Operation of Public Utilities," 3 vols., the indispensable report of the National Civic Federation Commission on Public Ownership and Operation, published in 1907.

TENEMENT HOUSE REFORM. The standard work on tenement regulation is L. Veiller, "Housing Reform." See also "Model Tenement-House Law," by the same author. De Forest and Veiller "The Tenement-House Problem." Consult the National Housing Association Publications.

PUBLIC HEALTH. T. S. Blair, "Public Hygiene," 2 vols., a large work covering the whole field. H. Godfrey, "The Health of the City," deals in a semi-popular way with all the aspects of municipal health, and gives in an appendix a bibliography on such topics as milk, food, sewage, ice, plumbing, and housing. J. Spargo, "The Common Sense of the Milk Question." G. Soper, "Modern Methods of Street Cleaning." The proceedings of the first annual conference of the mayors of New York cities are published under the title, "The City Healthful" (1911).

EDUCATION AND RECREATION. S. D. Snedden, "The Problem of Vocational Education." The Bureau of Commerce and Labor has published several reports on the subject of Industrial Education. L. P. Ayres, "Open-air Schools." E. B. Mero, "American Playgrounds." A. Leland, "Playground Technique and Playcraft." The annual report of the federal Commissioner of Education is the best source for general statistical data, and it usually contains a review of current tendencies in city schools. C. A. Perry, "The Wider Use of the School Plant." W. S. Cornell, "Health and the Medical Inspection of School Children."

CITY PLANNING. B. C. Marsh, "An Introduction to City Planning" (published by the author, New York), is sketchy but suggestive. C. M. Robinson, "Improvement of Towns and Cities" and "Modern Civic Art," two valuable works giving special attention to esthetic considerations. The most helpful general treatise is J. Nolen, "Replanning Small Cities," a recent work dealing with the concrete plans of a few smaller municipalities; includes also an excellent bibliography of books and periodicals. *Special Libraries* for May, 1912, contains an extensive bibliography on city planning. "The Report of the New York City Commission on Congestion of Population" (1911), gives valuable data on that city and the conclusions of the Commission. The "Annual Proceedings of the National City Planning Conference" are the chief source of information on current development in the United States.

INDEX

A.

Administration, municipal, 102 ff.
Albany, juvenile court, 179
Anthracite coal towns, 27
Appointment, methods of, 115 ff.;
see Civil Service
Australian ballot, 57

B.

Baltimore, population in 1789;
council, 88
Baths, public, 236; in tenements,
295
Bicameral council, 88
Boards, bi-partizan, 106
Boston, population 1789, 3; home
ownership, 10; foreign population, 24; propertyless voters,
55; criticism of direct primary, 59; recall, 72; United
Improvement Association, 76;
council in, 88 ff.; mayor, 98;
appointment of officers, 110 ff.;
collusion in contracts, 121;
debt, 130; budget-making, 146;
Finance Commission's work,
155 f.; sliding scale, 213;
school boards, 315; vocational
bureau, 322; playground movement, 338; recreational guide,
343; parks, 351; city planning,
362
Budget, exhibits, 150 f.; hearings, 152; making, 143 ff.
Buffalo, wages of Poles in, 9;
foreign population, 24; council, 88
Bureaus of Municipal research,
78

C.

California, home rule, 44
Canton, school expenditures,
312
Capitalization of public utilities,
194, 219; regulation of, 208.
Charleston, negro population, 24
Chelsea, foreign population, 23
Chicago, population in 1860 and
1900, 4; foreign population,
24; limits on state legislature
in favor of, 43; Municipal
Voters League, 76; ground
values, 136; Vice Commission,
162; juvenile court, 179; street
railway settlement, 203; electric plant, 238; sewage disposal, 269; health exhibit, 281;
plans for industrial training,
321; playground development,
339; social center movement,
346; city planning, 363
Cincinnati, juvenile court, 179
City planning, 356 ff.; conferences on, 356; in New York,
357, 365, 378; San Francisco,
357; Boston, 362; Chicago,
363; St. Louis, 364; Philadelphia, 366; Grand Rapids, 366;
Rochester, 366; Hartford, 367;
Washington, D. C., 367; New
Jersey, 368; Wisconsin, 368;
Pennsylvania, 369; methods
of, 370; and congestion, 375;
and the land, 378; see Appendix II
Civic centers, 344 ff.
Civil service, 108 ff.
Clean-up days, 245
Cleveland, home ownership, 11;
foreign population, 24; constitutional limitations, 33; long

415